COVERING VIOLENCE

CONTENTS

PREFACE

Bill Coté and I awoke to the powerful role of trauma in human experience in quite different ways. We had been newspaper reporters and had covered a wide range of news events, but we matured as journalists without knowing much about what the victims in our stories truly experienced. Our ignorance wasn't at all remarkable, though. Few of the reporters, editors, and photographers around us understood trauma, either.

Roger Simpson: I came to see trauma as integral to journalism practice as I designed and taught an ethics course at the University of Washington in the 1980s. I regularly invited advocates for sexual assault survivors to speak to the ethics students. Those talks led to classes that examine how news coverage might affect the emotional injury that accompanies the physical assault. Over time I began to realize how much I did not know about the experience of surviving violent injury. A Seattle conference that brought journalists and the families of murder victims together in the late 1980s found survivors venting their anger and showed usually confident journalists to be more defensive than sensitive when confronted with the families' complaints. A key that might have helped everyone in that session was missing; few participants said anything about trauma.

I pressed the journalism faculty at the University of Washington to change the reporting curriculum to make a permanent place for several hours of trauma training. Since the spring of 1994 nearly every journalism student at Washington has heard about emotional trauma and has practiced interviewing survivors (played by talented actors).

William Coté: I first observed the effects of trauma as a young reporter filling in on the police beat at a small Michigan daily in the 1960s. I noticed startlingly different reactions among defendants, family, and friends in a court hearing on a murder case. Some people showed shock, despair, or fury. Others appeared

ACKNOWLEDGMENTS

This book would not exist without the inspiration and insights of Frank Ochberg, M.D., a psychiatrist who has done more than anyone else to bring journalists and trauma experts into dialogue about their common interests. He guided Michigan State University and the University of Washington in implementing trauma education for their journalism students. He has been profoundly helpful to Bill Coté and me in the writing of this book. He continues to make us proud of our efforts.

The Dart Foundation of Mason, Michigan, has provided the money that enables the Dart Center in Seattle to take leadership in both trauma science and newsroom response to traumatic events.

I would like to note the support of Gerald Baldasty, chair of the University of Washington communication department, former chair Anthony Giffard, and the contributions of former colleague Kevin Kawamoto. The following members of the journalism faculty have infused the book with their own experiences and made their classrooms available for training: David Domke, Kathleen Fearn-Banks, Matthew Golec, Michael Henderson, Deborah Kaplan, Linda Lawson, Paul McElroy, and Doug Underwood. The book also reflects the uncountable ideas of graduate research assistants James Boggs, Cathy Ferrand Bullock, Jason Cubert, Elizabeth Koehler, Brennon Martin, Janice Maxson, Kristin Moran, Paula Reynolds-Eblacas, and Jill Wiske. I also acknowledge the contributions of E. K. Rynearson, M.D., and Fanny Correa, both on the staff of Separation and Loss Services of Virginia Mason Medical Center in Seattle. Dart Center associates, past and present, include Mark Brayne, Diane Bui, Jeffrey Cantrell, Christy Cox, Craig Kasnoff, Taso Lagos, Cait McMahon, April Peterson, Sharon Rigbi, Bruce Shapiro, Margaret Spratt, Jesse Tarbert, Adam Welch, and Larry Zalin.

William Coté thanks his former Michigan State associates: Stan Soffin and Stephen Lacy, former directors of the School of Journalism; Bonnie Bucqueroux, coordinator of the Victims and the Media Program; Kirk Haverkamp, who gave special help as a graduate assistant; Sue Carter, professor of journalism; and School of Journalism staff members. Linda Harkness, Dan Anderson, and Pat Anderson, officers of the Michigan Victim Alliance, gave their expert time and advice willingly.

Bill Coté gives his loving appreciation to his wife, Donna. She married him even after she knew he was consumed with writing and teaching about covering survivors of violence. She encouraged him greatly while he worked on this book, even if she's glad he's retired now.

Columbia University Press editors Ann Miller, the late John Michel, and Juree Sondker have offered unwavering support. Copy editor Polly Kummel has fine-tuned the manuscripts of both editions with informed care. Outside peer reviewers, whose names are not known to us, helped us focus the work. Helen Benedict and Migael Scherer gave us counsel on the sexual assault chapter. Donna Gaffney helped us address children's trauma.

Despite the efforts of all these good people, only Bill Coté and I are accountable for the content of this book. John Harris wrote the profiles of David Handschuh, Marley Shebala, Anh Do, Sharon Schmickle, and Fletcher Johnson. Migael Scherer wrote the profiles of Scott North, Sonia Nazario, Jane Hansen, and Debra McKinney.

We gratefully acknowledge the following for permission to reprint material in copyright that accompanies the journalist profiles:

For Sharon Schmickle's "A Little Boy, a Frantic Effort": Copyright © 2003 by the *Star Tribune*. Republished with permission of *Star Tribune*, Minneapolis-St. Paul. No further republication or redistribution is permitted without written consent of the *Star Tribune*.

For photographs by David Handschuh: Copyright © 2005 by the *Daily News*.

For Marley Shebala's "What Is a Navajo Leader?": Copyright © 2001 by the *Navajo Times*.

For Anh Do's "Caring for Newborns Inspires and Inmate to Start a Family— Bribing a Guard at her Husband's Prison So the Couple Could Be Together," an excerpt from "Camp Z30-D: The Survivors": Copyright © 2001 by the *Orange County Register*.

For the excerpt from Sonia Nazario's "Enrique's Journey": Copyright © 2002 by the *Los Angeles Times*.

For images by Fletcher Johnson: Copyright © 1992, 1994 by the American Broadcasting Co.

For Jane Hansen's "Selling Atlanta's Children": Copyright © 2001 by the *Atlanta Journal-Constitution.* Reprinted with permission from the *Atlanta Journal-Constitution.* Further reproduction, retransmission, or distribution of these materials without the prior written consent of the *Atlanta Journal-Constitution,* and any copyright holder identified in the material's copyright notice, is prohibited.

For excerpts from Debra McKinney's "Malignant Memories": Copyright © 1993 by the *Anchorage Daily News.*

For Scott North's "Family Supports Decision on Plea Deal": Copyright © 2003 by the *Herald* of Everett, Washington.

COVERING VIOLENCE

Introduction: Journalists and Violence

People in much of the world understand an American's shorthand reference to "9/11" and share indelible images of jet airplanes approaching, or exploding on impact with, the towers of the World Trade Center in New York City. The violence in Manhattan that sunny September morning replays in our minds years later, sometimes triggered by a flight on a jet or a quick glimpse of the towers in an old movie. No event in recent U.S. history has crystallized the experience of trauma as did the September 11, 2001, attacks. The Oklahoma City bombing in 1995 and the Columbine High School shootings in 1999 had made readers and viewers more familiar with the emotional shock that those communities had endured. Both events drew news teams from around the country and world, and the subsequent reporting showed the emotional strain not only on survivors and rescue and recovery workers but also on people some distance removed from the event. In time, journalists too began to acknowledge their own stress. By 2001 journalists and those in the news audience were gaining a vocabulary about traumatic violence and an understanding that trauma affects individuals and communities. On September 11 of that year the idea of national trauma entered American consciousness.

The 9/11 experience changed the practices of journalism in important ways. As the United States prepared to invade Iraq in 2003, many correspondents assigned to the conflict received training about trauma along with attending "boot camps" on how to survive in dangerous situations. News managers appointed stay-at-home reporters to keep in steady touch with the journalists sent abroad. Progressive managers looked for ways to ease the stresses on the returning journalists. Trainers and human resource personnel talked about the importance of training before dangerous assignments and support after risky assignments were over. To help assess the impact of the battlefield assignment, the British Broadcasting Corporation (BBC) put in place a program for periodic interviews with those journalists who covered the war. As the attention to journalists changed, so did the content of their reports. The Iraq invasion yielded compelling accounts of the traumas suffered by both military personnel and Iraqi civilians. The war reporting from Iraq for the first time placed emotional injury on the spectrum of wounds suffered by those involved in violence. Reporting about mental health incorporated the knowledge that scientists were gaining about how the human brain responds to danger and violence.

A sequence of tragic events since the 1990s continues to change the character of journalism for the better, Coté and I believe. Since the Oklahoma City bombing in 1995 the news industry has covered—and learned from—the horrors and bravery shown in school shootings, in the terrorist attacks of September 11, 2001, from the Iraq experience, and from the hurricanes that have devastated the Gulf Coast and Florida. These events captured public and media attention, and their repercussions continue to affect everyone. A significant effect of those years of violence is belated attention to the journalists who serve readers and viewers locally, where violence takes the form of a car crash, a rape, violence in the home, or a death or injury from gunfire. Reporters, photographers, and editors—just doing their job—interview and photograph those affected by violence, moving their pain to the front page or the evening newscast where everyone can see it. Many journalists find violence on their doorstep on their local news beat. Indeed, this book was planned with the local news reporter and photographer in mind.

For all the gains in understanding of the trauma of people who suffer violence, many in the public believe that journalism continues to exploit victims, milking their grief, shock, or fear to give their reporting a compelling edge. While some journalists are reporting on violence with extraordinary sensitivity, others do continue to treat victims as necessary props for stories about human cruelty but props without a chance to affect the way the stories are told. It isn't surprising that the public and the people in the stories complain about insensitive, callous, and excessive coverage. Anger drives people to throw rings of protection around children and other victims, defiantly shouting off or closing out the circling reporters. Journalists quickly become scapegoats for the discomfort that ensues from exposure to tragedy. Joann Byrd told me and Coté that in three years as ombudsman of the *Washington Post*, she "probably fielded a couple thousand calls from people angered by coverage—in the *Post* or elsewhere—of trauma." Other calls for change in media coverage of violence come from religious, parent, or women's advocacy groups. Many of the harshest critics of the news media were subjects of news stories, at once victims of the violence that drew newshounds to the area and of the media invasion itself. But other thoughtful people simply ask why a wealthy industry can't do a better job of reporting violence.

The American journalist stands in a whirlwind, grasping venerated news values in a desperate search for shelter. The storm swirling about the journalist gains force as mass media inundate viewers and readers with images and words about violence and disaster. Reporters and photographers go to the scene, see the effects of violence, and report to the public. Readers and viewers all too often complain about the media's exploitation of suffering people yet readily join in the country's gluttony for the violence-filled products of commercial entertainment. Media corporations, aided by dazzling technology that can set up live coverage from the devastation in minutes, build pain and injury into their news formulas, in the worst cases making sure that the first stories in the news program whack viewers' emotions. The mass-mediated world promotes our penchant for violence and nature's capacity for destruction, while news consumers go about their chores and pleasures out of harm's way. As crime rates have fallen across the nation, the media have projected a picture of escalating crime and violence.

Journalists, more than ever, express personal anguish about delivering the news of violence. Inside the newsroom is more alarm about this task than Coté and I have ever known. Today, journalists candidly voice the pains of news work, which once were disguised by a code of professionalism and a macho style that even some women in the newsroom felt compelled to adopt. We listened as a reporter on a small Washington State newspaper said, "Every day I get up and there's this river, this wild, raging river, and I take a deep breath, and I dive in and at the end of the day I claw out, and the next day I jump back in. I don't feel that I ever have time to think about what I'm doing." Rick Bragg, a former *New York Times* reporter whose beat and talent landed him regularly in tragedy's wake, writes about interviewing a minister in Alabama after a tornado destroyed her church and killed her daughter. "You hate this part, as a reporter, you hate to look into the eyes of a woman who has seen her child taken away forever," he says (1997:245). Journalists concede that they too suffer as they do their work—a thought that would have stunned the brash, cynical reporters of earlier eras. Journalists' suffering goes beyond mere distaste for some chores. Reporters and photographers emerge from covering horrible events with their emotions battered by the sights and sounds of the story.

And they are asking themselves and those who manage their organizations new questions: How does a journalist usefully report violence to people who gorge on violence? Why do the oldest kinds of stories—new only in the names and faces of the latest victims—now provoke anger at the messenger along with rapt attention? What are the personal and professional costs of trading in the injuries and hurts of other humans? Do such stories need telling? If the stories need telling, how can a reporter get a better purchase on their parts: the people, what they go through in violence and loss, how they recover, what the traumas of violence and disaster mean for them and for the rest of us? And what support do reporters and photographers need from the newsroom to be able to tell these stories effectively?

Journalists are facing the social ferment around violence and looking for solutions. Like them, Coté and I searched for a way out of the storm, a way to tell about life's worst experiences in ways that serve personal and social needs. We are both former reporters who have taught in journalism schools for many years, and we are convinced that the answers for the besieged journalist are close at hand, in the traditional skills and values of reporting. We have tried to respect the goals that define journalistic excellence. Among these goals are searching responsibly for the truth, keeping the public interest in mind, caring for the people in the story and others close to them, respecting the voices of people at the center of an event, knowing that the storytellers also are at risk, and doing no harm.

Skilled reporters put the individual's struggle with fateful events at the center of their professional concern. The personal story is their raison d'être. Events, they believe, are best perceived through the thoughts, words, emotions, and actions of the people swept before them. But we also have come to see the double-edged character of those stories, that the focus on the personal both serves and angers readers, viewers, and listeners. Through such stories we see how people suffer and endure, and we sense some of our own vulnerability and mortality. We recognize our penchant for voyeurism, the fragility of the shield of privacy that we hope will protect us in similar circumstances, and how easily fairness is sacrificed to a striking image: the tear or grimace that prods the emotions.

We have come to appreciate how much of the training of reporters and photographers, the day-to-day conduct of the business, and even the rewards of journalism reflect assembly-line thinking. On the news assembly line each person performs a set of tasks so that a finished product will emerge at a pre-set time—a television news program at 6 P.M., a newspaper on the porch at 5 A.M., a newsmagazine in the mail on the same day each week, or a bulletin on a Web site in minutes. The assembly lines of the news media squeeze both mundane and extraordinary events—even those that kill and maim people—into the same hourly, daily, or weekly production schedule. They push reporters to get more information at a faster pace, exposing the brutal surface reality of events but little of the truth about what will follow.

In these chapters we show how to supplement the assembly line with a quite different model of news gathering—one that is called for when either the emotions of close neighbors or the mass consciousness of the globe are shattered by a cataclysmic event. Our model traces the shock waves of the event. When something explodes or the earth shakes or a hurricane levels a community, it instantly affects those at the epicenter. Then the shock waves radiate outward in ever-larger circles from the detonation point. The waves may wound less severely at points far from the center, but they may wound nonetheless.

Half a century of research about emotional trauma has yielded new thinking about its social, political, and economic consequences. Exposure to traumatic events is extensive; studies estimate that 40 percent to 80 percent of the population has experienced a traumatic event. In that number traumatic injury is common—perhaps one out of ten of us has long-term emotional wounds. Many victims conceal their symptoms out of fear of the perpetrators or of social prejudice, their inability to obtain treatment, or ignorance or confusion about the causes of their symptoms. Sandra Bloom, a psychiatrist, sees trauma "as a central organizing principle in the formation, development, [and] maintenance of human society" (1997:212). Trauma, in other words, is more central to human existence than most people like to acknowledge. Indeed, one of its most insidious characteristics is the way it encourages people to deny it. Journalists also suffer lasting traumatic injuries, which puts the lie to the assumptions of some in the business that reporters and photographers are superhuman, somehow able to endure any kind of emotional shock. It is now clear that journalists suffer trauma and its most chronic form—post-traumatic stress disorder (PTSD)—at rates comparable to the general population's and that some journalists—those who regularly chase violence in big cities, war zones, or in civil conflicts—risk suffering PTSD at rates as high as 30 percent.

What researchers now know about trauma can make a difference in how journalists do their jobs and their relationships to the people they cover. Among the findings is that the interviews, stories, and photographs all have the potential either to add to the injury or to help in the recovery. To tell honest stories the journalist must know the basics of how violent acts and events affect people. We have written this book to support those who want to report about the victims of traumatic injury to help them and their communities in ways that do credit to journalism. We show how journalists can give the public vital information about calamities without further harm to the victims. The book is premised on the conviction that news can tie the victim and the public together constructively through the rigor of thoughtful reporting practices.

UBIQUITOUS MEDIA VIOLENCE

Nothing is at all novel about modern culture's addiction to violence and its fascination with victims. Tales of assaults, murders, rapes, robberies, earthquakes, and floods appear in the earliest surviving publications. The first newspapers in virtually every country told of human and natural violence as readily as they reported on affairs of state and commerce. The oldest-known preserved report of a current event in the Americas is a news booklet printed in Mexico City about a 1531 storm and earthquake in Guatemala. Early newspaper illustrations and, later, photography captured the sinister side of human nature along with its finer points.

That representations of violence have pursued humans through history leads to the speculation that horror—in art, stories, dramas, and plays—serves humans' struggle for survival, preparing our brains and bodies for the reality of a violent assault by another person or by nature.

But U.S. society and the media may have gone over the top in their preoccupation with violence. Violent acts abound in television programming—not just dramatic shows but also children's fare, talk shows, and, most critically, the news. Prime-time television offers five to six violent acts each hour. That rate is bad enough for adults, but the so-called children's programs are many times more violent.

Whatever the merit of any particular cultural depiction of violence, Americans have for decades been exposed to endless hours of television and movie violence and the echoes of it in other media, including newspapers, magazines, and recordings. Visually exciting media violence is a relatively new part of American culture yet already so ubiquitous that some people spend more time with it in a day than with any other single activity.

Depictions of violence may not be the gravest part of the problem. Careful studies of television programs, for example, affirm that violent acts occur in a context that is neither realistic nor informative. Indeed, the acts appear to be calculated to induce fear. Perpetrators are rarely captured or punished—the 1994–1995 *National Television Violence Study* (1997) says that those who commit violence in prime-time drama go unpunished most of the time, usually repeat their violence, typically rely on guns to maim and kill, and often act as though violence were a humorous action. Few programs offer any warnings about violence or any useful information about its consequences.

Television's portrayals of victims are just as unrealistic. In 58 percent of all violent interactions depicted on dramatic television, the study found, the victim did not experience any pain. In only 13 percent of the situations did the victim show moderate or extreme pain. Although the *National Television Violence Study* did not consider the traumatic aftermath of violence, researchers know that few, if any, depictions suggest how trauma has injured the person or how long a reasonable degree of recovery requires. The context, the study warns, is important because it tells people what to expect in violent interactions.

Television news commits many of the same errors. The emphasis is on crimes and events rather than punishment or other outcomes. The accused dominate the spotlight until the justice process ends. Victims and their survivors fade from view or remain marginal figures for both the justice system and the media. After Gary Ridgway pleaded guilty in 2003 to forty-eight counts of first-degree murder, ending a two-decade hunt for Washington State's "Green River killer," his victims' relatives had one chance—during the sentencing hearing—to speak about their travails.

Journalists too often trot out easy explanations or simplistic ironies to quickly summarize violent acts—small towns do not have murders, only poor parents abuse their children, immigrants kill because they cannot handle the fast-paced American culture, personal debts explain why people go berserk, a man killed himself because he was a war veteran. Journalism often lacks the patience to wait for a fairer explanation or the humility to say none is obvious.

At the same time the frantic rhythm of violence plays across television news and across the front sections of newspapers. The news industry scrambles to feed a system whose hunger for news and information is expanding at an extraordinary rate. Explosions in the number of cable channels and the capacity of the Internet to make every person, organization, and corporation a news provider offset the fairly stable numbers of newspapers, magazines, and television networks. As long-time news media and the upstart cable and Web services fight for attention, violence is the currency of the competition.

GIVING THE VICTIM "EQUAL SPACE"

Edna Buchanan, Pulitzer Prize winner and former *Miami Herald* crime reporter, is noted for vivid newspaper stories and books that depict vicious murderers and other assorted lawbreakers. As a reporter she sometimes went to great lengths to spotlight particular criminals in the hope of locating or bringing them to justice. She warns against the temptation to give too much exposure to criminals, no matter how intriguing they are. "Writers have to work at not glamorizing them. Crooks may be colorful, quotable, and even likable, but they are not nice people," she says. "When you tell their stories, it always helps to give the victims equal space" (1987:14).

It's no simple matter to give the victims equal space. Humane reporting does not simply call for equal time or column inches for victims in the news. It requires a new set of assumptions about the person who suffers trauma and new thinking about how to apply those ideas to the basic work of journalism. The most important of these is that the traumatized person has become a different person emotionally. If news practices take trauma into account, reporting their stories can help victims. That belief explains our commitment to teaching and writing about journalism and trauma. We do not contest the quest in the justice system and among mental-health specialists and journalists to know more about what drives some people to act violently. Half a century ago that interest drove journalists to focus on criminals to the nearly complete exclusion of those they killed or injured. We share Edna Buchanan's desire for fair reporting about victims and have planned this book as a practical guide to reporting about those who endure violence in any form.

BENEFITS FOR THE PUBLIC INTEREST

The public has a huge stake in the conflict between time-honored journalistic practices and new worries about people caught in the shock waves of disaster and violence. Better reporting about trauma can help readers and viewers gain empathy for the suffering of victims and enrich everyone's awareness of the powerful role that trauma plays in people's collective lives. The news does not often illustrate or explain Sandra Bloom's contention that trauma is the organizing idea of U.S. society. Yet so many public policy issues gain clarity when the reporting on them takes into account the implications of disasters, wars, and other kinds of human abuses.

The cutting edge of information about psychological trauma is the finding that it denies vital human values to those who suffer its effects. The immediate depredations (described in detail in chapter 1) of anxiety, unwanted memories, and numbness cost a person the vitality of life. Another devastating stage follows as the traumatized person moves into the margins and shadows of existence, unnoticed and little understood. If the ultimate benefit of the changes that we propose here is greater awareness of how others suffer from trauma, the public's renewed capacity to offer collective care and support will perhaps be the greatest public benefit.

In recent years public health officials have labeled violence as an epidemic that warrants the kind of response that has been marshaled against cancer, alcoholism, and HIV-AIDS. In 1993 the head of the federal Centers for Disease Control and Prevention told the *New York Times*: "Violence is the leading cause of lost life in this country today. If it's not a public-health problem, why are all those people dying from it?" (Stevens 1994:23). Violent deaths deserve and receive the greatest attention from people concerned about public health, but the costs of trauma also need massive attention. When reporters' work is informed by trauma, the public stands to learn about the epidemic, about those afflicted by trauma, and about those who find ways to cope with and minimize its abrasive assault.

ADDITIONAL ISSUES

This book identifies ways that journalists do—and can—act humanely toward victims while adhering to the traditional values of journalism. This guidance, we are well aware, may bump journalists up against contrary expectations about their work.

For example, approaching someone whose life has just shattered may lead a reporter to consider what some journalists still call an unthinkable option in journalism—"Should I not do this interview at all?" Most of this book is based on the premise that journalists will interview victims or family members, but we believe that sometimes contact is not justified. We think the choice not to interview or photograph is a fundamental one. Journalists should make that decision with care after initial contact with the person and after consulting with editors or coworkers. Concern for the traumatized person should sometimes lead the news organization to find an alternative approach to the assignment. In other words, if the journalist's actions are likely to harm the traumatized person, the reporter should back off. Not all such choices fall neatly on one side of the ethical divide. Some intrusions—or decisions not to intrude—plague the journalist long after. It is critical, though, that a deliberate decision replace a knee-jerk assumption that reporters must interview all victims, photographers must record all injured people, and pen and camera should capture all tears and screams.

When we make these points in conversations with reporters, we know almost to the word what we will hear next. "My editor told me to get that interview. How do I tell her that I just decided not to do it?" It's a fair question.

We answer in two ways. First, if all the news staff—editors, photographers, and reporters—learn about trauma and work out practical responses to the needs of those caught by the shock waves, editors, reporters, and photographers will face fewer such conflicts. But that won't help journalists today if they and their editors disagree about interviewing or photographing a victim. The burden is on the photographer or reporter to justify that decision in the field. This book offers a basis for decisions to leave someone alone as well as to interact sensitively. We are adding another obligation to the many that the journalist carries—the obligation to justify to oneself, to the editor, and to others a decision not to intrude in the suffering of others. This decision takes precedence over news value or competition because of a strong moral factor—the choice between preventing harm and causing harm. When the stakes are in the moral realm, personal integrity resides at the center of the decision.

Another matter often comes up when we talk to journalists about these ideas. Knowledge about trauma comes from psychology, psychiatry, and medical science and is applied in diagnosis and treatments by psychiatrists, other physicians, and therapists trained in psychology. Journalists are not physicians or therapists, they don't know the science that goes along with it, and they are not trained to see or draw out the symptoms of trauma. Journalists ask why they should think about trauma at all.

One doesn't have to attend medical school to be able to respect the suffering of another person. Empathy and sensitivity are human, not medical, traits. In addition, journalists can incorporate information about trauma in their work without invading the specialist's domain of diagnosis and treatment. Indeed, this book is an argument that reporter, victim, and public all will benefit from knowing more about trauma. No reporter would try to cover a World Series game without knowing baseball or try to explain a stock market rally without first studying finance and economics. Every beat in journalism demands special knowledge from the reporter. A crime reporter must be familiar with police blotters, snitches, arraignments, and plea bargaining. A government and politics reporter learns about caucuses, tax assessments, soft money, and polling. Sports broadcasters know about batting averages, first downs, dunk shots, hat tricks, and aces. Firefighters, police, and military personnel usually are not physicians, yet the application of trauma knowledge has transformed those vocations in recent years. The journalist can only do better work by learning about trauma.

Finally, we have heard the argument that some events are so cataclysmic, some people so well known, some situations so volatile that the public interest in knowing every detail will override even the best intentions to be sensitive to trauma victims. It may be tempting to invoke the "What a story!" side of journalism, that time when all bets are off, all rules are voided, and anything goes. What about violence against the president, scenes of massive destruction such as Americans saw on September 11, 2001, or moments captured by television and exposed instantly—without regard to individual sensitivities—to huge audiences? Such circumstances do not warrant ignoring the need for humane treatment of those in the story. We think that the public's interest in knowing about the event can generally be served along with due regard for the needs of people who have been harmed. The only certainty in such cases is that media competition will shape the outcome, making it more difficult to respect the needs of people caught in the middle. Yet the 9/11 news coverage yielded many, many examples of humane attention to victims and survivors.

Many journalists and their employers already have responded to the trauma crisis. Support, flowing from the public, some in the media, and the mental health professions, encourages such changes. An impressive momentum is behind this new regard for the ethics of covering violence.

As we prepared this book, we found many examples of excellent reporting of traumatic events and victims. We have incorporated many of them in these chapters and, in particular, in the profiles of nine journalists by John Harris, a talented journalist who teaches at Western Washington University in Bellingham, and Migael Scherer, a Seattle writer who for more than a decade taught journalism students at the University of Washington about trauma. Harris's and Scherer's profiles tap the values and experiences of these stellar reporters and photographers—Anh Do of the *Orange County Register,* David Handschuh of the *New York Daily News,* Jane Hansen of the *Atlanta Journal-Constitution,* Fletcher Johnson of ABC News, Debra McKinney of the *Anchorage Daily News,* Sonia Nazario of the *Los Angeles Times,* Scott North of the *Herald* of Everett, Washington, Sharon Schmickle of the *Minneapolis Star and Tribune,* and Marley Shebala of the *Navajo Times.*

A FINAL NOTE

Journalists routinely face and pass trying professional tests—writing or producing a story that will be read or viewed, making a photograph in an instant, and interviewing a person who is not prepared for the emotional stress of such contact. Although they make some mistakes, a huge corps of journalists regularly does its work with a high standard of ethical and professional excellence.

We have not written this book out of a sense of despair. Instead, we have written it with the confidence that the best work of skilled reporters, photographers, and editors can guide the efforts of others who are trying to report about violence. Since 9/11, we have witnessed a renewed commitment to sensitive, insightful reporting about trauma. We want to see more news that conveys in ethical words and images the experience of the people who suffer harm. We have been moved to write these chapters because so many journalists we know express the same hope.

SHARON SCHMICKLE

Finding Peace in Covering a War

Sharon Schmickle wasn't sure what she would write about when she arrived in Kuwait in February 2003. She was there as a war correspondent for the Minneapolis *Star Tribune*, but she'd never covered a war. Within weeks she was turning out gut-wrenching stories about the people caught up in the war's violence—soldiers and citizens, Americans and Iraqis, children and parents.

She wrote about a twenty-one-year-old marine who made his squad's first kill. He wasn't sure whether his victim was a soldier or a human shield, possibly a woman, and he couldn't sleep at night because he thought scorpions were biting him.

Sharon Schmickle.
Photo courtesy *Star Tribune*

She told about a two-year-old Iraqi boy whose lower legs had been blown off, presumably by a land mine, and about the U.S. military surgeons who worked doggedly, but in vain, to save his life.

She rode into Nassiriyah with marines who'd been assigned to search for human remains on a street where a bloody battle had raged the previous day. More than forty children gathered to watch as marines scraped human remains from a charred U.S. assault vehicle.

The subheads on a story that she wrote about the emotional toll of the war on U.S. soldiers could have summed up her first month in Iraq: *Reality Hits, Almost Surreal, "You Can't Complain."*

Schmickle, a grandmother of three and a veteran of more than twenty years as a journalist, had jumped at the chance to go to Iraq when her editors asked her. She offers two reasons. One, she says, was noble: "It's a fundamental duty of journalists in a democracy to cover government. I can't think of a more important time than when your government wages war." The other, she says, was less noble: "It's a big story, and reporters always want to get to the big story. There was a bit of professional pride there."

She prepared by training for a week in North Carolina with retired U.S. Army Special Forces soldiers, learning first aid and how to handle herself in dangerous settings. She researched Iraq and exchanged information with other journalists. She and the other *Star Tribune* reporters and photographers covering the war bought body armor from a police supply store.

That took care of the physical and intellectual preparation. She also needed to prepare herself emotionally. "I thought about it for about a month," she says. "I told myself, 'You must find some peace with this or you can't go.'" She thought about people whose work brings them into regular contact with pain and trauma—firefighters, police, nurses, and doctors. She considered the value of their contribution to society and drew inspiration from it. She would make her own contribution by going to Iraq and reporting on what was happening there. "Once I felt I had found some peace," she says, "I guess I was prepared."

Schmickle and photographer Mike Zerby initially worked independently of the military, but about a week before the invasion of Iraq they moved to a U.S. Marine camp in northern Kuwait. They were embedded with the First Marine Expeditionary Force and were assigned to a combat service support battalion. They worried that they would be too far from the action and begged the commanding officer to let them join troops in the first wave of the invasion. He relented, and she and Zerby hooked up with medical platoons whose mission was to provide frontline medicine. International law required that the medics also treat wounded Iraqis. Accompanying the medical platoons "seemed like our best chance at getting near the action and also getting a glimpse of both sides," she says.

Some embedded journalists complained that their circumstances limited their vision of the war, but Schmickle did not consider that a drawback. She reminded herself every day that what she was seeing was not necessarily going on elsewhere in Iraq. She determined to do the best job she could of reporting on what she was witnessing and to let her stories be tiles in the mosaic of the war's coverage. It was up to the editors and readers to make sense of the big picture.

She and Zerby camped in the desert about an hour's drive from Nassiriyah, which, as it turned out, was the site of some of most intense fighting of the early days of the invasion. Schmickle pitched her one-person tent beside a tent that was serving as an emergency room. Helicopters came and went throughout the night and day, dropping off wounded U.S. soldiers and Iraqis, and doctors alerted her when they expected an incoming chopper.

The situation allowed her to detail the effects of the war on a personal level, and poignantly. She interviewed a female marine whose duties included transporting and guarding wounded Iraqi prisoners of war. She told Schmickle about a teenage boy she had picked up with shrapnel in his face. He could not talk, but his eyes pleaded for help. Schmickle observed a Bedouin couple as navy surgeons treated their wounded sons. U.S. Marines had mistakenly fired on the boys as they chased after their sheep.

"I was in a position to see amazing detail," she says, "and certainly the human drama was the most important part of that detail."

In that sense her approach to reporting was no different in Iraq than it had been when she wrote about domestic violence in the 1980s. Back then, she had, in a sense, embedded herself with police, social workers, and others who were on the front lines of the story. She followed them into living rooms where a parent lay dying on the floor and children whimpered. She sat in courtrooms where juries wept at grisly testimony. The stories were about a broad social issue, but they always came back to the people affected by the violence. "It never quite leaves you," she says. "When I talk about it, when I think about it, it always gives me a chill. It gives me this burst of passion, and I'll call it anger too, about how we human beings live our lives. I don't think I'll ever shake that."

Schmickle cried at times in Iraq but drew inspiration from the other professionals around whom she was working—the marines who were preparing to go into battle or who were wounded, and the doctors and nurses treating them. "I became very tightly focused on my writing and reporting," she says. "I can't explain exactly what drives that or governs it. I didn't think about it; I automatically saw myself as the reporter whose job it was to gather as much information as I could and send it back home."

She returned to Minnesota at the end of April to resupply and regroup. Her laptop was full of sand and her satellite telephone was working sporadically. The *Tribune*'s top editors urged her and the others who had covered the war to seek counseling. Schmickle declined. "I'm not going to say I didn't need it. I will say I'm adjusting in a pretty healthy fashion," she says, adding with a laugh, "I sleep at night."

Schmickle says she left Iraq with the expectation that she would go back. A bout of pneumonia and an assignment to cover the Democratic primary race kept her home through the spring of 2004, but she held out hope that she would return. "The story isn't finished," she says. "The U.S. is the occupying force in another country. Our responsibility [as journalists] requires us to be there and see how our government conducts itself."

If and when she returns, she says, she will continue to cover the story as she did before, by showing how the war is affecting the people caught up in it.

A Little Boy, a Frantic Effort

SHARON SCHMICKLE

Sharon Schmickle's brief story about the determined, but unsuccessful, efforts of medics to save an Iraqi boy reflects her sense that covering the war required covering Iraqi civilians and combatants as well as U.S. troops. Her writing captures the critical details of the life-saving effort but also requires the reader to sense the emotions of the surgical team and the journalist watching them. This story was published in the Minneapolis Star Tribune on March 27, 2003.

CAMP VIPER, IRAQ—The small Iraqi boy was brought by helicopter to a military tent hospital Wednesday afternoon with his right foot missing and the leg mangled up to his knee. The other leg was too damaged to save.

The surgeons blamed a land mine, but it could have been some other form of ordnance. They didn't know for sure, just as they didn't know his name or who found and bandaged him and carried him to the medical helicopter that ferries battlefield casualties to this compound. It was the seventh such injury the surgeons had treated that day. Four arrived with legs missing.

"If this isn't a case for the abolishment of land mines, I've never seen one," said Navy Lt. Cmdr. David English, an orthopedic surgeon.

They guessed the boy on the table was 2 years old. He had enough fight left in him to push away their hands when they started treating him, but he was seriously dehydrated from blood loss.

The arrival of the plump-cheeked child clearly unnerved even the normally cool surgeons with the Navy's Forward Resuscitative Surgery System, who have seen more than their share of bodies mangled and bruised by weapons of war.

Within minutes of the boy's arrival, a 10-member surgical team was working feverishly over him. First, they finished the job the mine had made inevitable and cleanly severed what was left of his legs. Then they cleaned grime that the blast had embedded in his flesh.

Their job was all the more difficult because the operating room was designed for Marines, not toddlers.

"This is where we are going to get into trouble," someone muttered. "We don't have anything small enough for kids."

More trouble loomed. The child should have been evacuated immediately after the surgery to a pediatric hospital. But none of them within reach of the helicopters at hand would take him. The obvious choice was Kuwait, which has top-notch pediatric care. But Kuwait won't take any Iraqis, not even an innocent child.

"We may be able to save him, but we can't find any place to send him," said Julie Kellogg, a pediatrician who planned to care for the boy through the night in hopes a miracle would happen.

But Kellogg's duty proved to be shortlived.

Two hours after the operation, the child died.

CHAPTER 1

Trauma: Assault on an Essential Human System

For those who suffer violence, emotional trauma is a specific, devastating, and sometimes long-lasting wound. In this book we are not writing about the physical wounds that an emergency room might treat after an accident. Our interest is in the emotional wounds that may be related to a physical injury but that may also affect a person who has suffered no bodily wound. ERs do little for the emotional wounds that may afflict a person long after the broken bones or the internal organs heal. Emotional trauma is not confined to the single shock that comes with an assault. Some people suffer trauma from continuing attacks on their emotional stability.

Political prisoners and torture victims suffer trauma not from single acts but from months or years of having their sense of safety destroyed. A woman continually abused by a violent spouse and a child repeatedly exploited sexually will be trauma victims as well. The form of trauma that this book addresses is emotional injury, sometimes sudden and unexpected, sometimes taking place during a prolonged assault.

Reporters and photographers often are first responders—the first or among the first to arrive at an auto accident, house fire, shooting, or other violent event. Someone may be dead. Survivors may be bleeding, unconscious, or in shock. At other times reporters knock on doors weeks, months, or even years after an event. They may be covering a court action or following up on, say, the 9/11 anniversary. In all those cases the people with whom the reporter speaks may exhibit one or several of the many trauma symptoms.

It is also important that journalists know about and report about the innate ability of most people to endure traumatic conditions and continue their lives without lasting effects. Human beings are built to survive traumatic experience and remain whole. Relatively few suffer the most chronic form of emotional injury, but more are vulnerable to transient emotional pain. Knowledge and sensitivity are essential tools to counter the effects of trauma that may lead to depression and anxiety and abuse of drugs or alcohol or other attempts to stop the pain.

NATURAL DISASTER VERSUS HUMAN-CAUSED TRAUMA

Journalists certainly report on people who have been hurt in accidents and natural disasters such as tornadoes, hurricanes, and floods. Natural disasters may emotionally traumatize even those who survive them without physical injury. A person who watches a building collapse after an earthquake, hears injured people cry, or sees bodies of victims is likely to suffer from emotional trauma.

But what is even more traumatizing to many people is to be injured by a deliberate human act. In an accident or natural disaster, victims or their families and friends may find some comfort by telling themselves, "It's nothing personal. It just happened (perhaps to many others too). It wasn't my fault." A victim of violent crime usually sees it differently: "This was a deliberate attack on me personally—me! I'm angry. I'm bitter. I'm ashamed."

When a cockpit fire led to the crash that killed all 229 passengers and crew of Swissair flight 111 in Nova Scotia in 1998, surviving relatives and friends grieved. However, they did not suffer some of the pain felt by the loved ones of people aboard Pan Am flight 103 when terrorists blew the plane up over Lockerbie, Scotland, in 1988, murdering all aboard. The 1995 Oklahoma City bombing generated many of the same kinds of suffering that people would have experienced if the federal building had been destroyed by, say, an accidental natural gas explosion. But anger and bitterness characterized some survivors' reactions because the bombing was the work of terrorists, and homegrown ones at that.

WHEN JOHNNY CAME TRUDGING HOME

Journalists should not feel guilty if they fail to recognize and understand many aspects of trauma and victimization. Even psychologists and psychiatrists have only recently come to recognize, name, and devise specific treatments for what are believed to be the special after-effects of violence. Physicians traditionally were not taught to treat crime victims differently than accident victims. So it is not hard to understand why reporters working on deadline may not distinguish such differences or reflect an understanding of them in their interviewing and reporting.

Times are changing. Several trends combined to initiate a recognition of the need to understand victims' suffering and healing, according to Frank M. Ochberg, a psychiatrist who is the former director of the Michigan Department of Mental Health. He says that one factor was the end of the Vietnam War. The terms *shell shock* and *combat fatigue* have long been used to describe the lingering psychological effects of combat experiences. But during and after the ten-year U.S. involvement in the Vietnam War, many more returning veterans voiced such complaints.

Vietnam was a divisive war, and the United States did not win it. Veterans seldom got the public praise and respect accorded the victorious veterans of earlier wars. The Viet vets' arrival home by airplane within hours of leaving Vietnam also deprived them of the long cruise home that gave combatants of earlier wars time to swap tales and exchange experiences, ways of learning that what they were feeling or had seen or experienced was not unusual. And studies show that just talking about traumatic events relieves the symptoms of trauma. Moreover, some returnees encountered outright personal hostility. Although it may be a myth that many veterans actually were spat on at home, more than a few felt that way psychologically. "Many veterans suffered victimization syndromes," Ochberg says. "They were traumatized, and they felt like losers" (1987:12–13, 41).

For many veterans the lack of respect at home compounded a sense of betrayal at the hands of military leaders and services, according to Jonathan Shay, a psychiatrist who treats veterans' combat trauma. Negligent and irrelevant training, as well as such harmful policies as continually breaking up units, added to the psychological injuries of many veterans (Shay 1994:165–81).

Political terrorism also fostered new studies of trauma effects and new ways to treat the traumas of victims of terrorism. Since 1972 international terrorists have demonstrated a continuing fondness for this easy and especially disturbing form of warfare. The attacks on September 11, 2001, set off numerous studies of trauma among those close to victims, the first responders— including journalists—and those who worked at the attack sites in the ensuing weeks or months.

THE KEY CONTRIBUTIONS OF THE WOMEN'S MOVEMENT

Women's challenges to the medical establishment have contributed greatly to knowledge about trauma. Concerned and vocal women have forced male-dominated medical professions to recognize the specific and varied nature of rape trauma, reevaluate father-daughter incest, and to shelter battered women without stigmatizing them as mentally ill. In the early 1970s women moved from raising each other's consciousness through personal disclosure to shaping public and medical response through "speak-outs," research designed and carried out by women, and advocacy. The trauma syndrome that their efforts illuminated had striking similarities to that of the combat veterans. The consequences of the women's efforts were profound. Feminists helped establish a scientific basis for seeing rape as violence, not sex, and showed how it subordinated women through terror, the psychiatrist Judith Lewis Herman writes (1992:30). Studying rape in adults led women to see the unexamined tragedy of sexual abuse in children.

As experts have grasped the causes and effects of trauma, they have seen that it infects populations far beyond war combatants, rape survivors, and abused children. Those vulnerable to emotional trauma include refugees; torture victims; people caught in the devastation of natural disasters; political prisoners; individuals who endure severe poverty, prejudice, or oppression; people struck by technological disasters; and those caught up in war and genocide. A litany of such events as automobile and plane crashes, neighborhood riots, and apartment fires also belongs on the list. These events are the news media's stock-in-trade, and journalists can convey their meaning more clearly if they understand how trauma will affect those at the center, those first to experience the shock waves.

THE CRITICAL ROLE OF EMOTIONS

The journalist who would understand trauma must begin by learning about the powerful role that emotions play in people's lives. Journalist Daniel Goleman based his popular book, *Emotional Intelligence,* on the science of emotions. "All emotions are, in essence, impulses to act, the instant plans for handling life that evolution has instilled in us," he writes (1995:6). Emotions serve as the radar for both the human body and the confusing world around it, and they are central to humans' survival, psychiatrist Sandra Bloom explains (1997:44). Emotions register on people's faces and in their body language as they experience fear or pleasure. Emotional communication between baby and parent is critical to a child's development. Adults and children monitor each other's emotions constantly, even "catching" the hysteria of others or calming other aroused individuals. When people are threatened, their bodies provide an automatic heroic response, what is called the fight-or-flight response. Time and again this system saves lives.

The human emotional system—complex and resilient as it is—still can lose its balance and spin a person out of control. Judith Lewis Herman writes that some experiences "overwhelm the ordinary human adaptations to life." They threaten life or the body. "They confront human beings with the extremities of helplessness and terror, and evoke the responses of catastrophe" (1992:33). Emotions tell people when and how to act, but emotions sometimes convey the devastating message that a person cannot act. This makes a person the captive of horrible circumstances, and neither flight nor fighting back is possible. Then the emotional system itself may be torn apart or fragmented. Although the individual survives the assault, afterward that person's brain and emotional system will respond to life's challenges differently, and his body will not allow him to forget that he could not act. From that time on, he lives with the memory of an event that overwhelmed him.

Trauma injures its victims in several ways. It disables the early warning system—humans' survival radar. It confuses people because they can no longer keep the details of their lives in order. It not only inhibits the expression of some emotions but it may rob a person of the words she needs to talk about that loss. The injury may be more severe and costly in early childhood. "For children, every aspect of the self will be distorted and bent in the direction of the traumatic exposure," Bloom says (1997:72). People's ways of remembering change too, planting the traumatic experience deep in the brain. Sometimes the brain effectively suppresses those traumatic memories, but they may reach the survivor in horrifying nightmares or intrusive flashbacks to the event, a reliving that she actually "sees" but may struggle to translate into words.

POST-TRAUMATIC STRESS DISORDER AND ACUTE STRESS DISORDER

The medical profession has, quite logically, approached trauma in its most severe manifestation, the collection of symptoms that persistently troubles a person for a month or longer after a traumatic event. In looking at these long-lasting cases, psychiatrists gave the name post-traumatic stress disorder (PTSD) to the group of symptoms they observed: intrusive recollections, avoidance, and heightened anxiety. Even so, the formal diagnosis called PTSD originated only as recently as 1980. In 1994 the American Psychiatric Association added acute stress disorder to the official list of diagnoses, describing effects that last more than two days but not more than four weeks. A diagnosis of acute stress disorder is warranted when a trauma survivor has had three general PTSD reactions as well as several abnormal signs of dissociation (feelings of unreality or disconnection). PTSD and acute stress disorder are closely related conditions, almost indistinguishable to laypeople, except for timing.

HOW THE JOURNALIST ENCOUNTERS TRAUMA

Some people will act in stunningly inappropriate ways—separating the emotions of an event from other activities—which leads to the often reported anomaly of a "carnival-like atmosphere" at a scene of death or injury. Some observers will be amazingly focused on what happened, ready with the most minute details. Some people may be grieving or hysterical. Others may show no obvious sign of emotion. Police at a scene were "so shocked by what they found that they seemed to pass on [to others] their stress and dread," a reporter told us.

Writer Joan Deppa and her colleagues learned about an amazing range of responses from reporters who reached Lockerbie, Scotland, in the hours after the explosion in the air of Pan Am 103 killed its passengers, crew, and many people on the ground. Right after the crash many people spoke eagerly to reporters; over time more people became reticent and withdrawn. Some stories were incoherent and exaggerated, others tightly controlled. Reporters labeled some observers ghouls, folks who seemed to make an entertainment out of visiting the scene. Other residents were extraordinarily friendly and hospitable, repeatedly offering tea to the reporters. And a reporter found someone who saw the cockpit of the jetliner crash to the ground and bodies strapped in their seats. The young witness, who was "clearly haunted," readily told his story to a reporter whose emotions also were locked away (Deppa et al. 1993:69–99).

Reporters who work on such stories for days after the event may encounter people who display a range of responses, including not only disconnection from what is going on but self-destructive behaviors such as drinking, feelings of shame and hopelessness, fear of fairly familiar sights and sounds, and impaired relationships, as well the key indicators of long-term traumatic injury. Each person will present a unique array of responses. Reporters cannot make medical diagnoses of each subject, but they can be sensitive about their assumptions. The ghouls may be distancing themselves from the pain of the experience; the emotionless folks are not necessarily unaffected, and frenzied reactions often reflect more than excitement.

Finally, reporters are as likely to exhibit this range of responses as the people they encounter. At Lockerbie a reporter frustrated by his inability to get information from a press officer flew into a rage. Later he was able to tie his viewing of bodies on a hillside to his reaction (Deppa et al. 1993:76). In the presence of victims of traumatic injury, we argue, journalists must act in ways that acknowledge and respect the effects on victims—and on them.

PTSD

Emotional reactions to trauma have always been part of the human condition. That is why it is remarkable that an in-depth understanding of the emotions is relatively new and still developing. The term *post-traumatic stress disorder—PTSD*—often pops up now as journalists try to report medical explanations of the long-lasting traumatic effects of such events as the terror attacks on September 11, 2001, and the combat experience of military personnel in Iraq and Afghanistan. It is important for journalists to understand PTSD so they can alert their audiences to what trauma may be coming, as well as how to cope with what's already there. Journalists should keep in mind, though, that a PTSD diagnosis describes only the most serious effects of a traumatic event. Being alert to the spectrum of emotional injuries that do not constitute PTSD can enhance a journalist's reporting.

The basic PTSD diagnosis—revised by the American Psychiatric Association in 1988 and 1994—has three ingredients. All three reactions in this psychological witches' brew must be present at once and must be caused by an event that terrifies, horrifies, or renders someone helpless. Here's a distillation of the triad of PTSD responses:

- Recurrent and intrusive distressing recollections of an event
- Emotional numbing and constriction of normal activities
- A shift in the fear threshold, affecting sleep, concentration, and sense of security

In other words, the sufferers are so haunted by a terrible event that they cannot forget it. They are not mentally ill, even though victims sometimes erroneously think, "I must be going crazy." They aren't, but their lives are crippled.

By definition, a diagnosis of PTSD is not justified unless the three conditions last at least a month. It is understandable if, for example, a bank teller who is robbed at gunpoint feels frightened, angry, and nervous right afterward and for some time to come. It might even be a cause for concern if the teller did not seem to feel somewhat shaken for a while. But if three months later he is sleeping well, working normally, and not jumping or cringing at every loud noise, a reporter better not jump to the conclusion that the teller "had PTSD" after the holdup.

Indeed, journalists must take care in naming the diagnosis—PTSD—in stories about victims of violence. First, since a diagnosis of PTSD can come only from a trained professional, lay witnesses and even victims are not qualified to say that someone has PTSD. Second, since the PTSD label cannot apply unless the symptoms have continued for at least a month, no one can report immediately after a violent event that it caused anyone post-traumatic stress disorder. Third, a person diagnosed with PTSD has the same right to keep that information private as she would any medical condition. Disclosure should be the choice of the survivor, not the journalist.

Flashbacks

What especially distinguishes PTSD from more temporary effects is the first of the trio of conditions: recurring and unavoidable recollections. That is not just a lasting and unpleasant memory of a bad event but one that hits so often and so hard that the person cannot lead a normal life. Sometimes that recollection is so real that it is called a flashback, or a hallucination. The person repeatedly relives the event.

Flashbacks often are associated with combat veterans. A soldier wounded in combat may again see the shell exploding in front of him and hear the screams of a buddy killed at his side. In other types of trauma a woman may feel a rapist grabbing her; a man nearly killed by a drunken driver may "see" the car careening toward him again. In young children, psychiatrists say, the recurrence may take the form of playing out a frightening scene over and over—a boy repeatedly struck by his father may, in turn, pummel his teddy bear.

In some cases the trauma victim may not have such vivid images or perceptions in the daytime, but once the body tries to relax in sleep, the same terrifying dreams of the trauma erupt. On awakening the dreams may not quickly fade away but linger in the conscious memory.

The pain and sorrow someone suffers at the unexpected loss of a spouse or child may not be related to PTSD. As painful as such deaths are, psychiatrists do not put the responses into the PTSD category unless they are accompanied by haunting images of death. (And when death is expected and an individual can prepare for it, the emotional response usually is grief and not a symptom of trauma.)

All memories related to traumatic injury are not created equal. They also are not all signs of PTSD. A memory of seeing a loved one die in a drive-by shooting may be very painful, but it clearly remains just that, a memory, not a terrifying reenactment. Relating the painful memory under the right conditions can even help the eyewitness to reduce and eventually master the pain. Volunteers from the Michigan Victim Alliance tell Michigan State University journalism classes that retelling their stories to sympathetic listeners does help victims to heal. When a loved one dies violently and relatives are not present, the mind drives the person's survivors to imagine how death came. In the days after the suicide of his wife, psychiatrist Edward K. Rynearson writes, he could not help but imagine the last moments of her life. In time, he found the capacity to disengage from the imagined details of her death to a retelling that reflected how he had been changed by the loss (2001:3–11).

Numbing the Pain

PTSD also is marked by emotional numbing and avoidance. Psychiatrists say that it is as if the person's mind decides, "My memories are so terrible that I'm shutting down so I won't be overwhelmed." That may give human sufferers some protection but at the cost of robbing them of joy, love, and hope, says psychiatrist Ochberg. He tells of a national PTSD research project in which he interviewed Vietnam War veterans decades after their service. They didn't necessarily look sad or gloomy, "just incapable of delight." Furthermore, Ochberg explains: "They no longer participated in activities that used to be fulfilling. Why bowl or ride horses or climb mountains when the feeling of fun is gone? Some marriages survived, dutiful contracts of cohabitation, but devoid of intimacy and without the shared pride of watching children flourish—even when the children were flourishing" (1996:21).

Avoidance is a symptom of PTSD, although therapists caution that it may not continue for so long that a formal diagnosis of PTSD is warranted. Most survivors of trauma will avoid reminders and change their usual patterns for a while to prevent unpleasant recollections from surfacing. The key phrase is "for a while." Ex-hostages from a notorious train hijacking in the Netherlands avoided all trains for weeks, Ochberg says. Some avoided only the particular train on which they were hijacked. Others took that train but changed to a bus for the few miles near the site of the trauma. Most of these people gradually worked their way out of such mind maneuvers and resumed their former travel habits (Ochberg 1996:21).

Numbing and avoidance, then, can help someone up to a point. The concern in PTSD is that this aspect becomes a serious obstacle to recovery. A journalist interviewing a survivor may find that the person still is affected months or years after the violence happened. A man who seems calm, even casual and unconcerned, during an interview about the drive-by shooting death of his son may in fact be numb—and may have lost his wife, friends, and job as a result. The caveat for the reporter here is not to underestimate the effect of the trauma on the person involved, as the impact may well not be readily apparent.

William Coté wishes he had understood the numbing aspect of trauma when, as a fledgling police reporter for a small Michigan daily, he covered the preliminary hearing of three youths suspected in the knifing death of another teenager. Two of the youths and some of their family members and those of the victim were agitated, crying, or cursing. One youth and some relatives were so quiet and calm that they could have been at a hearing for a mere parking ticket. Cries of joy and, from the victim's family, of disbelief erupted when the judge found insufficient evidence to hold one youth over for trial. That young man, the quiet suspect, was released and—with shaking hands—lit a cigarette out in the hallway. Relatives who had been calm began sobbing with relief. They were not so cool after all. Relatives of the dead teenager variously continued to cry, swear, or look blank.

When the two other youths appeared at trial on murder charges several months later, Coté was a bit perplexed to observe similar behavior in the courtroom; even after a lengthy time, some people on both the victim's and defendants' sides appeared amazingly composed. Others sometimes had to be warned by the judge to quiet down or be expelled from the courtroom. One defendant finally was convicted, the other acquitted. If Coté had understood then what he knows now about trauma and victimization, he would have tried to go beyond the hard news story. How were the family members of the victim and the defendants really coping? Were they suffering more than some appeared to be? Was anybody helping them? If so, how?

Detecting such invisible trauma can be even more difficult in a telephone interview than in person. A former *Lansing (Mich.) State Journal* editor recalls assigning a reporter to call the father of a murdered child whose body had just been recovered: "The father seemed fairly calm and willing to answer our questions about his child and the murder. Yet, when the story appeared in the next morning's paper, he called, very angry, and demanded to know where we'd gotten the information and comments. He'd been in such shock the day before that he literally didn't remember even talking to the reporter, much less what was said." Reporters do well to expect that either immediate shock or persistent trauma can suppress memories.

The numbing aspect of PTSD includes forgetting with a vengeance, as well as memories that cannot be suppressed. Called *psychogenic amnesia,* this kind of forgetting originates in the mind or in mental or emotional conflict, rather than from physical injury. In this situation the sufferer does not forget the horrible details of the bad experience but cannot remember all of what happened. In fact, the missing pieces lie beneath the protective cloak of forgetfulness, too terrible or painful to be exposed to the daylight of consciousness.

High Alert

The final PTSD ingredient is a physical, not emotional, condition. Caused by the mental trauma, it takes the form of greatly aroused bodily reactions and gives new meaning to the term *jumpy.* The person shudders or jumps at unexpected noises, not necessarily those that are similar to noises that occurred during the original trauma. Apparently, the body's normal alarm mechanism is on a hair trigger, set off by things that really are not dangers. Consider, for instance, a classroom where a professor is lecturing when a student accidentally drops a book on the floor, causing a sharp bang. Most students will check where the sound came from, determine it is a harmless action, and, the instructor hopes, refocus on the lecture. Someone with PTSD, though, may be so shaken by the noise that concentrating or taking notes is impossible. Carried to extremes, that sensitivity can set off so many false alarms that the person cannot concentrate or sleep restfully and is irritable or withdrawn. The ability to enjoy intimacy may fade, making a normal sex life difficult.

One of the scariest variations of the heightened startle response is the panic attack. In this case, though, no loud noise or other obvious trigger is evident. The person simply has a sudden, overwhelming feeling of fear or dread. It may feel and look much like a heart attack: dizziness, light-headedness, perhaps a sensation of choking or smothering.

Coté witnessed those signs when he was working with a volunteer group that was serving coffee and donuts to weary travelers at a freeway rest stop during a summer holiday weekend. A young man approached from a car and asked in a trembling voice whether someone could call an ambulance for him. He was shaking, wobbly on his feet, and said he was cold even though he was sweating. "I think it's a panic attack," he said. "I've had them before, but I'm out of medicine in the car and I feel so terrible." Someone called an ambulance. He was given a blanket and a place to lie down while volunteers comforted him. He returned several hours later, after treatment at a nearby hospital, and continued on his journey.

Actually, the young man did better than many panic sufferers. A comparative few are so afraid of having an attack that they will not even leave their houses, much less set off alone on lengthy highway trips. A larger number avoid supermarkets, church services, and theaters so they will not be embarrassed if they have an attack.

People Who Can and Cannot Cope

Some experienced journalists may wonder why one person they interviewed appeared to have obvious trauma symptoms while another victim of the same event did not. In other words, is one person more vulnerable to such trauma than another? Researchers who wondered about such situations framed a definition of coping long before the American Psychiatric Association defined PTSD. Copers, the researchers observed, are likely to be people who achieve four goals when they face major life disruptions and transitions. They successfully accomplish necessary tasks, maintain relationships with significant others, preserve their self-esteem, and keep their anxiety within tolerable limits.

The study examined many groups of people for their coping abilities, including students who were adapting to out-of-town colleges, children entering puberty, and soldiers with third-degree (the most serious) burns at an army hospital. Some of those who coped the best were not necessarily those who faced up to their problems with the most realistic expectations. Instead, they sometimes denied the injury, fantasized, or used their imaginations to focus on other things during the trauma. For instance, soldiers with burns over 50 percent of their bodies had a better rate of survival when they denied to themselves that they would be disfigured and have a painful recovery than when they recognized grim reality early on. They eventually accepted the seriousness of their injuries, but the delay somehow gave their bodies time to start physical healing.

Similarly, Ochberg cites interviews he had with two employees of the U.S. Information Agency six months after they were released from eighteen months of isolated captivity by terrorists near Lebanon. "The one who coped occupied his mind in captivity by visualizing the designs for a house, down to the last detail," Ochberg told us. "And he categorized favorite restaurants, anticipating future menus. He exercised and kept his spirits up. I recall our conversation as pleasant for both of us."

The interview with the second man was very different, Ochberg recalls. "This man spoke guardedly, fearing foreign agents would overhear. He had no sense of humor and smoked nervously. During captivity he counted bricks in his cell and paced. He had no way of occupying his mind." The terrorists treated the two men equally and released them the same week. One celebrated his freedom. The other still felt chained by memories and fears. The one who did cope used denial of danger, imagination, and positive thinking to pull him through the ordeal.

Born for PTSD?

Why do some people cope so well with trauma and others do not? Nobody knows. Not for sure, anyway. Most current research shows that the more intense and lasting a traumatic event is, the more likely it is to cause PTSD. That does not seem surprising, but people exposed to the same injury or horror will vary greatly in their response. One speculation from therapists is—to use an old saying—that people should choose their parents and grandparents very carefully. In other words, heredity may play as important a role in traumatic injury as it does in the propensity to many physical diseases.

Some children are born shy and some are born with a bolder temperament. Similarly, some people are born with a brain pattern that keeps horror alive, whereas others have a brain pattern that allows them to recover quickly. That is not necessarily a bad thing, Ochberg offers: "As a varied, interdependent human species, we benefit from our differences. Those with daring fight the tigers. Those with PTSD preserve the impact of cruelty for the rest of us" (1996:22).

Continuing studies of trauma are trying to determine why people cope so differently with the same set of circumstances. One idea under study is that coping successfully with minor traumas in childhood protects against major psychological attacks later in life. Other theories about what helps feed or ward off PTSD emphasize the presence or absence of social supports, sustaining religious and spiritual beliefs, use of drugs and alcohol, simultaneous physical and emotional disorders, and the age of the trauma survivor.

OTHER RESPONSES

In addition to being aware of PTSD and related disorders, journalists should have some knowledge of other emotional conditions that are not listed in the official psychiatric diagnostic manual. We have already touched on one—shame—and it deserves some more attention because of its prominent place in the lives of victims of human cruelty. As we mentioned earlier, trauma survivors often feel shame. At first glance that seems backward. Shouldn't it be the attackers who feel shame? Yes, but they rarely do. Instead, the people who have been shot, robbed, or raped often feel ashamed. They may even feel ashamed of feeling ashamed. The shame triggered when people see themselves as helpless, weak, or incapable can itself scramble their thinking abilities, a serious condition that psychiatrist D. L. Nathanson (1997) calls "cognitive shock."

Survivors' understandable anger at their attackers often quickly turns into blaming themselves. Why didn't I see it coming? Why didn't I defend myself better? Why didn't I stop them somehow? How could I let such a thing happen to me (or to my partner or child)? Such reactions may seem reasonable, but if they are carried too far, long, and deeply, they can eat into a person and cause serious depression.

Another powerful emotion is anger. Again, people can easily understand why the victim would be angry, although often the victim's parent or spouse is most angry and after revenge. They can be considered victims as well. Take the situation of the Andersons of Michigan. Dan Anderson was shot by a prowler, nearly died, and has since endured more than thirty surgeries. Still, he tells journalism students that he has forgiven his attacker (who never asked for forgiveness during the trial or while in prison since). "I've never ever felt anger toward my attacker; I still don't," he says twenty years later. Anderson says the shooting "completely turned my life around" by deepening his religious faith and concern for others. He sometimes worries that he might have intended to hit the prowler with a flashlight just before the man shot him. But now listen to Pat Anderson, normally a gentle woman: "Dan's more forgiving than I am. I can't do that, not yet anyway. I'm working on it, but I'm still angry."

Anger can be turned into constructive actions. Many of us know of someone who has started or joined a campaign to wipe out a deadly disease after losing a loved one to the ailment. Perhaps for similar reasons, relatives and friends seek ways to find and punish a perpetrator and, often, to bring to justice other similar attackers.

MADD (Mothers Against Drunk Driving) has led fights in several states to toughen penalties for driving while under the influence of alcohol or drugs. A Massachusetts father whose young son was abducted and murdered hosted a national television series devoted to capturing criminals in unsolved crimes. Family members and friends of four Michigan women murdered by a confessed serial killer formed an organization that worked successfully to find ways to keep him from being paroled. The group also helped get state legislation that bars the early release of inmates for good behavior.

Journalists need to be able to recognize signs of anger or shame because those emotions may greatly color how a victim reacts during an interview, especially in the hours and days after a traumatic event. The interviewee may displace anger from the prime target, the attacker, onto the immediate and convenient target—the reporter or photographer. Similarly, any question or comment that implies that the survivor should have acted differently may turn underlying shame into anger directed very specifically at the journalist.

Having said that, some psychiatrists and psychologists caution that reporters should not necessarily stop an interview because someone is crying or appears to be angry. The journalist might hand the person a tissue or turn off a recorder or camera for a while; if the person wants to continue, the reporter should respect that decision and the individual's desire to have the story told. Trauma victims often feel hopeless, hostile, withdrawn, threatened, ineffective, or powerless. A thoughtful, accepting interview at the right time may help survivors regain some sense of security, control, balance, and power in their jumbled lives. Letting survivors choose how they talk about their experiences is a great prescription, many mental-health experts agree—one way journalists can aid trauma sufferers.

THE STOCKHOLM SYNDROME

Many trauma reactions noted here at least seem plausible. Many people, however, have difficulty understanding how a victim can express friendship, affection, or even love for an attacker or kidnapper. That response is called the *Stockholm syndrome.* The term comes from a robbery in Sweden in 1973 during which the hostage taker and a bank teller fell in love and had sex in the bank vault during the siege.

TINCTURE OF TIME

Many things can help people recover from trauma, and one of the best medicines often simply is time, experts say. After a natural disaster people begin to feel like their old selves in six to eighteen months, according to Dr. Bruce Hiley-Young of the U.S. Veterans Administration's National Center for Post-traumatic Stress Disorder in Palo Alto, California. Recovery is likely to take longer, however, when crime is the cause, cautioned Hiley-Young in an interview by the *Daily Oklahoman* (Painter 1995:8); Hiley-Young advised state health officials after the Oklahoma City bombing. The anger, frustration, and loss of the feeling of security that result from deliberate violence often complicate and lengthen the healing process. Many times, Hiley-Young said, survivors benefit from learning what to expect by talking with other victims or trained professionals. Just learning that others have similar reactions can help victims.

Journalists can help in the recovery process by pacing their actions to the expectations of the injured person. That may include carefully explaining your intentions, pausing when the interview terrain gets too rocky, regulating your physical movements and space so the other person is not threatened, and by seeing the story as an element in the recovery process that could be either harmful or helpful.

One Survivor's Responses

Seldom does one person's experience encompass the wide range of trauma reactions that we have described. One survivor's story, though, may be helpful because it does reflect several emotional responses common to victims. The person happens to be a journalist. Bruce Shapiro, then a contributing editor of the *Nation* magazine, was among seven people stabbed and seriously wounded when a deranged man attacked customers and employees—all strangers to the attacker—in and outside a coffee bar in New Haven, Connecticut.

The man's two lunges with a hunting knife into Shapiro's back and chest caused pain that "ran over me like an express train," leaving him screaming on a sidewalk (1995:446). Police and emergency medics arrived quickly, summoned by bystanders, but at the time Shapiro thought no one was trying to help him. "I was really aware of just wanting people to help me," he told us. "I was feeling quite frightened. People didn't seem to be there for me. . . . I really perceived these bystanders as not having acted in my behalf."

In an article in the *Nation* Shapiro explains his response this way: "For weeks I thought obsessively and angrily of those minutes on Audubon Street, when first the nameless woman in the window and then the security guard refused to approach me—as if I, wounded and helpless, were the dangerous one" (1995:449). However, the woman had called police, and a few minutes later the guard helped police chase down the assailant. As Shapiro was loaded into an ambulance, he told us, "My heart was going a mile a minute and I was aware

I was in a lot of pain. I described to them what I thought had happened. I also was just trying to understand myself what had happened. I kept asking them, 'Just tell me where we're going; what happens next?'"

Shapiro's reaction to the reporters who interviewed him or tried to in the next few days helps journalists to understand early traumatic reactions of assault victims. On the first day after his life-saving surgery, he felt very weak and turned aside two interview requests from newspaper and television reporters. It was too soon, and he did not sense that either reporter truly was concerned about him personally. Two days later he did give an interview to another local reporter he knew. "His first concern was human," he told us. "It made all the difference, especially when he said beforehand that if I decided after the interview that I didn't want any of it to run, it wouldn't."

Details in other interview stories struck him as callous in some cases and careless in others. One that published the names and addresses of the victims "just invited potential burglars to come and steal from their houses while they were hospitalized," he said. He was upset by the coverage of two friends who, sent home to recover, were ambushed by a television crew as they left their physician's office. Like many victims, he was angered by errors in the stories. Although he was single at the time, a *New York Times* reporter "even invented a wife for me." Shapiro told us that "it seemed more humorous later, but I was very irritated at the time."

Over time, Shapiro placed the press coverage in the context of his emotional injuries and ways of coping. The anger he mentions was part and parcel of the trauma he endured. The triggers for some of that anger were provided by journalists through carelessness or ignorance of the likely effects of their work. "Such press coverage inspired in all of us a rage it is impossible to convey," Shapiro writes. "To the victim of violent crime the press may reinforce the perception that the world is an uncomprehending and dangerous place" (1995:450). He also recognizes the frequent association of violence with anger and actions calculated to reap revenge. A better answer, he argues, is to strengthen the emergency agencies that saved his life and sheltered him from greater injury within moments of the assault.

THE HUMAN FAMILY

Journalists may be able to help in some ways, but they should not be expected to act like psychologists, psychiatrists, or social workers. That is not their job,

even if they have the necessary training. What journalists can do is learn enough about trauma to understand what people may feel when subjected to traumatic circumstances. As more becomes known about the effects of violence, both medical and journalism professionals can use that information to enhance their traditional skills and values.

If journalists treat victims of human cruelty with respect and informed attention, they can ease the effects and channel them into pursuits that are constructive for the victims and everyone the media cover. Journalists should recognize that they are part of the human family and that social support may boost someone's psychological and perhaps even physical recovery from severe stress. In that way journalists may help victims become something different, as envisioned in the "Survivor's Psalm" by Frank Ochberg:

I have been victimized.
I was in a fight that was not a fair fight.
I did not ask for the fight. I lost.
There is no shame in losing such fights.
I have reached the state of survivor and
am no longer a slave of victim status.
I look back with sadness rather than hate.
I look forward with hope rather than despair.
I may never forget,
but I need not constantly remember.
I was a victim.
I am a survivor.

(1993:782)

CHAPTER 2

The Journalist: At Risk for Trauma

Journalists can suffer trauma simply by doing their work—by visiting scenes of destruction, and talking to, and photographing, people who have been injured or traumatized. Sometimes journalists feel the effects after seeing dead and injured people and the debris of deadly events. In other cases, by hearing tragic stories and by trying to ease the pain of others, journalists join disaster workers and others who experience what therapists call *compassion fatigue,* the result of absorbing information about the suffering of others. Not all reporters and photographers are affected by covering traumatic events; the kind of exposure and traits of the person are variables that can mean that some journalists are scarcely affected, if at all, whereas others may experience trauma symptoms.

A few years ago we sometimes encountered skeptical editors and even reporters who doubted that our interest in emotionally healthy journalists matched the reality of their workplaces. Some believed that journalists suffer little more than momentary effects from doing stories about violence, if they are affected at all. They believed that all but a few journalists—those who are already troubled—manage to cover the most trying assignments with professional polish and immunity to emotional shock.

Although the number of doubters has declined in recent years, we still hear these comments and see these assumptions expressed in journalism textbooks that treat violence only as a category of assignment, not as work that might harm the journalist. And we learn about callous editors who have sent reporters into violent situations without training, adequate backup, or later attention to the journalist's emotional needs. Similarly, novice journalists on college campuses are too often exposed to searing events in the name of getting them early experience. This chapter challenges those conventions and shows how recent research requires new ways of supporting journalists who cover violence.

HOW DO TRAUMATIC EVENTS AFFECT JOURNALISTS?

Journalists talk about detachment, focus, being desensitized, being in control. A few actually use the word *compartmentalize*. They echo the words of a famed World War II correspondent, Marguerite Higgins, who reported from the newly liberated German death camp at Buchenwald in 1945. Years later she wrote a memoir in which she talked about feeling no emotion on seeing the dead and dying at the concentration camp. "My condemnation and disgust were of the mind. And I believe that [it] is generally true that a journalist covering a war, a train wreck, a concentration camp, or some other disaster, tends to compartmentalize his emotions and isolate them from professional reactions. He feels no more personal involvement than does a surgeon performing a delicate operation or a regimental commander ordering a comrade into battle" (1955:76). As she ended the memoir, however, Higgins wrote that the death of someone close to her had helped her understand that her efforts at suppressing her emotions had in fact buried her natural compassion for those she saw.

Consider how Peter Maass, a *Washington Post* correspondent who covered the war in Bosnia in the early 1990s, talks about his work in *Love Thy Neighbor*, a book about the war published in 1996. Maass captures powerfully the plight of people he covered: "Refugees who saw friends or family members killed or raped—they exposed their brains to the radiation of tragedy. . . . They would wake up at night screaming and shaking, or they would not wake up at all, because they could not sleep. These people were haunted by a war that was inside of them, lodged somewhere in their brains in a spot that a knife could not get to, nor the soothing words of a best friend" (103–104). And then Maass invokes the argument about the journalist's compartmentalization and promptly contradicts it. "Journalists rarely overdose on tragedy," he declares, before writing that he could not clear his head of his dreams, even on breaks to London or Budapest. "I could spend two weeks in London and still, every night, I would dream of Bosnia. It was inescapable" (104). He was relieved to find that the commander of the first British troops in Bosnia also had such dreams.

Other combat correspondents and photographers tell of such effects. Bob Gassaway, who covered the Vietnam War in the 1960s for the Associated Press, wrote in the late 1980s that the war's effects still pursued him. Still startled by helicopters and car backfires, he resolved to avoid fireworks displays on the Fourth of July: "The bright lights and the loud noises are too real for me" (1989:348).

When an entire newsroom is hit by the shock waves, as was the staff of the *Daily Oklahoman* (now known as the *Oklahoman*) after the 1995 bombing of the Alfred P. Murrah Federal Building in Oklahoma City, the strain is noticeable. Charlotte Aiken, then a reporter at the newspaper, wrote in 1996: "In the past year, throughout the newsroom, personal relationships have been shaken or ended. Eating disorders and other emotional problems have developed. Use of sick time has skyrocketed" (31). Although the newspaper's management quickly brought in a counselor to help the reporters, only a few women reporters responded. Most of the men, including the editors who "experienced the same fatigue and tension reporters had," stayed away from counseling. Aiken recoiled from the steady need to do stories about the bombing. "I began to dread the endless bombing stories that we wrote every day for an entire year. Enough was enough. Every time I wrote something, I heard that woman screaming for her dead babies" (31). Too often, reporters, photographers, and editors are asked to recall that day and recount their place in its coverage. Invariably, some have intrusive memories and sleep restlessly afterward.

The bombing in Oklahoma City, the war in Bosnia, the Iraq war, and the attacks of 9/11 were profoundly troubling events. But tragedies in small towns also deeply affect journalists. Virtually every news staff, no matter the size of its community, at some time faces an event that severely taxes its members. A newspaper reporter who had covered crime news for a decade witnessed the fatal shooting of a drug suspect by police officers. "I saw the body moments after he had been shot, the legs dangling there, and I saw the shocked look on the cops' faces," the reporter recalls. His presence at the shooting required his testimony at the inquest. "Somehow you feel responsible. You are this man's last living witness on Earth," the reporter says. Within weeks he began to suffer sleeplessness and found himself responding angrily to coworkers and friends. "I became irritable. I began waking up at three or four in the morning for no explicable reason." As he showed signs of depression as he worked his beat at police headquarters, officers commented that the reporter was acting like any officer who had been involved in a shooting. "Why don't you see the police psychologist?" one officer suggested. His editors had not suggested that the reporter talk to a counselor.

Few reporters actually witness a fatal shooting. Immersion in a drawn-out story about death, though, may cause responses similar to those of the police reporter. Ginger Casey, a Providence, Rhode Island, television anchor and writer, writes about covering a series of child killings in Los Angeles some years ago: "I couldn't understand why I found myself a few weeks later unable to get out of bed, sleeping 12 hours a day. In my dreams, I kept seeing those tiny faces, even though I did the 'professional' thing and showed up for work every day, ready to deliver my reports without a shred of emotion. I didn't want my boss to know these stories were ripping my heart out, lest she think I wasn't up to being a 'real' reporter" (1994:38).

Other reporters who cover crime have described in print their drift from excitement to dull routine. Mark Pinsky, a *Los Angeles Times* reporter, writes that his career as a journalist began with bracing investigations in local courthouses in the southeastern United States. His reward, he says, was rescuing people who were suffering injustice. Later, his preoccupation with trials led to exhausting coverage of murder cases and, in time, a resolve to give it up. A job offer from the *Times* put him back into courtrooms for a long period. "Four days a week I listened to testimony, looked at evidence, and interviewed tearful parents and siblings after the verdicts. On Fridays, sentencing days, I listened as friends and relatives of the slain and maimed told the judge why murderers should be executed or sent to prison forever. Gloom turned to depression. Sleeping became difficult. My home life was affected" (1993:29). Pinsky points to the source of his stress: "If you protect yourself too much by screening out the unpleasantness, you cheat the reader by failing to convey the horror, which is, after all, your job. On the other hand, if you allow yourself to absorb the reality of what you see and hear, you run the risk of destroying yourself emotionally" (29).

Finding the right balance is difficult, as Pinsky says. One of my colleagues left television news reporting in the late 1960s after covering two major murder cases; until recently, she had not linked her urgent request to her employers to transfer her out of news to the experience of being at the scene in both cases. Now it is clear that reporters, like the rest of humanity, risk traumatic wounds from what they see and hear.

WHAT RESEARCH SHOWS

Although journalists' stories about trauma symptoms are numerous, little systematic study of such effects had been done before the late 1990s. The only research published before 1999 studied fifteen journalists who witnessed a gas chamber execution of a murderer in California in 1992 (Freinkel, Koopman, and Spiegel 1994). The research argues that traumatic effects appear in those who observe violence, such as the journalists, as well as in direct victims of violence. Although the executions were an official act, socially sanctioned, the journalists were not immune to its short-term effects and had no special shield against emotional pain. The lesson for journalists is that while they may think that by concentrating on taking the pictures, getting the facts, or interviewing victims they are escaping the shock waves, some of them will be wrong.

That study covered only a few journalists and wasn't concerned with lasting effects of exposure to violence. The next question asked—one that had never been studied—was whether the journalists who toil in local newsrooms bear residual effects from exposure to violence throughout their careers. While a few people in newsrooms may never report on a violent incident, a high percentage of journalists have seen violence and its effects. Eight-six percent of the newspaper reporters surveyed in one study had covered one or more violent events at the scene (Simpson and Boggs 1999:10). A later study of photojournalists found that 98.4 percent had covered an event in which people were hurt or killed (Newman, Simpson, and Handschuh 2003:9). The exposure to violence is high. How are journalists affected by being close to the causes of emotional injury?

Boggs and I surveyed 130 newspaper reporters, editors, and photographers in several newspapers in Michigan and Washington State in 1996. Editors were included because they often have had extensive reporting experience. The group of journalists disclosed a level of symptoms similar to that found among public safety workers recently engaged in a traumatic event (Simpson and Boggs 1999). Other important findings emerged from the survey. The longer people had worked as journalists, the more likely they were to report trauma symptoms. This was true of intrusion symptoms, such as unwanted recollections, as well as avoidance mechanisms associated with trauma.

One type of assignment was often linked to trauma symptoms. Judging from our experience and that of recent graduates who give us feedback, it is not unusual for cub reporters to be sent to the scene of a fatal highway accident. In that survey that I conducted with Boggs, journalists who had gone to crash scenes were likely to report intrusive recollections, in some cases long after the event. Survey respondents offered vivid and detailed accounts of those crashes, some many years and even decades earlier, underlining the power of such events to produce recurring memories over a long period. One reporter said that thirty years later he still sees the image of the dead victims in the car, and another described victims in the road and in the car on a "very cold and windy night" while long lines of cars detoured slowly around the crash. Another remembered the smells of a crash scene. A photographer called his picture of a man who was holding his injured girlfriend in an ambulance "a touching moment, a callous shot." Another recalled "the awesome violence of an auto crash, the blood trails of victims who later died, the scalp left behind by the ambulance crew, the un-eaten box of donuts in one car, the half-finished bottle of vodka in the other." The reporters and photographers had covered many tough assignments, includ-ing fatal fires, airplane crashes, and even a deadly charge by a circus elephant, but the auto crash was mentioned most often. Although the fatal auto crash is a common assignment, it is not a benign one for many reporters and photogra-phers who witness its results.

We are convinced that news reporters are at some risk of trauma symptoms as early as their first violent assignment. Research suggests that continuing to cover such stories without dealing with the symptoms may affect the reporter adversely. Friends, relatives, and coworkers will find themselves absorbing the fallout. The survey asked reporters in the two states what they had observed about the behavior of others in their newsrooms.

The reporters said they notice friends who anger quickly or develop and sus-tain irritable personalities. Others show sadness, occasional crying, and what coworkers take to be depression. Anxiety and nervousness appear in others. Some reporters see or learn about excessive smoking or drinking and link those behaviors to the stresses of the job.

How do journalists cope with such stress? Some use drugs, alcohol, or to-bacco, while others give in to anger and anxiety. Their answers, though, also provided more helpful remedies. Some newspeople isolated themselves until they could work more confidently. Conversations with friends, at lunch or after hours, helped some. Talking about hard stories was the remedy they mentioned most often. A few others were known to take long walks, listen to music, pray, and share their job stresses with their families.

The symptoms that journalists report may be related to the general stress of their work, but they also may reflect exposure to scenes and images of personal suffering that threaten the emotional stability of the reporter. Of course, rarely would the emotional effects be diagnosed medically as a trauma disorder, but a high level of symptoms can nevertheless be damaging to health and productivity.

News photographers get closer to death and grief than most other journal-ists. A 2003 study asked how photojournalists are affected by their work. Mem-bers of the National Press Photographers Association answered a survey about their work experience, personal exposure to violent events, and the support they get from their employers. The percentage of those 875 respondents with indica-tors of chronic traumatic stress roughly matched the estimated lifetime preva-lence of PTSD in the general population, among men of 5 percent and among women of 7.8 percent (Kessler et al. 1995). The factors that increased the risk of

PTSD included the number of traumatic events covered, personal trauma history, and degree of social support. The life experiences most likely to put the photographers at risk for PTSD included sexual coercion or attempted sexual assault, sexual abuse as a child, kidnapping, domestic violence, physical abuse as a child, involvement in car accidents, and witnessing domestic violence (Newman, Simpson, and Handschuh 2003). The photojournalists said most were not warned of the emotional or physical dangers of their work, and the majority thought that their employer did not offer counseling, leading the authors to propose that newsroom managers give out information about trauma and training for covering violence as ways to boost staff morale and resiliency. "It may be especially useful to warn individuals . . . with personal exposure histories that they are at greater risk for the development of PTSD," the researchers write. (11)

Although researchers now know that journalists are widely exposed to violence, and that a small percentage of them are at risk for PTSD, researchers have only begun their work. In 2002 a study of war correspondents provided a benchmark reading for those few journalists who dedicate their lives to chasing conflict. Feinstein, Owen, and Blair (2002) looked at self-report questionnaires from 140 war journalists, compared those responses with those of 107 journalists who had never covered wars, and Anthony Feinstein, a psychiatrist, then interviewed 20 percent of the correspondents in both groups.

Feinstein and his associates learned that war correspondents carry heavy emotional burdens into the battles they cover: "Their lifetime prevalence of PTSD was 28.6 percent, and the rates were 21.4 percent for major depression and 14.3 percent for substance abuse" (1570). The PTSD rate was close to that of combat veterans, yet the journalists were not likely to receive treatment for their traumatic injuries. The findings, the authors say, should be "a wake-up call to the news organizations that all is not necessarily well with the men and women who, at considerable risk, bring us news of the world's conflicts" (1574).

The psychiatrist wondered whether the experience of covering wars was at all similar to that faced by New York journalists who witnessed and covered the attacks of 9/11. In a 2003 book Feinstein observed: "Domestic journalists of all types post–September 11 had significantly more PTSD symptoms than domestic journalists pre–September 11. Now their PTSD profile resembled more closely that of the war journalists" (Feinstein 2003:189).

Journalists interview people about the traumatic losses of family and friends. How do those interviews affect reporters?

Charles Figley, a psychologist, and others have labeled indirect traumatic exposure as compassion fatigue because it draws on the empathy of a person who works with those who suffer trauma. The journalist absorbs the trauma effect in the same way that a family member shares the emotional upset of a person who has been severely hurt (Figley 1995). Some spouses appear to share a psychiatry patient's mental illness; a man may exhibit symptoms of pregnancy out of empathy for his wife. Hysteria may sweep through a group, leading to a mass response, presumably conducted by the capacity of each group member to absorb the emotions of others in the group.

The relationship of a traumatized person and a reporter is somewhat like that of a therapist and a client. If the victim's story is compelling and painful to tell, some of the emotional burden will fall on the listening reporter. Some victims want a caring listener, someone who will recognize their pain. Journalists try to limit their emotional responses, in part to protect themselves and in part to honor the journalistic value of objectivity and detachment. Other journalists, though, cannot limit their empathy; they care too much about the other person and her story.

A good number of the journalists surveyed in Michigan and Washington State spoke readily about their empathy for victims (Simpson and Boggs 1999). Sixty-eight percent of the journalists said they found some stories emotionally difficult. Stories about children troubled them the most. Several reporters said that interviews with relatives of people who had been killed were most difficult. "The classmates of a teenager who was shot were obviously touched," said one reporter. Another wrote that after interviewing pregnant high school students, she was "drained emotionally." She added, "I kept thinking how hard it was going to be for these young women and they really had no clue." Another person wrote: "The sister of a man who died of AIDS really opened up to me. She was sobbing and I was holding her hands, crying with her." Yet another reporter told of going to a swimming pool where a three-year-old boy had drowned. "I ran into the child's parents. They wanted to talk about it, but it was emotionally hard on them and I had trouble covering the story because they were portrayed as irresponsible by the police, but they were visibly devastated."

How do these conversations mark the reporter? In part, journalists are like trauma therapists, police, aid workers, and others whose work summons a high degree of emotional intensity. Empathy is the resource everyone brings to such demanding situations, yet showing empathy and sharing with a victim may leave secondary effects with the reporter. The stories may remind him of a similar experience. It is not uncommon for a reporter who has suffered a trauma, such as rape or combat violence, to have traumatic memories during or after an interview. The effects can be particularly strong if the reporter has not worked out the personal trauma. Stories about children, as we have suggested, often arouse deep feelings in the listener, in many cases because they evoke thoughts about the journalist's own children. Psychologists describe an effect called *identification*—a person becomes emotionally involved in the plight of others because of similarities in their circumstances. A West Coast reporter who recently had lost a child drew an assignment to fly to Oklahoma City right after the bombing. Covering that explosion, which killed many children, left emotional wounds that the reporter and his editors had not anticipated.

Several journalists in the survey mentioned guilt feelings that followed covering certain traumatic events (Simpson and Boggs 1999). Guilt may be a potent factor for some journalists because their work usually denies them the chance to help people. Reporters who covered the Oklahoma City bombing in 1995 say that guilt feelings plagued them as they observed rescue efforts but could do little to help. They found their news work wanting, compared with the dogged and sometimes heroic efforts of those at the site. Editors wisely reminded them that the news media play a key role in keeping the community informed during a stressful time.

WHAT TO DO ABOUT TRAUMA

The symptoms of anxiety, intrusive memories, and avoidance of unwanted reminders give the journalist an extra burden to carry through a day's work. But when reporters speak of that burden, they use images that suggest that the burden gets heavier over time. The news industry has paid little attention to the sense of helplessness that may increasingly trouble reporters exposed to trauma.

We believe that the stresses of covering violence in some cases will drain a reporter's energy and commitment. We strongly suspect that some journalists who leave the craft do so because of trauma. We also believe that many who stay in the business respond to the stresses in unproductive ways. When Boggs and I asked the newspaper journalists how they and coworkers deal with traumatic events, many mentioned excessive smoking and drinking, anger, hostility, excessive talking about the event, loud talk in the newsroom, and cynicism.

Over time the repetition of such behaviors changes the journalist's outlook toward work. Roger Rosenblatt, a magazine and television news columnist, described this change after a visit to the troubled African nations of Rwanda and Tanzania in 1994. Journalists respond at first to the suffering around them with shock and "perhaps a twinge of guilty excitement" (16). As they grow accustomed to atrocities, they "get bogged down" in its routine nature. Finally, "embittered, spiteful and inadequate to their work, they curse out their bosses back home for not according them respect; they hate the people on whom they report. Worst of all, they don't allow themselves to enter the third stage, in which everything gets sadder and wiser, worse and strangely better" (16).

Here are some suggestions for dealing with the traumatic symptoms of news work:

• Acknowledge that you may see and hear things for which you are not prepared. One reporter answered the survey from me and Boggs by saying that her first assignment would have been less shocking if she had spent a few minutes talking to an editor about what she should expect. Two out of three reporters say they were not prepared for what they saw on their first assignment that involved violence. In some cases the details of that first event—the physical wounds to dead and injured people, for example—prevented reporters from getting information. One reporter confused the order of events. A photographer at the scene of a fatal accident "just went automatic, snapping away like a robot" (15). The first events flood the journalist's senses; the scene may seem like chaos until the organization of the public safety response becomes obvious; the collision of emotions and fact gathering may seem incongruous to some; journalists will not be aware of their dissociation. Although some people are ready for that first event, others need to talk with an editor, another reporter, a friend, or a counselor.

• Bring a trying assignment under control to some degree by concentrating on the tasks at hand: shooting the photographs, asking the questions, observing the details of the scene, and taking notes. Many reporters speak gratefully of the anchor that those routine tasks gave them during a trying event.

Some reporters and photographers take their time getting used to the scene, circling the site for a while and observing it carefully before trying to talk to or photograph anyone.

While interviewing people at the scene or later talking to family members, neighbors, or friends of victims, try to monitor your own reactions. Some reporters become robotic at such times, pumping out the questions without remaining sensitive to the person with whom they are speaking. How can you keep a balance between the task and the emotions of the other person? Our advice is that reporters should seek ways to connect with the traumatized person. Put down your notepad and camera from time to time and talk without benefit of those job-defining props. That simple act will enable you to sustain eye contact as the other person speaks. As you maintain eye contact, you will communicate some of your own emotion, empathy, and, surprisingly, calmness. That humane sharing will help both the traumatized person and the journalist. Reporters and photographers should never forget that the other person's emotions also are under siege.

• Do not ignore what you have just experienced. After police officers and firefighters endure a traumatic event, they may discuss what they have seen and felt. In some cases psychologists meet with officers, but police agencies are increasingly training officers to serve as peer counselors. If your newsroom does not have a therapist or a staff member ready to help, talk to a coworker or friend. Sometimes a conversation allows nothing more than a gradual winding down from an intense experience. It may help to write for a few minutes about your thoughts and emotions that are tied to the story. Acknowledge unexpected or unwanted responses.

Coté and I encourage newsroom management to give staff members information about possible reactions to trauma; how they can care for themselves, their families, and others in the community; and how to find additional help if they need it. Use of support should be voluntary.

No formal intervention should be mandated for everyone exposed to trauma, according to guidelines from Britain's National Institute for Clinical Excellence and the recommendations of leading experts on psychological trauma in the United States.

Even without a willing listener, you can care for yourself in ways that will lessen the effects. Take guidance from experienced journalists who understand the emotional reactions that accrue after covering a difficult story. Reporters often talk to spouses or partners, but some say that such conversations have limited value. "I fear I sound like a broken record," one reporter says, "so I don't talk very often." Another says, "It's hard because no one wants to hear the gory details, and often those are the ones you need to express." In the absence of a willing listener, journalists can take care of themselves by seeking private time and space, exercising, listening to music, bathing, praying, and crying. Some reporters ask for time off when their stress is obvious. Thoughtful managers and editors encourage reporters to rotate out of stressful assignments periodically, shifting to reporting on positive themes.

• Understand that efforts at self-care may not prevent the onset of trauma symptoms. The insurance and health care programs of many corporations provide counseling as part of employee benefits. We know many journalists who have sought help from a psychiatrist or psychologist and found it to be a rewarding and useful experience. But too often journalists avoid getting help. One respondent to the survey from me and Boggs wrote, "There is little recognition of stress in a business that focuses not on what you've done but on what you are doing for tomorrow. My employer makes counseling available as a benefit, but nobody has ever suggested that it be used" (1999:17).

Some reporters deal with personal stress by joining a support group of journalists who have similar concerns. After a workshop on trauma and news coverage, a reporter in one part of the state formed an e-mail friendship with a reporter on a newspaper a hundred miles away. E-mail enabled them to tell each other about their experiences and reactions and to offer help to one another.

Our intention is not to tell anyone how to deal with trauma, whatever form it may take. We are convinced, though, that many journalists who need such attention fear disclosing it or acting on their need. The best working environment is one in which everyone agrees that journalistic work can harm journalists, and each person is alert to signs of distress among coworkers.

• Be aware that sometimes many workers in a newsroom are exposed to trauma. A reporter kills himself, stunning and shocking coworkers. A shooter penetrates a newspaper plant, gunning down employees as they work. The horrors of a plane crash or bombing devastate a city, affecting everyone in the newsroom.

The *Oklahoman* in Oklahoma City is a good model for sensitive handling of the newsroom effects of trauma. Management support fully and fairly matched the staff's extraordinary commitment to telling the story of the 1995 bombing of the federal building (see chapter 12). Other newspapers have responded in thoughtful ways that helped to validate the fears and doubts of journalists. In some cases, though, the traumatic event passes unnoticed within the organization. As symptoms become evident among workers, some news organizations have sought outside help.

News media in several states have asked our journalism schools and the Dart Center for Journalism and Trauma to provide workshops on trauma for their newsroom staff. In sessions lasting one to several hours we have invited reporters, photographers, and editors to describe the event, air their responses, and discuss ways to make coverage both sensitive and effective. In one case the staff of the *Wenatchee World*, a daily newspaper in central Washington State, spoke openly about the pressures of covering an extraordinary series of local events, including murders, forest fires, and accusations of an adult-child sex ring. A few days later Steve Lachowicz, an editor, wrote in his column:

Reporters and editors are so busy meeting daily deadlines that they have never taken time to recognize that they, too, can suffer from the cumulative emotional strain that comes with tragic stories. Too many come to believe that feeling distant and numb and groaning about their job is a normal state of affairs. In reality, it may be the result of a psychological reaction to the pressures of dealing with death and destruction.

This is not to suggest that we will be able to avoid writing about families who lose their children or about victims of sadistic killers. There will still be those tough morning phone calls to make to the survivors, when the right words are so hard to come by.

But we got a little more education this week in ways we might approach those stories without doing unnecessary harm to the victims or to ourselves.

That shield of invincibility we carry around sometimes protects us. But the weight of it can eventually also drag us into despair.

(1995:2)

CHAPTER 3

9/11: Lessons from a Sunny Morning

In the months after four jetliners were commandeered by terrorists, then crashed, on September 11, 2001, American journalists' understanding of their role changed dramatically. Most U.S. journalists—the exceptions, of course, were those who covered the 1995 bombing in Oklahoma City and the first bombing of the World Trade Center in 1993—had not been consciously covering terrorism and domestic security. All that changed because of the events of that beautiful sunny morning on the East Coast.

News media in midsize communities have terrorism and "homeland security" beats now, or at least one staff member who monitors the many layers of planning and activity by municipal, state, and federal agencies. Indeed, the government antiterrorism efforts, orchestrated by the U.S. Department of Homeland Security, have refocused the efforts of public safety and public health agencies. Journalists and news organizations have had to pay attention to this relatively new, huge component of government.

But the legacy of 9/11 goes beyond government to the mental world of each person, what psychologist Jeffrey Kauffman calls the "assumptive world." We define terrorism as acts of violence directed at the civilian population with the intent to undermine resolve, create fears, and destabilize life. The world, he finds, is made up of "assumptions or beliefs that ground, secure, or orient people, that give a sense of reality, meaning, or purpose to life" (2002:1). As surely as 9/11 shattered Americans' belief in the nation's safety from terrorist attacks, related events challenged their assumptions about the routines of their lives and the ordinary details of their days. Air travel ceased to be a routine activity as security agencies imposed rigorous checks of luggage, purses, and laptops and forced U.S. travelers to shed their shoes and jackets before passing through electronic surveillance equipment. Purchasing a ticket to fly on a jet ceased to the rescue efforts. He saw me as a human being and not as a journalist. I think he trusted I could get the story right" (Bull and Newman 2003).

Santana, who had been enlisted by officers to help with the rescue effort when he showed his press pass, said he drew strength from Foster's dedication. "You can't help but wonder whether you would be as strong." The *Post* article caught Foster's hopes and fears and spoke for those of thousands more who were waiting for word of their loved ones in the first hours after the attack. "For the rest of the first day, through the night and then past the dawn of the second day, Foster focused on an open door in the distance, one he was sure could eventually lead to his wife. He knew she was there—somewhere down a long, smoky corridor and up three flights of stairs, waiting to be rescued" (Santana 2001:A01).

Near Shanksville, Pennsylvania, Michael Reed, a cameraman for WWCP/WATM-TV in Johnstown, recoiled at what he saw after the crash of the fourth hijacked plane: "Nothing but a smoldering hole, nothing left to even remotely identify as a plane, and the terrible realization that dozens of souls, lives, had come to a horrific end. What was in front of me was a graveyard, hallowed ground. What was I doing, running there, and trying to get a big story?" Reed later said that what he saw in that Pennsylvania field changed his way of thinking about the victims: "It was the lack of evidence of the plane's existence that got me—the lack of anything human. That shocked me. The total obliteration of all those lives prevented me from ignoring them" (Gilbert et al. 2002:137, 139).

JOURNALISM OF EMOTIONS

Journalists who were there on 9/11 wanted to share their stories and contributed readily to anthologies of first-day accounts (Gilbert et al. 2002; Bull and Erman 2002; Sylvester and Huffman 2002). The outpouring of personal experience by journalists was unusual; journalists defied the expectation that they would keep their emotions to themselves lest disclosure imply weakness or inability to perform. The events that day upset that traditional idea, enabling journalists to speak openly of shock, fear, grief, and anger. "I knew I needed more interviews," wrote Eileen Lehpamer, a radio reporter, "but I felt frozen and I wasn't sure what to do next. . . . I had never felt so alone as at that moment, but I also knew I would not quit" (Gilbert et al. 2002:115).

Across the nation all hands turned for the next few days to reporting a story about human emotions, a topic usually delegated to those specialists in personal stories, whether those of tragedy or of transcending barriers. No matter what the beat, journalists caught the story through observations, quotes, and personal reflection. "All traditional beats covered this story," said one newspaper editor. "Reporters didn't have to be told, 'Here's your assignment.'" At the "family center" near Ground Zero, Fox News reporter Heather Nauert interviewed people live about their missing relatives. "It struck me that before the attack, the missing had all been full of life, making plans to buy a house or start a job," she later wrote. "The photos that their relatives had brought to help identify them were of their happiest of times: at a wedding, on a night out with friends, holding a newborn baby, or cooking at a summer barbecue" (Bull and Erman 2002:163). Nauert came to recognize that the interviews required emotional responses from her, responses that gradually wore her down. "I showed empathy to the families but at home, I had no energy or emotion for Scott [her husband]." For two weeks she watched rapid mood changes in the family centers, "from frantic and hopeful to anger and depression." At last, she gained a weekend off and traveled with her husband to a rural community that provided the calm and comfort that allowed the two to speak openly about their emotions (165). Reporters around the country shared with Nauert both the burden of hearing emotional stories and the need to find a calm place to retreat from the stress.

Rose Arce, a Cable News Network producer, had raced toward the World Trade Center that morning, using her cell phone and pay phones to provide some of the network's first eyewitness descriptions of the crashes and collapse of the towers. She and thousands of other journalists followed the story relentlessly, both informing readers and viewers and staving off the emotional impact of the work. Three months later, during the holiday period, the symptoms of stress caught up with her and with many journalists in the affected cities and in many other places (Bull and Newman 2003).

COPING WITH THE AFTERMATH

Using missing-person flyers that relatives and friends left at Ground Zero, *New York Times* reporters began writing that week about the lives of those who died at the World Trade Center. Between September 15, 2001, and February 5, 2002, the paper published more than eighteen hundred profiles of victims. "Portraits of Grief," as the series was called, became a source for reflection and grief by readers, as reporters offered honest glimpses of a human life in a way quite distinct from that of obituaries. In 1995 the *Daily Oklahoman* had published its

"profiles of life," one for each of the 168 people who died in the federal building bombing. The *Times* applied that idea to those who died on September 11
and later collected the portraits in a book, pledging to add to the book as the
paper learned about additional victims (New York Times 2003). Tina Kelley,
one of several writers of the portraits, said she was humbled by the project.
"We are confronted with very surprising glimpses of average people who would
not likely ever appear [in the paper] if the planes hadn't fallen out of the sky.
The survivors told us things we didn't know. We couldn't say 'I understand.'"
Relatives of victims taught Kelley about fairness. "I dreaded talking to mothers,
and I avoided it, until one told me how she felt left out when no one asked her
about her daughter." She learned too to look beyond the clichés that people use
to speak about a departed friend or relative. She also noticed how her empathy
with victims played back in her emotions. "Sometimes, after a hard interview, I
would get up and announce I would no longer do these stories, but few people
were around to hold me to it. When I felt the need, I took a week or so off to
work on other stories. With each interview I learned a new version of sadness"
(Kelley 2003).

Not all journalists found it possible to get away from the stress of that story;
for journalists in cities and towns where victims lived, the work took a heavy toll
on energy. Many editors and managers recognized the strain, and a few found
creative ways to bolster staff morale. In Asbury Park, New Jersey, the *Press* assigned two reporters who had attended a seminar on reporting about trauma
and emotion to be watchful for staffers suffering from the stress of covering
death in a community hit hard by the World Trade Center attacks. Dubbed
"staff ombudsmen," Elaine Silvestrini and Carol Gorga Williams helped shape
coverage, intervened to press for sensitivity in reporting, and kept watchful eyes
on the staff. The latter role "included everything from pointing out to managers people who were being overused and in danger of burning out to those
who weren't being included and were eager to help," Silvestrini told us (she
has since joined the *Tampa Tribune*). She and Williams took food and praise to
the newsroom and the bureaus. The two reporters also scrutinized errors that
showed up in print, seeing some mistakes that could be symptoms of stress.
"We persuaded managers to issue memos thanking the staff for their work and
encouraging them to talk about their feelings," Silvestrini said. "After it was all
said and done, we were told by reporters that we had made the experience much
more bearable than it could have been."

No one has done a study of the emotional states of New York journalists
since 9/11. Belatedly, a program that screened rescue and recovery workers

at the Ground Zero site for mental and physical symptoms offered to add journalists who volunteered to be included. And reporters and photographers themselves have found opportunities to tell other journalists about their lives since 9/11 and have expressed gratitude for that experience. Handschuh, the New York *Daily News* photographer and former president of the National Press Photographers Association, and Adam Lisberg, a reporter for the *Bergen County (N.J.) Record*, organized several gatherings of journalists whose only agenda was to share their personal stories. "This is organized by a reporter and photographer who went through the same things you did that morning, and who believe there haven't been enough places for all of us to get together and just talk," Handschuh wrote in his invitation. Liz Margolies, a therapist who helped with the sessions, said of one of the off-the-record dinners: "Some people cried, some people got drunk, some people claimed they were absolutely fine. But they all showed up. That is more telling than anything they may have said" (Lisberg 2003).

New York journalists, especially those who worked in some Manhattan media centers, also endured anxieties caused by the discovery that letters containing anthrax spores had been sent to media organizations, individuals, and public officials a few weeks after 9/11. One letter infected an assistant to *NBC Nightly News* anchor Tom Brokaw. Robert Windrem, a senior investigative producer for the program, later wrote about the intense anger and raw emotion of staffers who suddenly became part of the anthrax story in New York. "All this talk about 'terrorizing' us and 'trying to instill fear in the city' was beside the point. 'They'—whoever they were—wanted to kill us. I became anxious and then increasingly angry. I threw things. I felt like a victim and I didn't want to" (Windrem 2001:19).

Since 2001 Americans have moved beyond 9/11, perhaps incorporating its emotional residue into daily efforts but recovering and responding as people can after horrifying events. People deal with such shocks in their own ways and in their own time. In writing this book, Coté and I realized that we were surprised by emotional reactions to things that trigger the shock of that day—for me, any bank of television monitors in a retail store is a reminder of my first awareness of the attacks. As others have found, watching documentaries about 9/11 can be stressful and troubling. Those emotional hits are natural to the process of learning to live with violent events. Americans also recognize that their sense of the world that they travel has changed; they have come closer to the sense of reality of people all around the world who confront life day by day in places that invite violence.

THE NEW BEAT OF SECURITY AND TERRORISM

News companies and their employees will cover terrorism into the distant future; we can say that with some confidence. In some cases terrorism merits a beat assignment, but most editors and producers now recognize that threats against civilian targets and civilian morale are an on-going component of life since 9/11. Unlike more traditional beats such as police, fire, and natural disaster coverage, where coverage is usually focused on a community or region, security reporting involves politics, international relations, business and the economy, technology, government, criminal justice, religion, education—nearly every beat already in place. We understand why some newsrooms emphasize teams and teamwork across beats as necessary responses to the wide range of counterterrorism activities and terrorist linkages that might merit coverage in giving readers and viewers a sense of what "homeland security," the new defining phrase of this decade, entails.

Good coverage of security and terrorism requires the fullest possible knowledge of all areas of life. It also requires flexibility and resourcefulness on the part of editors, producers, photographers, and reporters. If nothing else, terrorism uses and thrives on surprise and shock, traits calculated to challenge news practices built around routines and predictable events. However, absent attacks, journalists can pursue the threads of security and terrorism in conventional ways, keeping in mind that they must look in numerous places to do their work adequately. Traditional investigative and reporting methods remain useful but may confront barriers that are themselves a product of an era of anxiety about terrorism. In the wake of 9/11 and during subsequent military actions in Afghanistan and Iraq, the U.S. government limited access to information in ways that made journalists' work considerably more difficult than in previous decades.

Recent events—some the result of terrorism, some of old-fashioned criminal violence—have given journalists new guidance in approaching the unexpected. The World Trade Center attacks in 2001, for example, showed that neither photographers nor reporters should rush blindly toward the site of a disaster. Immediate dangers included debris and bodies falling to the ground, the horrendous ground-level clouds of polluted materials caused by the building collapses, and the possibility that working journalists would inadvertently interfere with rescue activities. Only later did anyone understand that the clouds that enveloped fleeing people contained toxic materials, including asbestos, that might only later begin to show their true effects. If the attack itself had used biological or radiological agents, the risks and harm would have been substantially greater. In the aftermath of 9/11 journalists challenged their own ages-old assumption that a good reporter or photographer rushes toward the scene. They began to listen to veteran officials at public safety agencies and those who had begun to train journalists about personal safety. Paul Rees, director of Centurion Risk Assessment Services, Ltd., a British firm, told *American Journalism Review,* "Our advice is to get the hell out of there. If [reporters] are adamant that they need to be there, look for a vantage point that is away and out of the immediate danger area." He added that the option of remaining works only for personnel equipped with appropriate protective gear (Smolkin 2003:54).

People tend to forget that terrorists first attacked the World Trade Center in New York in 1993 with explosives set off in its lower-level parking garage, a blast that affected several stories deep in the base of one tower. That attack led authorities to develop federal standards for terrorism response training. Those standards designated zones around contaminated areas—the close "hot (exclusion) zone" considered dangerous and even life threatening, an intermediate "warm zone" that trained personnel could enter, and a "cold (support) zone" that would pose no threat and would be the site of command and support activities. Both hot and warm zones would require protective gear, the standards declare (Virginia Department of Fire Programs 2000:V-1–V-6).

Because journalists sometimes cannot tell whether they are in a "warm zone" or a "cold zone," agencies advise finding a command post by approaching the site upwind and from uphill while looking carefully for signs of chemical or radiological attack. Signs of exposure may include difficulty breathing; reddening, burning, or itching of the eyes and/or skin; irritation of the nose and throat; runny nose or salivation; coughing; pain in the eyes or head; vomiting; and seizurelike reactions or convulsions (Virginia:II-6–1). Look for other people who are showing those signs, as well as vapor clouds, dead plants and animals, peculiar smells, loud pops, and the smell or sound of gas or vapor escaping. Some of those signs suggest that the reporter may already be contaminated. Experts advise against eating, smoking, drinking, or chewing gum in those situations.

First responders from public-safety agencies may have equipment that tells them from a safe distance about chemical or radiological risks. Journalists who also may be first at the scene are unlikely to have either the technical means to identify the danger or the right gear to protect themselves from the danger. Although some newsrooms bought protective gear after 9/11, experts have identified problems with its use. First, without equipment to detect the specific risk, it won't be clear how to use the protective gear. Second, the gear provides protection only if it is used properly. In some cases journalists won't have time to put on a protective suit (Smolkin 2003:56)

In the event of an attack that apparently involves nuclear radiation, experts say, journalists should cover their mouth with a handkerchief to keep from breathing radioactive dust, and they should wash as soon as possible. "They also should attempt to put a shield—such as a vehicle, concrete or even dirt—between themselves and the source of the radiation," writes Rachel Smolkin, a contributing writer for *American Journalism Review* (2003:56). Biological agents, which are usually inhaled or absorbed through the skin, may not show their effects immediately. Terrorists disseminate biological agents by using heating and cooling systems, aerosol devices, foggers, or sprayers. Injury from inhaling radiological agents also may not be evident for some time.

The science and technology of weapons available to terrorists is changing rapidly, just as the technology used in response gear, detection instruments, and decontamination is evolving. Editors and managers should consult with agencies and companies familiar with disaster and terrorism training, provide the best current information to staff journalists during frequent training sessions, and regularly evaluate and compare responses among media organizations.

We close this chapter by discussing an issue that has troubled many journalists since 9/11: What are the obligations of the media in regard to presenting news of real or potential terrorist threats? Many have rated Homeland Security's color coding of potential terrorist threats since 9/11 as of little value, because each shift in level of concern carries no precise information about the nature or location of potential threats. Repeated warnings to the public in the absence of any evidence of actual threat have fostered skepticism about their value. The media contribute to that skepticism by playing such warnings as though attacks were imminent in every community in the land. Howard Kurtz, media critic for the *Washington Post*, told an interviewer, "I think it's entirely possible to write about potential terror attacks and suggested precautions without in effect yelling from the rooftops, and yet that's something that modern media or today's media seem to have great difficulty with" (Robertson 2003:19).

As the United States struggles to respond to terrorist threats, Americans are learning from many other parts of the world, places accustomed to both the dangers and the reality of attacks. Journalists here will find it necessary to recognize that news work will require an understanding of the evolving nature of political violence.

TOOLS FOR JOURNALISTS

Let us summarize what journalists should keep in mind as they respond to a terrorist attack:

- Remember that the terrorists want to undermine resolve, create fears, and destabilize life in the civilian population.
- Bear in mind that of all the images that television showed on September 11, 2001, those of people falling or jumping from the towers were most closely associated with self-reported symptoms of PTSD or depression.
- People who die or are injured in terror attacks deserve sensitive accounts of their lives; those who interview survivors and write about the victims should anticipate the emotional toll of their work.
- Recognize the changes that 9/11 made in Americans' assumptions about life and safety. Be aware of those changes in yourself and the people you report for.
- Keep warnings about terrorism in perspective but provide as much information as is available.
- Avoid "scare reporting" of incidents that may reflect terrorist actions when the evidence is not definitive.

ADVANCE PREPARATIONS BY MANAGEMENT

- Have a plan for moving a newsroom when it is damaged or threatened; all members of a staff should know alternative contacts in case a newsroom is damaged or unreachable.
- Make advance plans for alternative means of communication. Because cell phones may not work, the staff will need another way to stay in contact with editors and managers. Have a plan—or at least enough fresh batteries on hand to power those walkie-talkies in the closet.
- Identify in advance staffers who would be suited to the task of monitoring their coworkers' emotional state. Prepare for ways to gain relief for overworked reporters (have meals delivered to the newsroom) and to provide activities that can contribute to staff morale (staff gatherings to show how challenges were handled).

- Keep available up-to-date copies of the *Emergency Response Guidebook, 2004: A Guidebook for First Responders During the Initial Phase of a Dangerous Goods/Hazardous Materials Incident,* prepared by the U.S. Department of Transportation. It lists chemical hazards, recommends distances from the chemical, and provides first aid instructions.
- Arrange for advance safety training and lessons on self-care for reporters who may be sent to assignments in a distant place. These reporters should also be discussing effective ways to cover a changing event with editors and other reporters.

The Meaning of Being There

David Handschuh has spent the morning photographing a chef who is making peanut butter éclairs at Fauchon, an upscale bakery in Queens. The other day he photographed the cast of *The Sopranos* as the actors lunched on pasta and red sauce. Handschuh works for the New York *Daily News*, a newspaper proud of its tradition of spot news photography. But Handschuh does not cover breaking news; in fact, he refuses. He prefers to photograph food.

This is the same David Handschuh who built his reputation shooting car crashes, fires, and murders, who started listening to police scanners when he was thirteen and hopped buses to get to the scene or splurged for a cab if it sounded like a big story. He was a modern-day Weegee, the cigar-chomping photographer of the '30s and '40s who estimated he covered five thousand murders. When Hollywood decided to make a movie based on Weegee, the producers enlisted Handschuh as a consultant. "That was my life," he says. "I ate, drank, and breathed spot news."

David Handschuh.
Photo by Jeffrey Cantrell

No longer. As Handschuh describes it, "I went out in a blaze of glory" on September 11, 2001. He was headed to New York University that morning to teach a photojournalism class and, as always, had the police and fire radios chattering away in his car. He spotted smoke billowing into the blue sky above Lower Manhattan, and a moment later a fire dispatcher yelled for all available apparatus to head downtown. A jetliner had crashed into the World Trade Center.

One tower was ablaze when Handschuh arrived—he had tailed a fire truck south in a northbound lane of the West Side Highway—and he started making photos. He realized debris was falling around him but wasn't too concerned about his safety. Then he noticed it wasn't just building debris in the street; it was body parts as well. Bodies began crashing down, people who had decided it was better to jump than to burn to death. "The sound of the bodies hitting the sidewalk will never leave my mind," Handschuh says.

The south tower fell first. Handschuh's first reaction was to lift his camera and start making pictures. A voice in the back of his head told him to run. *Run. Run. Run.* For the first time in his career he turned and fled from the news. He ran as fast as he could, but a wind he likens to a tornado picked him up and threw him under a vehicle. Choking on debris, he was sure he was going to die there in the gutter. He reached for his cell phone. He wanted to call home and tell his wife and children he loved them. His phone, his pager, and his glasses were gone, but he'd held on to his cameras.

He cleared debris from his mouth. His right leg was shattered and he couldn't walk. He called for help, and three firefighters dug him out and carried him to a delicatessen about a block away. Among those who had sought shelter there was Todd Maisel, a fellow *Daily News* photographer. Maisel photographed Handschuh lying on his back on the floor of the deli, covered in a yellowish soot, his legs bent under him, his arms upraised, his mouth agape. The *Daily News* published a half-dozen photos that Handschuh took that morning and another two that Maisel took of him.

Handschuh returned to work in March 2002, hobbled physically and scarred emotionally. He told his editors that he no longer would cover news and, with a few exceptions, has not. On those occasions he approached the assignments with trepidation, fearful of what he might see and what it might trigger inside him.

Handschuh realizes that few journalists have the clout to tell their bosses that they won't cover news. Most cannot even admit publicly that they sometimes suffer from the trauma they encounter in their work. "Not only can we not admit it to ourselves, we can't admit it to our management," Handschuh says,

9/11

Top: (Tower)} Handschuh snapped this photo as the second plane flew into the south tower of the World Trade Center.   Photo by David Handschuh, *New York Daily News*

Bottom: (Crowd running from hotel)} Guests flee the Marriott Hotel next to the South Tower.   Photo by David Handschuh, *New York Daily News*

Top: (Firefighters)} A bystander assists New York firefighters as they move an injured woman to safety.   Photo by David Handschuh, *New York Daily News*

Bottom: (Park ranger)} A park ranger and other bystanders try to help a woman burned by flaming jet fuel. She died forty-one days later.   Photo by David Handschuh, *New York Daily News*

Food

(Chef with seafood dish)} Chef Jeff Raider delivers another seafood plate at Sea Grill in Rockefeller Center. Photo by David Handschuh, *New York Daily News*

(Hand with plate)} A chef at Pigalle, a midtown Manhattan French bistro, sprinkles rosemary on a seafood plate. Photo by David Handschuh, *New York Daily News*

"and the main reason for that is fear there will be career reprisal for admitting that covering the news might affect us."

When he's not taking pictures of food, Handschuh speaks to journalists, journalism students, rescue workers, and anyone else who will listen about the effects of trauma on those who deal with it for a living. He tells them that it's not enough to look after their physical health and safety. "We need to take half as much time worrying about our mental, spiritual, and psychological health," he says.

Half as much time?

"I'd be happy with half," he says. "Half would be a huge improvement."

More and more journalists are joining the chorus, men and women who were touched profoundly in their own ways by covering September 11. One told Handschuh about halting in rush-hour traffic on a New York highway, frozen in fear as an airliner made its final approach to LaGuardia. Another journalist showers three or four times a day, trying to scrub off the smell of Ground Zero. Picture editors who lived hundreds of miles away, who never heard a body smash against the pavement, were traumatized by poring over hundreds of still images. Tape editors suffered similarly by viewing and re-viewing video images of the horror. "It was an epiphany for our community, our industry," Handschuh says. "It allowed people who didn't think they were affected, or that others weren't affected, to understand that wasn't the case. Now, all of a sudden, it was OK to raise your hand and say, 'I'm affected by this.'"

It's not enough for journalists to simply acknowledge that they have work-related problems, Handschuh says. They must do something to address them: take a walk, meditate, work out, and/or talk to a colleague, clergy member, or psychologist.

"I'm not a therapist, but I highly recommend scuba diving," he says. "It is calm, it is peaceful, it is suspended animation. It's like returning to the womb. And cell phones and pagers don't work under [water] yet."

September 11 taught Handschuh to appreciate everyday life and every day. That's something else journalists need to remember and to incorporate in their personal and professional lives, he says. Blue skies can fill with terror, but dark skies always turn blue eventually.

CHAPTER 4

Reporting at the Scene

The reporter, photographer, and field producer at the scene have unusual power to shape what people remember about searingly violent stories, and what they tell or show their audience may remain in people's minds forever. Thoughtful reporting can prepare readers and viewers to respond intelligently to subsequent events; repeating myths and errors will confuse and undermine personal and community efforts in a crisis.

The journalist at the scene must avoid the traps that such events set for the unwary. Reporters and photographers rarely are prepared for what they face. Journalists may hear themselves voicing the effects—venting—along with the other people there. Clichés about human behavior come too readily: People panicked. The victims need everything. Everyone is angry.

THINK ABOUT GOING TO "THE SCENE"

As journalists plan for that unexpected event, they need to give some thought to the meaning of "the scene" in twenty-first-century journalism. Oklahoma City reporters faced bomb destruction, fatalities, and hundreds of injuries among the living. At Columbine High School in Littleton, Colorado, reporters found deaths, injuries, shocked and frightened students and families, and a sprawling complex whose walls masked horror long after journalists got there. In New York and Washington, D.C., on September 11, 2001, "the scene" shifted mercilessly as planes struck buildings, rescuers worked in desperation, and bystanders tried to process what they had seen. "It was as though I were watching a movie," everyone said. Perhaps only survivors of a tornado could have anticipated the angry wave of metal, glass, gravel, and cement that swept through streets near Ground Zero.

Even those horrific recent events fail to capture the complexity of preparing to go to the scene. What was the scene as a tsunami swept in deadly rage across the Indian Ocean in South Asia in December 2004, killing more than 200,000 people? When a bomb exploded in an airplane over Scotland in 1988, the scene was a huge area around the city of Lockerbie. Other planes have crashed into water, making a nearby land base the only scene a journalist can readily reach.

No two scenes are alike. Unfamiliar places challenge the most ingenious journalists. "Parachute reporters"—those sent from distant cities to the site of a crash or natural disaster—and local reporters often have different objectives. But to some extent it won't matter whether the journalist comes from two blocks or two thousand miles away; the disaster or accident will require quick and sensitive action.

Thinking about what might happen ahead of time can equip reporters or camera crew for what they find. A news staff can plan for local and regional disasters that could place unusual demands on it. On the Pacific Coast earthquakes are familiar events; hurricanes try cities on the Atlantic seaboard and on the Gulf of Mexico, whereas tornadoes are common in the Midwest and inland South. On the coasts and along the Gulf of Mexico boating and shipping accidents are common. Planes crash anywhere. Planning for these events can make a great difference in the quality and accuracy of the reporting. Failing to plan will certainly test the talents of journalists, who may well bumble about as they simultaneously deal with their own emotions and try to make sense of the scene.

When journalists go to the scene, they join other first responders—police, firefighters, emergency medical teams, and others trained and equipped to go to a disaster. All too often the first responders who are journalists confront the same ethical and professional questions at the scene that face the others but often do so with less training, no equipment, and far less guidance about what to do.

When a sky bridge in a Kansas City, Missouri, hotel collapsed and killed 111 people during a packed, festive event on a hot night in July 1981, Roger McCoy, a television reporter, was nearby. He had just come home exhausted from work when his assignment desk called to say the hotel had suffered some sort of structural collapse. He got there ahead of firefighters, ambulance crews, and other aid workers. Near the hotel the first person he saw was an elderly woman who was walking into the street. McCoy led the woman, who was in shock, to people nearby and asked them to watch her.

"Inside, it was utter pandemonium. There were dangling wires, showering sparks, broken water pipes spraying water, and all the dust generated by the collapse of the concrete and steel skywalk in the lobby atrium. You could see that some people were dead, with arms and legs hanging out from the rubble. There were pools of blood and cries for help from people trapped under the fallen concrete," says McCoy. He told us that the first fire truck arrived a few minutes later, followed by every available ambulance and fire vehicle in the city. The medical examiner set up a makeshift morgue in a hotel conference room. McCoy stayed at the hotel until 3 A.M., doing live reports for his station and occasional feeds to CBS network news. He told us, "I had an overwhelming sense of chaos and loss and an overwhelming sense of helplessness. That's trapped in my mind, and I've accepted that it's one of those things that will be with me for my life." Of his later reporting, McCoy says, "I did take some comfort in hoping that when I couldn't help physically, I could help bring about the healing process, help them understand the crisis, and maybe give people tools to deal with it all."

Experienced reporters and photographers know there are dangers in any disaster scene. Joe Hight and Frank Smyth list some of the risks facing a reporter who arrives quickly at the scene:

- The perpetrator is still in the area.
- A threat of violence continues or anything dangerous is near.
- An area is still contaminated in the event of a biological accident.
- Terrorists plan for a secondary bomb or attack.
- The journalist may suffer emotional effects as well.

(adapted from Hight and Smyth 2003:32, 33)

American news media have covered accidents involving hazardous chemicals for decades, often relying on databases available to fire units and police about the risks of particular chemicals. Even so, the impulse to rush to the scene ought to await a check on risks. Journalists who were close by when the World Trade Center towers collapsed suffered exposure to a toxic chemical mix, a hazard that persisted for weeks as the site cleanup continued.

A terrorist attack involving the Tokyo subway system in 1995 points up the importance of planning for journalists. Five men carrying packets of liquid sarin, a potentially deadly nerve agent, punctured the packages at a predetermined stop and left the train. Eleven people died that day, and many others were affected by exposure to the agent. A sad reality of modern times is that not all dangers are immediately identifiable, one reason to be careful about going to the scene.

TRAINING FOR COVERING THE SCENE

Hospitals, police and fire departments, and emergency agencies often hold disaster drills, testing each department and person to see how rapidly and productively each responds. Whereas news media sometimes report on the drills, planners rarely include journalists. News organizations can be crucial to accident and disaster relief; leaving them out of the planning may worsen the situation.

News organizations might benefit from what has been learned in "critical incident" programs that bring together specialists from various academic disciplines to evaluate and plan responses to devastating occurrences, such as earthquakes, plane crashes, and hazardous materials spills. Journalists could prepare for an event by learning how various agencies would respond, identifying locations where information would be available, and evaluating news coverage of similar events.

Every newsroom should have a plan for the unexpected. Some journalists assigned to cover U.S. military action in Afghanistan and Iraq received training for coping with biological and chemical hazards. When domestic newsrooms deem that such training is too costly, managers should provide some training to alert journalists to potential risks and to emphasize the importance of communication among reporters, photographers, producers, and editors.

But sometimes the only planning time that a journalist has is the time it takes to reach the scene, and preparing even for that eventuality is possible. First, no amount of planning and little prior experience will fully prepare journalists for what they are about to see. Some people they will see or meet will be injured physically and suffering psychological shock. Public safety personnel will be under stress that will manifest itself in different ways, ranging from an intense focus on the job at hand to obvious grief or distraction. Journalists also should prepare themselves for seeing bodies and physical mutilation and for the emotional responses that they and others may have.

One of the most common assignments for newspaper reporters is the highway crash that causes injuries or deaths. First-time reporters are rarely prepared to see the injured and dead victims. They should be ready to step back from the scene and think about how to help themselves deal with the experience. They should be prepared to help if needed, but they should not interfere with medical, police, or firefighting efforts. They may be of more assistance in traffic control. They should be careful not to touch or move objects.

Journalists must think about the nature of trauma. They may see signs of traumatic stress in nearly everyone around them. Taking a few moments to reflect on the possibility that nothing will seem ordinary for a while can help. Like the aid workers, witnesses, and survivors, journalists may get an adrenaline rush just from being there. Their own senses and emotions may seem alien. They may find themselves on automatic pilot, working away at a furious pace without taking time to process all that is going on around them. At some point, probably after they leave the scene, their emotions may take charge. Reporters and photographers have no genetic or other immunity against the beating that trauma can deliver to the human emotional system. The event is likely to mark their memory, just as it will become unforgettable to others at the scene. Daniel Goleman, in the book *Emotional Intelligence,* writes that part of the brain primes the body to react to a stunning event, while another part creates an emotional reaction, "stamp[s] the moment in memory with vividness," and stores the memory (1995:20).

Hope Tuttle, who worked on Red Cross disaster response teams for many years, told us of an afternoon interview she did with a young radio reporter soon after the Loma Prieta earthquake in northern California in 1989. Three hours later the reporter was on the phone to Tuttle, sobbing and begging for help. She had gone back to work when another of the many aftershocks hit. "I need someone to help me," the reporter told Tuttle. "I can't stand it anymore. It just keeps shaking." The reaction is a common one, but it's safe to say that the reporter's training for emergencies did not include the likelihood that her own emotions might get in the way of finishing the story.

Remember that the scene will change steadily in the hours and days after an event. The scene may change quickly from the site where shock waves left instant victims to other venues—hospitals, morgues, hotels, briefing rooms, sites of press conferences, courts, and so on. For planning purposes it will be useful to think in terms of an immediate scene—the chaotic site where the unexpected has occurred—and the other sites where facets of the story will be revealed over time.

Journalists should also have a communication plan in mind. They should know how to reach several editors and staff members, and they should carry those telephone numbers in written form in case their cell phones are not useable, as was the case for a time in New York on 9/11. Journalists should know how to reach backup locations if their newsroom, printing plant, studio, or transmitter is affected. Staff members should know whom to call in an emergency about their location, personal safety, and availability for assignment.

Journalists should also think about what they are preparing to cover. Is it an accident or a disaster? Earthquakes, volcanic eruptions, forest fires, floods, drought, war, and famine are likely to be called disasters. In contrast, most air crashes, shipping mishaps, fires, and building collapses are usually called accidents, even though investigation may eventually show that they were intentional.

We make the distinction between accidents and disasters here only to point out that journalists usually can go to the site of an accident, speak to witnesses and public safety people, and gain a fair sense of what happened. Journalists will likely learn what agency or person has vital information about the event, such as the names of those hurt or killed, hometowns, and where they were taken for medical attention. A photographer will have a fair chance of capturing many important facets of the event with relatively little movement.

A disaster, by contrast, does not yield its evidence readily. A central place to obtain information often does not exist. The effects of a disaster are widespread and not readily known, even to agencies with responsibility, such as federal or state governments. Joseph Scanlon comments, "When disaster strikes, there is no site and it may be hours, days, or even weeks before there is a comprehensive picture of the extent of impact. It is unlikely that any agency, no matter how competent, will have a feel for all that has happened" (1998:47).

WHAT TO LOOK FOR AND DO AT THE SCENE

Finding the scene may be the first challenge.

When Pan Am flight 103 exploded over Lockerbie, Scotland, in 1988, journalists immediately headed for the town from such nearby cities as Glasgow, Edinburgh, and London. The plane blew up a few minutes after seven on a December evening. As reporters got close to the town in the next few hours, they encountered highways that were closed to all but emergency vehicles. One reporter pulled his car in at the rear of a convoy of ambulances and police vehicles and managed to drive into Lockerbie. Joan Deppa's detailed description of Lockerbie that evening includes the tale of a Glasgow *Daily Record* reporter who arrived at the city in darkness. A man with a flashlight offered to take him to the site of the crash. Deppa writes, "Following his escort through back gardens and streets, the newsman soon found himself near Sherwood Crescent, staring at a huge, burning crater. Nothing in his long career could have prepared him for this or any of the many sights he would see in the hours ahead. It was as if he had arrived in the middle of a war zone" (1993:71). Three teenagers escorted another reporter across several fields littered with crash debris until they arrived at the crater. The image of the crater was burned into the early stories, but reporting in the next few hours took place on city streets, in local pubs, and among the damaged houses. Through the night, as reporting crews continued to arrive, the scene spread over a wide area. By the next day reporters also were focusing attention on the headquarters for search teams and police. And as international news crews reached Lockerbie, authorities restricted access to headquarters buildings and to the areas with crash debris.

A photographer and reporter from the *Daily Oklahoman* were the first journalists to reach the bombed federal building in Oklahoma City in 1995. The photographer had to find places to take the pictures that would effectively tell the multiple stories of damage, injuries and deaths, and rescue efforts. The reporter simply stayed a good distance from the rescue effort, watching the activity and listening to witnesses, survivors, and emergency personnel. News teams sent from distant places found the bombing site under fairly tight control. Reporters who wanted to talk to families of the bombing victims had to go to a church several miles from the federal building where, under the close watch of national guard troops, they waited for interviews.

In the attacks on the World Trade Center in New York, a city where working journalists number in the thousands, photographers and reporters rushed toward the inferno, shooting as the second plane hit the tower and the mayhem that followed. The *Wall Street Journal*'s newsroom was destroyed by the explosions; a photographer died as he walked inexorably toward Ground Zero, and another was injured by falling debris. Until access to the site where the two towers collapsed was put under control, journalists observed and photographed freely.

Lockerbie, Oklahoma City, and New York City each was the stage for the inevitable meeting of local reporters and the news teams from national and international media. The two groups often have different goals in mind, and their accounts of the events reflect those differences. Reporters who parachute in would do well to remember the visit of CBS anchor Connie Chung to Oklahoma City a short time after the bombing. Chung arrived at the federal building in a limousine and later angered many in Oklahoma City by asking an assistant fire chief whether the city could handle the crisis.

Are there injuries and deaths? How extensive is the damage? Reporters will want to find emergency response and public safety people who are likely to have credible information later. Journalists should determine what other places someone will need to check, such as hospital emergency rooms and field hospitals, temporary morgues, and agency public information offices. Finally, reporters should stay out of the way of rescue and relief work, and coordinate their reporting with their city or assignment desk.

As journalists adjust to the scene, they should think about the phenomenon that disaster specialists call *convergence*. In the immediate aftermath of a major event, people may rapidly arrive at the scene by foot, cars, or other vehicles. Convergence also occurs in terms of a storm of communication about the event and a rapid assembly and movement of supplies and equipment. Official movement of personnel, equipment, and information is expected, if not always efficient and coordinated. Journalists and those dealing with the event often do not expect what is called informal convergence—the lookie-loos. Sometimes convergence causes additional deaths and injuries. After a tornado struck a school, a child died in the traffic frenzy as parents rushed to the building.

Crowds of observers may make the scene seem more confusing and disorganized than it is. Early broadcast reports that urge people to stay away and to not use telephones may render an important public service. Reporting the precise location soon afterward may draw people to the scene, but it may reassure others that people they know are not affected. Once the word of what happened is out, callers will try to phone to learn whether relatives are involved. When a bomb was set off in a park in Atlanta during the 1996 Olympics, people from around the world tried to call the city to learn about casualties. Although Atlanta created an emergency number to handle those calls, phone traffic was heavy.

PUBLIC SAFETY PERSONNEL

Police, fire, or other emergency personnel will try to quickly mark the boundaries of the scene to protect relief and investigative activity. Although reporters and photographers have moved among emergency workers at scenes that have not been marked, police expect journalists to stay clear of the boundary markers. A command hierarchy will take shape in the first hours. Police and fire agencies, hazardous materials teams, rescuers, and medical personnel may appear to be working independently, but coordination will eventually be imposed. In many situations a public information person will be designated to handle press questions.

The speed and complexity of public safety control of the situation will vary, of course. State troopers or local police will quickly take charge of an auto accident scene. Similarly, police and fire personnel will promptly take control of a fire scene. A plane crash site may be a large area, some of it inaccessible or difficult to control. Authorities quickly called in the national guard to enforce boundaries after the Oklahoma City bombing. Sometimes a federal agency, such as the FBI or the Bureau of Alcohol, Tobacco, and Firearms, may be in charge. More often a state or local police agency will oversee all rescue and investigative efforts. Journalists will need to identify key personnel with these agencies and stay in contact with them.

A 1998 story illustrates the way a scene becomes the focus of both public safety agencies and the press. Two male students at a middle school in a Jonesboro, Arkansas, killed four female pupils and a woman teacher and wounded nine other students. A study by the Freedom Forum (1998), a foundation that investigates media issues, showed what happened in the first hours after the noontime shooting.

The shooting began moments after 12:30 P.M. when a fire alarm at the school was tripped to send children rushing outside into gunfire from a wooded area nearby. The first call to 911 came in at 12:38, and the sirens of responding ambulances, as well as police messages on the newsroom scanners, alerted local media. A *Jonesboro Sun* reporter with a camera arrived by 12:50 and immediately photographed students on stretchers, tearful classmates, dazed bystanders, and "teachers and police walking across bloodstained concrete sidewalks" (Freedom Forum 1998:5). By that time sheriff's deputies had found the two boys who later were convicted of the shootings. By 1 P.M. the newspaper reporter, a local television reporter, and the "live truck" supporting him had moved behind police lines. The regional medical center had been on alert to receive shooting victims for fifteen minutes.

In Jonesboro the immediate scene of the school was relevant to reporters for a very short time. Within an hour no victims were at the scene, and the boys believed responsible had been taken into custody. The school was a scene that the media could exploit for interviews of other children, parents, and teachers. While reporters pursued those interviews, the critical centers for information were becoming the hospital and police offices. Even so, the television reporters who were arriving in the city by the dozens stayed close to the school, using it as visual backdrop for their reports. The sheriff allowed the media to stay at the school that day and night, then asked them to move to a nearby school bus yard or to the county jail. Other officials wanted the media moved from the school sooner. A year later the high school in Littleton, Colorado, where two male students killed several other people and themselves, was the center of news interest for hours as police established safety and then slowly reconstructed the murderous trail of the two shooters.

THE RED CROSS

At nearly every accident scene and in the unfolding of a disaster, such as a hurricane or earthquake, journalists will encounter people from the American Red Cross and its local chapters. The Red Cross has a congressional mandate "to provide prompt services to disaster victims to meet their disaster-caused basic human needs and to assist disaster victims without resources to begin and complete their disaster recovery efforts." Although the language refers to disasters, reporters will often find the Red Cross helping a family whose home has burned. The organization provides free shelter, food, first aid, mental health assistance, and comfort to victims and disaster workers. When recovery begins, the Red Cross can provide the means to buy food, clothing, shelter, furnishings, medical services, funeral services, and some supplies needed for work. Such support may continue for months.

After TWA flight 800 exploded near New York City in 1996, the Red Cross agreed to coordinate some services previously managed by airlines and other corporations involved in such crashes. Since that TWA accident, the Red Cross has coordinated mental health and public affairs efforts at accident scenes, in addition to its relief and recovery efforts.

As the event unfolds, journalists are increasingly likely to be working with a volunteer who works on a Red Cross rapid response public affairs team. After the first day reporters covering the Oklahoma City bombing talked with family members of victims through Red Cross team members. The Red Cross asked family members to volunteer for the press interviews; as reporters in small groups talked with the family members, Red Cross personnel stood by to assist. Beforehand, they had coached the families on the voluntary nature of the interviews and reminded them that they could end the sessions if they felt the need to do so. Although reporters and photographers often can roam accident scenes fairly freely, national guard troops limited the movement of the reporters in Oklahoma City, keeping them together near a church where family members were gathered. After TWA flight 800 exploded, family members stayed in a hotel where their privacy was guarded. When family members were willing to talk to the media, Red Cross volunteers assisted them.

The public affairs teams generally get high marks from journalists. Members are experienced professional people working both inside and outside the Red Cross. When they are on alert, they have their bags packed so they can be on a plane to the scene within four hours of a call. They often are the principal intermediaries between the press and those most affected. They are not sources of official information about an accident or disaster, but they often provide invaluable support to journalists. When a network television crew needed to have a live story about floods near Houston, Texas, on the air at 7 A.M. in the East, the Red Cross found high school students who wanted to help and a homeowner who literally needed mud shoveled out of his house. All were in place by 4:30 A.M. for the 6 A.M. transmission.

INFORMAL CONTROLS

As police, military, and other agencies gradually bring the chaotic nature of information about what happened under control, reporters and photographers may encounter unofficial but important efforts to limit access. After a school shooting in Springfield, Oregon, in 1998 students and the high school staff created a buffer zone for their grieving. Media personnel were told to respect that claim of privacy. The action was similar to that taken in Dunblane, Scotland, after the killing of several students at a school there. After an initial frenzy of reporting from Dunblane, the community acted to separate its children from the media. After a seven-hour siege at a Melbourne, Australia, preschool in 1989, four wounded children were taken to the nearby Royal Children's Hospital. To meet reporters' demands for details about injuries and treatment, the hospital staff convened a press conference the next morning. The staff gave reporters information about the injuries and educated them about trauma and the recovery process for children, including how the children might react to the many strange experiences they were confronting. Challenged by hospital personnel to stay away from the children and their families because of the likelihood of aggravating their trauma, all media representatives chose to stay away and adhered to that decision even through later legal proceedings.

When deaths occur, funeral homes and family representatives may seek to limit the media presence. Although these actions often keep journalists at a distance from funeral ceremonies, family gatherings, and grieving, many print and broadcast reporters have gained access to morgues, funerals and burials, and family gatherings against the wishes of survivors. But the best approach for the news media is to plan coverage of funerals and memorial ceremonies with the survivors and their representatives and to respect requests by families to stay out of funerals. No good will follow a reporter's intrusion into a private viewing of a body or electronic eavesdropping on a grieving family. When funerals and memorial services are intended for the community as well as the family, and offer opportunities for collective recognition of the people who died and of the value of their lives, journalists have a stronger case for being present. After the shootings in Jonesboro, the local newspaper, the *Jonesboro Sun,* devoted long stories to the funerals of the girls killed at the school, including the minister's remarks and photos of mourners. When eight thousand residents attended the Service for Hope and Healing several days after the shootings, the newspaper reported on the music, tributes, videotaped comments of President Bill Clinton, and details about the mourners. The Freedom Forum report added, "The stories are written in ways that reflect the power and emotion of the evening while avoiding maudlin language" (1998:20). Camera and sound technology allow photographers and television cameras to work some distance from the people gathered at a funeral or a gravesite. Even so, it is easy to underestimate the sense of intrusion that funeral participants may feel when they see a swarm of media people with their equipment. The policies of some media companies instruct the newsroom to forgo reporting on funerals but do allow coverage of community memorials.

PEOPLE AFFECTED BY THE EVENT AND THE MEDIA

Chapter 5 addresses ways to interview people at the scene. It is important that journalists remember that the people they are likely to encounter there are responding both physically and emotionally to a startling event. Some will be on a kind of high alert that may enable some to act heroically and others to persevere at horrifying work. A medic probably would find that these people have a rapid pulse and an increased blood volume in the heart. A reporter who is able to ask questions moments after an event might find people relaying some details with crystal clarity while others were greatly distorted. As time passes, both victims and rescue workers begin to adapt to the prolonged anxiety they must endure. They become accustomed to the increased flow of adrenaline and think more critically about what they heretofore grasped automatically. At this time reporters may also see acts of heroism and sacrifice. People readily help each other, managing to balance hope and exhilaration with their fear and grief. To some degree this description will fit reporters and photographers at the scene.

Such conditions are often present in tumultuous situations that have come to be called media feeding frenzies. Journalists drive for every fact, face, and facet of the scene, unaware that they manifest some of the same psychological signs as those they are trying to photograph or interview. As the numbers of reporters and cameras multiply, a common occurrence at violent events, the frenzy grows—those in it feed off the emotional highs of others. Each reporter wants a unique piece of the story. Consider what children and parents encountered at the school the evening of the day of the shootings in Jonesboro. Satellite vans for the television reporters lined nearby streets. "When a child and a family would get out of the car to come to the gymnasium (for counseling), there'd be cameramen and people . . . shoving [microphones] in their faces," a social worker told the Freedom Forum (1998:35). Helicopters hired by television stations from Memphis and Little Rock were circling the school grounds.

At 10 P.M. on the day of the shooting a counselor leaving the school noticed that the press had separated parents from children and one reporter was plying a little boy with questions. "I understand that that's their job, and he [the reporter] was doing what he needed to do, but he wasn't taking into account that this child had no parents there. The little boy was very scared and didn't know what was going on. They were asking him his phone number and where he lived," the counselor told the Freedom Forum (1998:8). At a nearby candlelight prayer vigil for the victims, television camera operators stood in the middle of the prayer circle photographing the faces of those present, including children. Whether such zeal reflects competitive tenacity, an emotional rush, or insensitivity to others is not clear. In any case these actions intrude on those who are attempting to recover from the event.

While those most affected by the event and bystanders are often receptive to being interviewed or photographed soon afterward, journalists must balance what they gain against the harm that they may do. Suffering is an arresting facet of such scenes, but it does not tell the full story. Jane Harrigan, a former editor and AP reporter who now teaches at the University of New Hampshire, happened to be in Kobe, Japan, when the earth shook on January 17, 1995. She later wrote,

> Journalists who cover disasters need to remember one crucial fact: The survivors aren't thinking straight. They ricochet constantly from hysterical elation at being alive to abject fear of imminent doom. These mood swings don't leave a lot of brain cells free for remembering the basic tenets of journalism. So treat disaster survivors gently. Inquire after their well being. Listen to their responses. Explain what you're doing and what you hope they can contribute. Ask specific questions, and give them time to organize their jumbled thoughts. You may be rewarded with a quote that, unlike most of what's re-

ported from disaster scenes, is actually worth printing or broadcasting. And if you get a quote, quote it correctly.

(1997:46)

Radio interviews introduce another kind of reality issue. Trauma sufferers, especially witnesses to crime, often do not want their real voices on the air. An answer to that—if using a sound bite of a source is absolutely necessary—is to use electronic scramblers that distort voices enough to ensure identification is impossible. (Some scramblers even can make a female voice sound male and vice versa.) As with cameras, sometimes the best move in taping a radio interview when a victim is upset is to turn off the recorder. Sobs may make for "great sound bites," but they also cause pain for concerned listeners. Interviewees who are given the opportunity to compose themselves when the recorder is off may be more able, and more inclined, to keep talking later.

AVOIDING DAMAGING CLICHÉS

People who work in accident and disaster relief have been heard to say that some reporters they have met could have informed their audiences just as poorly if they had remained in their newsroom. Consider some of the examples they offer.

After the 1989 Loma Prieta earthquake a news report carried a northern California shelter manager's response to a question about what was in short supply. "We're always running out of disposable diapers," he said, not mentioning that the diaper supply was replenished every morning. Within twenty-four hours trucks filled with diapers began to arrive at the shelter, occupying space, requiring attention, and frustrating relief efforts.

During Hurricane Andrew CNN flew a reporter and satellite broadcasting equipment by helicopter to Homestead, Florida, the hardest-hit town, right after the storm passed. The reporter interviewed people who had broken into a school for shelter. They had no food. The media presence fed the emotions of the people being interviewed. CNN broadcast nationally their angry accusation that their plight was being ignored. The reporter did not explain that the people had been ordered to evacuate before the hurricane hit. They had broken the law by staying there. Homestead had not set up shelters because city officials were aware of the potential for significant damage. Because of the likelihood of damage from hurricanes, Florida residents are advised to have three days' supply of food and water. This group did not. No matter. The story inspired thousands of people to try to take food, clothing, blankets, and jugs of water to the victims at Homestead. Because of the traffic jams emergency response feeding vans that provide hot meals could not get into the area. The Red Cross could only send in military MREs (meals ready to eat) by military helicopter.

Media across the country want to be helpful, so they collect things. They then pay to have the goods transported to the scene. They don't stop to think that the same thing is being done in thousands of cities across the country. The results of this are impossible to imagine without seeing a football field ten feet deep with unneeded and unwanted items being bulldozed under in southern Florida. No storage was available, it had rained, and then the heat had rotted the supplies.

Outside the prime area of impact most stores and businesses were open and needed business. People could buy most of the supplies they needed locally. Yet donors paid a lot of money to transport unneeded things across the country. As the trucks arrived, they completely overwhelmed the recovery system. Items had to be sorted, sized, and often cleaned, but relief agencies were too busy providing essential services. Many items were ludicrously inappropriate. Thousands of heavy wool blankets arrived in southern Florida.

Reporters also easily find people who are angry, grief stricken, or appear to be in shock—all signs of the emotional turmoil wrought by the event. Without context, quick visual impressions of such people can create a compelling but false sense of the mood and resilience of those being interviewed. In Seattle an apartment manager angrily complained to the media that undeserving people had crashed food lines after a five-alarm fire had displaced several hundred people from her building. Viewers' blood might have boiled at the callous insensitivity of those people. But in that case a reporter did some checking before the story was broadcast; the so-called line crashers were people who had been ordered to evacuate homes threatened by the apartment blaze. The station did not use the interview, and the apartment manager later apologized for her remarks. Angry people sometimes capture the essence of a scene, but just as often their emotion needs context and explanation. Grieving people also trigger emotional responses in viewers and readers, yet sometimes such examples eclipse stories of aid and relief. People who appear too stunned to even speak may help a reporter show that everybody at the scene is "in shock." But some of those people "in shock" recover from their weariness moments later. Relief workers and disaster researchers say that those stunned survivors, far from being incapacitated, generally get relief and cleanup efforts going well before relief agencies arrive.

Such clichés as the shocked survivor are part of what disaster specialists have come to call *disaster mythology*. Henry W. Fischer III, a sociologist, offers this version of the mythology based on numerous studies in sociology, anthropology, psychology, and other fields:

> Most of us assume that individuals cease to act in a predictable, orderly fashion.... They are expected to flee in panic, suffer from psychological dependency and disaster shock. It is often believed that evacuation of these people must not be called too soon for fear of causing massive flight behavior. It is believed that shelters overflow beyond capacity with organizers unable to deal with the mob mentality. Both survivors and those converging to the scene are believed to be driven by base, depraved instincts. These individuals are commonly perceived as likely to loot property, price gouge one another, and generally behave in other selfish ways—most of which are imagined to spread from individual to individual in a contagious fashion.
>
> (1994:11–12)

These behaviors are myths precisely because actual experience contradicts them. Reporters at the scene can avoid perpetuating the myths by describing and carefully considering only what they see. Joseph Scanlon criticizes journalism textbooks that include frequent exhortations to budding reporters to look for examples of panic at the scene. Scanlon comments, "In fact, panic is so rare it is almost impossible to study. During the crowd rush at Hillsborough soccer stadium [in Liverpool, England, 1989], those who died did so while helping others over the fence that stopped spectators from going onto the field. Similarly, at the Beverly Hills Supper Club fire in Kentucky [1977], many victims helped each other even at the cost of their own lives" (1998:49). Studies of other high-fatality fires have recognized that those who died had tried but failed to find an escape route. Rather than being irrational and panicked, the victims' last efforts were logical and focused, if desperate and finally futile.

Other parts of the disaster mythology similarly fall apart when subjected to close scrutiny. Fischer's study of media coverage of Hurricane Gilbert, which struck the south Texas Gulf Coast in September 1988, showed this in detail. He and an associate studied both broadcast and print media in the region, interviewed journalists and local officials, and observed behavior during the hurricane (1994:38–71). The study credits the media with accuracy in reporting rational preparation for the storm while criticizing reporters for perpetuating such myths as looting, price gouging, and panic. Reporters exaggerated evacuation rates and shelter populations. The researchers noted greater accuracy in the local broadcast media than in network television. Fischer speculates that some exaggeration was the result of the journalists' own belief in the elements of disaster mythology (1994:69).

E. L. Quarantelli, a student of the reporting of accidents and disasters, offers these conclusions based on numerous published studies of the behavior of people under extreme stress:

> They seldom engage in antisocial or criminal behavior such as looting. Similarly, on the whole victims neither go "crazy" nor psychologically break down, nor do they manifest severe mental health problems as a result of disasters. Those officials and others with community responsibilities do not abandon their work roles to favor their family roles. In the aftermath of the disaster impact, survivors do not passively wait for outside assistance, but actively initiate the first search-and-rescue efforts, taking the injured to medical care and doing whatever can be done in the crisis. Mass shelters are avoided. Those forced out of their homes go overwhelmingly to places offered by relatives and friends.
>
> (1989:6)

Although victims are often unfairly reported as irrational, Quarantelli notes that the relief agencies are generally portrayed—equally unfairly—as more rational and better organized than they are (1989:7). Journalists seem eager to show that emergency agencies have accomplished a good deal; the weight of research suggests that the convergence of relief and emergency agencies at the scene may complicate, rather than ease, the suffering. In the 1995 Kobe, Japan, earthquake, authorities failed to restrict highways to official use, leading to delay in the arrival of police and fire vehicles. Officials also were slow to ask for support from the armed forces. A reporter ought to be looking in a fair but critical way at the overall management of the scene rather than seeking to convince the audience that whatever agencies responded have matters firmly in hand, a misleading message that those agencies will strive to reinforce.

An equally serious problem in reporting on events that are not natural disasters is the pressure that reporters will experience from editors and other media to find an explanation. James Carey, a commentator on the character of American journalism, writes: "How and why are the most problematic aspects of American journalism: the dark continent and invisible landscape. Why and how are what we most want to get out of a news story and are least likely to receive or what we must in most cases supply ourselves" (1987:149). Carey says that journalists faced with an unexplained event will try to attribute it to some rational reason (188–89).

Carey's analysis was exemplified by a series of shootings in schools in several states in the closing years of the 1990s. When boys killed other students, reporters vied for such instant explanations as racism or gender difference. Some reporters focused on troubles between the shooter and his parents, while others tried to show that a "gun culture" led to their actions. Other media, eschewing a ready cause, made their stories fit the "believe it or not" formula—the shootings happened in small towns where such things just do not happen.

After the Jonesboro shootings in 1998, all three national newsmagazines— *Time, Newsweek,* and *U.S. News & World Report*—emphasized the gun culture explanation. *Time* and *Newsweek* ran cover photographs of one of the suspects holding a firearm. Although some accounts disavowed the explanation or noted the anger of Jonesboro residents about repetition of the theme, network coverage reinforced the idea. A CNN correspondent, speaking about the funerals, speculated that mourners were wondering whether the familiarity of youngsters with guns "may have had something to do with this" (Freedom Forum 1998:25). While some details about the boys' use and knowledge of guns were relevant, these quickly became the single answer or explanation that eclipsed other possibilities. A year later, in Littleton, Colorado, the media looked for the "why" in evidence of enmity between athletes and other students and in an inaccurate reference to the shooters as members of a marginalized clique.

Here are some tips for reporting at the scene:

- Be aware that local public safety planning for tragic events should consider who will respond, what needs will be urgent, and what long-term help the community will require
- Train for safety and self-care, as well as effective ways to cover what happened, for assignments to a distant place.
- Discuss with peers and editors how to respond to those in need at the scene.
- Recognize the dangers associated with dispersal of chemical or biological agents. Learn about the risks before approaching the scene.
- Be sure that communication equipment is working and available to reporters and photographers, and the media organization should have a plan for how staffers in the field will communicate with editors and other reporters.
- Take note of your own emotional reactions, appreciate that the intensity of reporting may delay those reactions, and know ways to address emotions when they surface.

- Respect the impact on people at the scene; they may be disoriented and have difficulty expressing themselves.
- Check with authorities before telling viewers that a devastated area has particular needs; one person's cry for a blanket can lead to mountains of donated but unneeded blankets.

MARLEY SHEBALA

Adding Context to the Scene

Marley Shebala's *Navajo Times* colleague showed her a photograph he had taken of a blood-soaked mop at the scene of a domestic dispute. A man had beaten his wife and then ordered their teenage son to mop up the blood. The photographer wanted Shebala to write a story about it and use the picture. She declined; she was busy with other stories, and she saw no point in writing a "flat news story" about the beating.

Shebala believes that such stories do not serve her readers or her community. They tell that a woman was beaten, or that someone shot someone else, but they lack context. They are presented as moments but with no explanation of their broader emotional and economic impact. "The media start desensitizing the community," Shebala says. "I don't believe that's what a newspaper is supposed to be doing. That doesn't really challenge us as writers."

Marley Shebala.

Shebala's coverage of tragedy and violence goes beyond simply collecting facts. She analyzes what happened, considers whether it is indicative of an underlying problem, and thinks about solutions. When she decided to write a series of stories about how domestic violence affects Navajo children, she told the photographer the time was right to use the picture of the bloody mop. It no longer illustrated an isolated incident but showed poignantly what children experience when ensnared in domestic violence. "When you show that, that a child had to clean that up," she says, "that's taking the story a little bit further."

Shebala's mother was a Navajo and her father a Zuñi, and she grew up on the Navajo Nation's reservation. She began working at the weekly *Navajo Times* as an intern in 1983, moved on to the tribal radio station, and also worked at two daily newspapers before returning to the *Times*. She was a teaching fellow at the University of California, Berkeley, and serves on the board of directors of the Native American Journalists Association. She is one of just a few news reporters at the *Times*, the *only* one when times are tough, as they have been lately. She has had opportunities to work at larger papers, but she always says no. She is a storyteller in the Navajo tradition, and she cannot tell the stories of her people if she leaves them behind.

"Some reporters zip in and zip out, and they don't have to be responsible," she says. "If you stay in a community, your reporting becomes so much more accurate and you are so much more responsible, because the community knows who you are."

Shebala's duties require her to chase all kinds of news stories, including tragedy and violence. When she arrives at the scene, chances are she knows the people involved. She grew up with them, or her daughter did, or her grandchildren do today. She tells the people she's there to do a story *for* them. She explains that others will learn from their experience, whatever they decide to share.

She wishes she always could report good news, because she wants a healthy community for her family and neighbors, but she knows she must present the bad with the good. To do otherwise would be to discount her people's storytelling tradition and to ignore their history. "The stories are there to help people to grow and to heal," she says. "That's tradition; that's what we're taught."

Shebala sometimes is criticized for writing stories that portray her people in a bad light or expose problems on the reservation. But, she argues, the Navajo tribe has always been an open society, and censorship of any kind has no place in it. The stories she tells relay a message; they are what she calls "teaching stories." They show people how to conduct their lives and what happens when they act in ways that are harmful to themselves and others. "When I look at these stories, they are like Aesop fables," she says. "Down deep, reporters don't really enjoy covering tragedy, but that's part of life."

Shebala makes sure she maintains a personal distance from her subjects, because she often is tempted to reach out emotionally. She reminds herself that she is there to write a story and forces herself to slow down. She looks at everything—her watch, where people are standing, the sun, the clouds. She gets it all, and she gets it as truthfully as she can. "That's for your readers," she says.

Shebala learned this lesson early in her career, and dramatically. A political dispute had ripped apart the Navajo Nation in the summer of 1989, and she was covering it for the *Farmington (N.M.) Daily Times*. "It really was a civil war," she says. "It was a civil conflict that had broken out among the Navajo people."

She heard about a demonstration at the tribal administration offices, and she and a reporter from the *Gallup (N.M.) Independent* decided to go together, for safety's sake. They posted themselves on a hill above and watched as a crowd of about three hundred people surged toward one of the buildings, menacing a tribal police officer.

Someone stole a shotgun from a police car and shots were fired. A smoke bomb exploded, enveloping the rioters in haze. Shebala and the other reporter raced down the hill into the melee and began "doing what journalists do—writing down what we saw was going on." She spotted an emergency vehicle and ran to it. An elderly man in a western shirt, Levis, and boots lay on his back and stared into the sky. "I remember writing that he looked so peaceful in all this chaos," she says. "And his eyes started turning gray, fogging over, and I was writing. And I wrote that he was dying."

Two men died that afternoon, and two police officers were among the injured. Shebala realized she had witnessed an important event in Navajo history, and she was determined to write about it, although she did so through tears. "Anything I write, if I have difficulty, I make a prayer," she says. "I talk to Creator and ask Creator to help me. Of course, I'm human, so if that experience I'm writing about hurts me, the tears come. But I think that helps any writer, whether it's anger or sadness or joy."

She prayed that day. "Watch over me, Creator, and watch over the People," she said. "Take pity on us."

Not long ago, a young *Times* reporter overheard Shebala talking about how she had covered the riot, and he approached her afterward and said he wanted to know the story. His aunt had been in the building that day, but he never knew the details because his family wouldn't talk about it.

But Shebala had been there, and she had had the strength to report and write about what happened. It became a part of her people's history. A part of her history.

What Is a Navajo Leader?

MARLEY SHEBALA

When President Bill Clinton commuted the sentence of former Navajo tribal chairman Peter MacDonald Sr. in 2001, Marley Shebala told her editor at the Navajo Times that he should write an editorial. MacDonald had never apologized for the bribery for which he was convicted, nor for his connection to a 1989 riot that left two people dead, a tragedy that Shebala covered. She gave her editor her notes from that day and told him he could use them to help write the editorial. She was not going to write it because she was recovering from surgery for a detached retina. Her editor told her that it was her responsibility. "You're not dead yet," he said. "You still have one eye."

Shebala wrote the following editorial, published on January 25, 2001, relying on her notes and summoning memories from more than a decade earlier. "You don't forget it," she says. "You just can't."

ONE SUMMER DAY

Two People Lost Their Lives When MacDonald Supporters and Police Clash

What is a Navajo leader? Is there a difference between a Navajo leader and a Navajo politician?

I was told that a Navajo leader or Naataani became the head of the people because he knew the traditional prayers, chants and ceremonies that protected the people, the land, animals—all of life between the Four Sacred Mountains.

On July 20, 1989, two of our people lost their lives in a riot at the financial services building in Window Rock. Several police officers were also wounded.

I was there. At the time I was a reporter for the *Farmington* (N.M.) *Daily Times.*

It was a beautiful summer day and I was riding in a pickup truck with then *Gallup* (N.M.) *Independent* reporter and photographer Richard Sitts.

We were driving back from the executive offices when we saw a Navajo police vehicle race past us. It was headed to the executive offices.

Of course, we spun around and followed the police vehicle. But then it quickly turned around and headed to the financial services building.

The power struggle

The Navajo Tribal Council and Chairman Peter MacDonald Sr. were embroiled in a bitter political dispute that had become physically and verbally abusive, in and around the council chamber.

A demonstration on April 7, 1989 outside the council chamber became violent after Navajo police failed to keep supporters of MacDonald and the majority council separated.

The MacDonald supporters at the time were occupying the executive offices in a 24-hour standoff with the majority council.

The council on Feb. 14, 1989 had called for the removal of MacDonald amid allegations of kickbacks, fraud and racketeering and also possible violations of the Ethics in Government Act and the Election Code involving the purchase of the Big Boquillas Ranch for $33.4 million and other business deals.

But the council soon found that they had a power struggle on their hands.

Over the 12 years that MacDonald was chairman, the council had delegated much of its authority to the chairman. Council records show how MacDonald eloquently convinced the council that the movement of their power to him was in the best interests of the people.

MacDonald presided over the council. He handpicked members of the various council committees, including the now defunct Advisory Committee, which had the power to act as the council when the council was not in session.

He also selected the chairmen and vice chairmen of the committees.

MacDonald decided what resolutions and individuals came before the council. And since he presided over the council, he decided what council delegates spoke on the council floor.

MacDonald's power to make political appointments was not limited to division directors and executive staff assistants. His reach went down to department and program directors.

So it was no easy task for 49 of the 88 council delegates to literally stand up on the council floor to make their voices heard.

Council records reveal passionate calls by the "49ers" to their colleagues to remember the oath of office they took on Jan. 13, 1987, which included the protection of the people's resources—money, land, buildings, equipment, coal, oil, timber, workers, etc.

Violence escalates

I was there when these elected leaders of the people were locked out of the council chamber and the legislative offices by the Navajo police on the orders of MacDonald.

The majority council finally had no choice but to meet at the Education Center, and the MacDonald supporters threw rocks at them, spit on them, shoved them, pulled their hair and publicly degraded them as men.

During the April 7, 1989 demonstration in front of the council chamber, I saw the Navajo Fire Department aim high-powered water hoses at our elders. Navajo police beat men, young and old, with their clubs.

The *Navajo Times* still has a photo of a police officer with his club held high over the head of Council Delegate Tom LaPahe, who is sitting on the ground with his arms over his head.

This week, several people, including a few council delegates, have talked to me—off the record—about former President Clinton's commutation of Mac-Donald's sentence.

But only one Navajo leader, LaPahe, went on record. On Jan. 23, in the council chamber, LaPahe stood up and reminded his colleagues that not everyone is happy about MacDonald's return. LaPahe did not want the council to forget the family members who would not see the return of their loved ones.

I can still remember standing at the top of the hill and looking down at the financial services building on July 20, 1989.

A lone police officer jumped out of his police car in front of the two-story building. A group of MacDonald supporters with large sticks in their hands raised them over their heads and walked towards the officer.

He held his arm out and put his hand up in a motion to stop them. His other hand went to his side, where his gun was holstered.

And then the crowd was upon him. I saw him fall from sight. His car blocked my view. But I could see people raising and dropping their sticks.

They were beating him.

A couple of other police vehicles arrived but the mob outnumbered them.

A police van became stuck in the sand on the north side of the building. The driver, a lone officer, ran down a ditch as the mob ran towards him.

One of the demonstrators got in the police van. When he exited the van, he held a rifle over his head.

I was running down the hill.

More police officers arrived and smoke bombs began exploding. People were yelling and screaming.

And then I heard gun shots.

I broke through a crowd of people and saw a man lying in the dirt. He was staring straight up into the blue sky, where white clouds billowed.

A soft breeze moved the smoke around him. His eyes were glazing over. I knew that he was dying.

I looked past him. Another individual lay on the ground.

Emergency medical technicians arrived and tried to save the men. But the crowd was acting like wild dogs.

"Only a demonstration"

The few police officers that were on the scene tried to surround the EMTs to protect them because people began jumping out of the crowd and lunging at them.

One of the EMTs, a young Navajo woman, was visibly scared. Her hands were moving quickly but each time someone jumped out of the mob and yelled or screamed, she'd freeze.

The EMTs finally got the victims into the ambulance and sped off.

I looked up at the hill and saw another crowd of people. This group was yelling at the MacDonald supporters to go home. They were angry.

A woman in her mid-30s walked by sobbing and shaking her head. I asked her why she was crying.

She said they told her it was only going to be a demonstration. She said she didn't know about the two-by-four clubs and baseball bats.

As I walked through the parking lot of the financial services building, I saw several people, including an elderly Navajo woman and a young Navajo woman, throwing the clubs and bats into the trunk of a vehicle.

The two women were smiling and laughing. . . .

I was at a pro-MacDonald rally in front of the parking lot of the executive office one night when I and a television crew from Italy heard then Vice Chairman Johnny R. Thompson tell the crowd that the only way for MacDonald to regain his power was to take back the "purse strings."

Thompson pointed towards the financial services building.

No guilt, remorse or compassion for victims

The council, during the short-lived administration of President Albert Hale, voted 51 to 14 with six abstaining on April 21, 1995 to pardon MacDonald and 13 of his supporters, who were convicted in tribal court in 1990 and federal court in 1991.

Tribal documents show that about $2.5 million of the people's money was spent on investigating and prosecuting MacDonald.

Federal and tribal records revealed that the Big Boquillas Ranch cost the people $33.4 million and that MacDonald shared a $7.2 million profit from that land swindle with two non-Indian buddies.

When the council was deliberating on the MacDonald pardon, then Chief Legislative Counsel Claudeen Bates-Arthur and then Attorney General Herb Yazzie cautioned the council about opening up old wounds.

Bates-Arthur and Yazzie, in written advice to the council, explained that in the traditional Navajo way, the victims of a crime must not be forgotten.

They said that this could only be accomplished when the offender expressed guilt, remorse and asked for compassion from the victims.

MacDonald, in an April 5, 1995 letter to Hale, Vice President Thomas Atcitty, Council Speaker Kelsey Begaye and the council, appealed to their kindness, love and compassion to pardon him of any and all convictions.

In 1995, MacDonald had served four years of his 14-year federal sentence.

MacDonald also stated, "I wish it was possible to suffer alone but that isn't possible. When one is serving time in prison, family members, relatives, and friends serve time with you.

"They suffer, they experience pain and deprivation. I dearly regret what happened to so many of us; resulting in so many tears and hurt," MacDonald stated in his five-paragraph letter.

He also talked about his age, 66, and physical illnesses, which included pain when he walked and a broken wrist.

MacDonald also spoke about the traditional Navajo way of life.

"Ours (Navajo way) is not a society of revenge or extended incarceration; ours is a society of khe' (clan relationship); ours is a society of harmony (Hozhoona'has'dlii); ours is a society of a'joba' (kindness); and ours is a society of love (Ah'yoo'o'o'na')."

The MacDonald letter is part of the council's April 21, 1995 pardon and nowhere does MacDonald admit guilt, show remorse or ask for compassion from his victims.

The day after the bloody July 20, 1989 riot at the financial services building, MacDonald held a press conference at the Navajo Nation Inn. He was asked by the media if he planned to discourage his supporters from becoming violent again.

MacDonald's answer, which was recorded by several members of the press, was that his supporters do what they want to do.

What is a Navajo leader? Is there a difference between a Navajo leader and a Navajo politician?

CHAPTER 5

The Interview: Assault or Catharsis?

Interviews with people caught up in traumatic events are standard fare for both television and newspapers. The interview is an old fixture in news, used for more than 160 years. In the beginning the interview offered a way for leading figures of the day—politicians, church leaders, and explorers—to offer their stories. The novelty of direct access to celebrated people helped establish the interview as a newspaper staple. By the end of the nineteenth century the interview—once branded "a thing of ill savor in all decent nostrils" (Snyder and Morris 1962:106)—was passing from a device as likely to be fraudulent as real to an essential tool of the journalist, a ready complement to the reporter's eyewitness account. In that transition common people joined celebrities as subjects of interviews, particularly if they were swept into suffering or loss by events such as fires, floods, earthquakes, and sensational crimes. The reporter could descend on any scene, ready both to observe its details and to question anyone in sight with a shred of information about what had happened. When Marguerite Higgins, then a correspondent for the *New York Herald-Tribune*, entered the newly liberated German concentration camp at Buchenwald in 1945, she was staggered by the sights of death and suffering but remembered some of the false atrocity stories blamed on Germany in World War I. "So at the concentration camp I questioned and cross-questioned the miserable inmates with a relentless insistence on detail that must have seemed morbid," she later wrote (1955:74–75).

Today many news interviews are brief encounters with people who have no interest in the spotlight; they were simply in a bad place at a bad time. Some of these brief interviews provoke angry public reaction, whereas others simply feed our fascination with extraordinary experiences. Some people say they appreciated a reporter's questions at a time of crisis; others remain angry about such interviews long afterward.

Reporters face a dilemma when they try to interview victims of violence. When does it make sense to interview someone caught in the shock waves of a violent event, and when is it best to leave the person alone? This chapter discusses what a journalist should consider before doing an interview. Now is a better time to examine these ideas and to make decisions than that dicey moment when the city editor or the assignment editor points toward the door and sends a reporter to the scene.

Few practices seem as contradictory as interviews of people in a crisis situation. On one hand, people carefully read the stories built on such interviews; on television, interviews with victims command audience attention. People close to those involved are deeply affected by the event and follow any news about it closely. Strangers also eagerly consume reports about the victims and the violence. In the *Nation* Bruce Shapiro describes being stabbed while he was in a New Haven, Connecticut, coffee shop. Friends, neighbors, and strangers told him that they were shaken by what had happened. "The reaction of most was a combination of decent horrified empathy and a clear sense that their own presumption of safety was undermined," Shapiro writes (1995:448).

Coté and I believe the interview with a person caught in a violent event is a staple of news because it puts people in touch with the voice, face, and emotions of a person who is suffering. Life sometimes offers an unsettling array of threats and opportunities. The threats alarm people, but they gain some information about the threats from the misfortunes of others. People learn about the risks in their lives from hearing about the mishaps of others, and some are reassured by the illusion that they are safe because the other person has suffered misfortune. People's reasons for reading and watching are diverse and not so simple as a desire to be entertained by another person's misery.

Journalists know that every story needs a "who," a person who will humanize the event, and stories about violence and victims of crime and disaster are no different. Violence stories let us read about and see relatively unknown people, people whose stories are not shaped by predictable formal roles such as business executive, politician, or expert. One could argue that violence news is journalism's way of linking the public with ordinary people.

The victim and the reporter are connected by intimate communication—intimate because the reporter enters the victim's life at a moment of extraordinary stress. The reporter's duty to inform the public may well coincide with the needs of the victim, but the reporter cannot use that duty to excuse exploitation of victims for other reasons, such as better ratings or awards.

The reporter and victim both bring to the interview assumptions about the other person, her or his needs, and the skills that doing an effective interview requires. In the hours after a violent event a victim, survivor, or witness may want to help apprehend a violent person, stop a pattern of violence in a community, or simply give voice to the emotions aroused by the devastating fire, flood, or earthquake. Family members of victims may be eager to help police identify and arrest a perpetrator or get help for a relative left homeless by a natural disaster. And some people, because of their heightened awareness, will be ready to speak to anyone who is interested. A journalist may find a willing interviewee who won't know whether talking to a reporter will be helpful or unsettling. A reporter's presence alone may persuade some victims and witnesses that they should ignore their discomfort in order to help the reporter. Others will act as though they have a duty to speak to the press.

As time passes, victims of violence may want to keep public attention focused on the crime, the search for suspects, pending legislation, or the needs of others. Some survivors will eagerly take on the role of public advocate, even seeking out journalists to give quotes or suggest story ideas. In contrast, some who have experienced physical or psychological wounds will react to stressful case developments, such as arrests, arraignments, trials, executions, or paroles, by avoiding contact with the media. Journalists should never view that other person in a simplistic or stereotypical way; an individual's reactions to media attention will depend on many factors and may change frequently.

The journalist carries a heavy ethical burden into an interview. The press, columnist Walter Lippmann wrote, "is like the beam of a searchlight that moves restlessly about, bringing one episode and then another out of darkness into vision." The news media place the violent event in the spotlight briefly, usually with interviews of survivors and bystanders. Such news may offer a rich and complex idea of how an event affects a community: aid services; public safety responses; the workings of the criminal justice system; relief and recovery for victims, families, and friends; and how individuals cope with harm and violence. Often, though, the event is only a brief reminder of perils, and the interview yields too little about the person, the context of the event, or information about how others can deal with the perils.

Interviews also serve the need of the television station or the newspaper to attract and hold an audience. Mayhem not only leads but also often dominates the first several minutes of television news shows. Television audiences appear to be more likely to watch news programs that emphasize violence, an echo of what newspaper circulation managers learned back in the days when most newspapers were sold on the street—stories and photographs of crime scenes and survivors of violence draw an audience (Dorfman et al. 1997). Although crime rates have been declining in urban centers for some years, a number of studies of local television news affirm the industry's consistent penchant for news of crime and violence.

The willingness of suffering people to talk to the news media does not give reporters a license to interview anyone right after a traumatic event. Reporters should not hesitate to decide that it is not a good time to interview a victim of violence, a child witness or friend, or a family member. Some effective reporters observe the scene but stay away from those affected by the event. Others introduce themselves, offer a business card, and ask for a chance to talk sometime in the near future. Bruce Shapiro, the journalist who was a stabbing victim, thinks fondly of the newspaper reporter who arrived at the coffee shop just minutes after Shapiro and others were attacked. "Instead of trying to interview anyone, he saw that the incident was causing instant gridlock on the nearby streets and began directing traffic," Shapiro told us.

Each interview needs a deliberate judgment about the capacity of the other person to understand what an interview entails, including potential ramifications for the interviewee, family members, and friends. It is not enough that a person agrees to the interview. The ethical burden is not on the interview subject but on the journalist. Reporters are not trained to assess the emotional state of a person, but they can take pains to assure that the people being interviewed know who is asking the questions and understand why the interview is taking place.

"Journalists have an obligation to disclose to their sources, at a minimum, the implications, advantages, and risks involved in agreeing to an interview," Sandra Borden writes (1993:222). Neal Shine, former publisher of the *Detroit Free Press,* proposes that victims be "read their rights," something like the *Miranda* warning that police give suspects, and be told that they don't have to do everything reporters ask. Frank Ochberg, the Michigan psychiatrist, suggests bringing up some of the harmful effects of doing the interview, something like: "Remembering, however, may be painful for you. And your name will be used. You might have some unwanted recollections after we talk and after the story appears. In the long run, telling your story to me should be a positive thing. Any questions before we begin?" Ochberg adds, "From an ethical point of view, you should afford your interviewee as much control as possible and as much foreknowledge as possible. You can do this by explaining your journalistic objective. For example, you might begin, 'I'm really interested in the facts of the robbery. I know this may be upsetting right after it happened, but I won't be reporting on how he made you feel'" (1996:24–25).

Some journalists oppose these suggestions. In their thinking the reporter ought to control the interview. Reporters have learned by trial and error how to get information from reluctant sources; reporters fear compromising an opportunity to elicit as much information as possible by using this form of negotiation with the victim or witness. In some interviews the information at stake is so important that it should not be compromised away. Some sources have eyewitness details to reveal or may turn out to be a suspect. But gaining informed consent does not detract in any way from what the reporter might pick up in the interview. It does, however, offer the journalist's subject useful knowledge about what an interview may entail.

Careful listening can provide the journalist with information about the other person's readiness to talk. Does this person understand that revealing certain details in an interview may later be cause for regret? With an assailant at large does the person realize that comments offered in a moment of excitement may place people's lives at risk? Will revisiting a trauma reopen emotional wounds for the person or for others?

BEFORE THE INTERVIEW

A familiar definition of *empathy* is that it is the capacity to walk in someone else's shoes, to appreciate what the other person is enduring. An empathetic reporter need not have suffered in the same way as the person being interviewed. Coté and I define empathy as a way of thinking that enables an individual to get a better understanding of the feelings and experiences of another person. The more empathetic the journalist, we believe, the better the resulting story will be and the less likely it is to result in harm to another person. We believe that empathy is revealed in the work of journalists who encourage people to tell the story their way, who balance expert voices with the voices of those who were hurt, and who listen carefully when another person speaks honestly about what she or he has experienced.

The first step to an empathetic interview is preparation—as much as time will allow. The pages that follow are interspersed with guidelines for reporters who are interviewing people whose lives have been disrupted by a traumatic event.

In most types of stories the reporter's gender does not—or should not—matter much in terms of the openness of communication between reporter and subject. There usually is no reason a reporter cannot do a professional, ethical job in gathering information and writing stories, regardless of his or her identity.

But when the news scene turns to more personalized and traumatic stories, gender sometimes can be important. There usually is no time to consider gender when reporting breaking news about violence. If a serial rapist strikes again, the police reporter—man or woman—probably will do the story. If the reporter is male, however, he should be very wary of trying to directly approach a rape survivor.

Reporters—male or female—do not, thankfully, routinely knock on rape victims' doors. An interview may be appropriate occasionally, though, in special circumstances such as when police are seeking a serial rapist and a woman wants to encourage other victims to come forward. Another interview situation might be months or years after a rape when, for example, a victim talks about coping and recovery programs available in a community. Whatever the time lapse, think about how the survivor may react to a reporter. "In the first few days afterward, I was very squirrelly around any men," says Memyo Lyons, a Michigan radio reporter and rape survivor. "That's unfair, but there it is." It would be better to have a woman interview a female rape survivor when what happened is very fresh, says Lyons, now a television news assignment editor. For that matter, she believes it is wrong for a reporter, male or female, to approach a recent rape survivor without first telephoning. "If someone, anyone, had knocked at my door for an interview a day or two afterward, I'd have lost my mind. The phone is a critical link then." After months or years, Lyons says, whether the reporter is a man or woman does not really matter "as long as they're respectful."

Even when years have passed, some stories about sexual crimes may be difficult for men to cover. The three women in the "Malignant Memories" account of childhood incest (see the excerpt that follows chapter 10) say they would not have talked freely if the reporter and photographer had been men. Many details in the prize-winning story by Debra McKinney came from observing what the women were doing or saying while McKinney and photographer Fran Durner accompanied them. Even so, time, patience, and mutual respect can bridge many gender-sensitive situations.

The reporter needs to respect the other person's efforts to regain balance after a horrible experience. The man, woman, or child whom a reporter faces in an interview will someday be an expert on surviving a violent, devastating experience but probably does not yet know how to communicate that knowledge. It may be hard to appreciate what the victim is enduring or to understand exactly what he wants to say. Sometimes he won't be able to find the words he wants. The reporter may be too busy asking questions to notice that he is having trouble answering.

The reporter should offer as much support to the interviewee as conditions will allow. Suggesting that the interviewee ask a friend, neighbor, or relative to be present may reassure her and may help her to speak more usefully. This will be especially important if there are barriers to communication, such as different language skills, ages, genders, classes, and cultures. The reporter also should give some thought to where the interview will take place. The setting should not force the victim to look at damaged vehicles, covered or uncovered bodies, and tense rescue workers while talking to the reporter. A better approach is to find a place away from the activity of the scene and give him and his companion a chance to sit. The reporter should maintain eye contact as the victim talks and should not stand if the other person is sitting.

Reporters also should watch what they say.

At this stage their words carry a lot of weight. They can lead the victim to seek promises from the reporter, to exaggerate what the reporter will be able to do, and to assume that the reporter is willing to be a friend as well as a reporter. This is a difficult balancing act. The reporter will be speaking to a person who needs support. By listening carefully, by keeping the line of questions close to what the person truly knows, and by not looking for past history or theories about why something happened, the reporter will maintain trust without opening the way to unrealistic expectations. People who have suffered violence sometimes speak about reporters whose sincerity, body language, and obvious concern suggested empathy. Yet when they saw the videotape or read about themselves in condensed and tightly edited stories, they found avoidable errors in the facts, or failed to find their comments at all, and felt betrayed.

People at the scene will not be ready for what some reporters call their "con." Reporters quickly learn how to act fascinated with someone's story and how to build rapport through eye contact, facial expression, and body language. Some people they interview do not appreciate the extent to which the reporter's manner may be a professional pose.

As soon as possible, reporters should let the other person know who they are, not just their name but that they are a reporter and the name of the publication or station for which they work. A reporter may have to repeat this information, but that is far easier than having to explain later how someone's confidences wound up in a newspaper article. A Michigan newspaper reporter said she had identified herself clearly to a man whose murdered child had been found. The next day, after her story was published, the man complained bitterly about some of the information; he did not remember that he had talked to the reporter. Forgetting such details goes with trauma, but the reporter could have mentioned her profession a second or even a third time.

The reporter's manner and first words will tell the other person whether he should trust the journalist and how sincere the journalist is. Those first impressions may decide whether the reporter is ever again able to interview that person. Reporters who are talking to someone who has just lost someone close to him should express their condolences. Martin Symonds, a former deputy commissioner of the New York City Police Department who later became a therapist, says that at least one of three comments always will be appropriate: "'I'm sorry this happened to you.' 'I'm glad you weren't killed.' 'It's not your fault'" (Ochberg 1987:12–13, 41).

The words "I'm sorry," spoken sincerely, can be reassuring and calming. The same words tossed off casually so that the reporter can start asking questions will leave a lasting negative impression. Reporters should not try to announce their empathy by saying they know how the other person feels or by relating one of their own ordeals. Journalists often are tempted to bring up their own terrible experiences because they have just been reminded powerfully of them. They may want to share their hard-earned wisdom about the length and difficulty of recovery. But they should, by all means, keep those insights to themselves.

Reporters also must respect the other person's need to focus on her circumstances. And they should avoid the question that drives some victims and survivors to distrust reporters: "How do you feel?" Marc Klaas, the father of Polly Klaas, who was kidnapped and murdered in California in 1993, says reporters never stopped asking the question from the time of the kidnapping through the trial of the murderer. "'How do you feel?' Don't ask. I felt like shit. We feel awful and we'll probably always feel awful. Don't ask how we feel. Ask us what we need," he told a group of reporters and editors at a conference in Oklahoma. The question is used so often that it is a painful cliché in newscasts. Reporters will swear they never use it until a close look at their tapes or stories shows that they have. On rare occasions, though, a thoughtful question about someone's feelings may open the way to a story that readers or viewers will understand and that will help the one who tells it.

Reporters also must prepare themselves for the time when they will be the first person to announce a death to a survivor. Reporters often have run into a family member near an accident scene or appeared at a home for a "death knock" interview, only to find that family members have not been informed. An Ypsilanti, Michigan, reporter called the widow of a man killed in a traffic accident for facts about his life. "I want to express my sympathy," the reporter said. "About what?" the woman asked. The reporter, startled, awkwardly suggested the woman call the police. After that, the newspaper made it a policy to call the home of an accident victim only after the police had notified the family. A call to the local police (or another agency that handles notification of next of kin) would have helped another reporter, who invented a story on the spot when he learned that the woman he was interviewing was unaware of her husband's death. He told her that he was seeking details for a story about an award. Compare his relief at not having to bear the bad tidings with the hurt the woman must have felt when she read in the newspaper the details she had volunteered. (Coté and I do not endorse "death-knock" interviews, although they are commonly done by both print and broadcast journalists.)

And if the reporter's intent is not to reveal a victim's identity until police have notified the family, paying attention to details is important. A Seattle television reporter planted himself in front of an accident victim's highly visible law office sign to report his death and to say, evidently quite sincerely, that the name was being withheld until the family was notified. The lawyer's wife, who did not know that her husband had died, was watching the news.

If an act of violence is involved, the story may require information about how someone was killed or injured, about what might have led to the violent act, about the possibility of a pattern of such attacks, and so on. Reporter should direct questions about these matters to the police; such details may only harm the survivor if a reporter brings them up during the interview. Reporters also should avoid speculation about what caused someone's death. Family members often say they are plagued by mental images in which they try to imagine the moments before their loved one died. News stories that include such details often are troubling to survivors, and mentioning such details in an interview soon after a death can also cause relatives to suffer unwanted and unexpected images of the death scene.

It certainly is permissible to give out any information that might help the person being interviewed to get in touch with friends or family members and agencies such as the police and fire departments, American Red Cross, or medics. But reporters must think carefully about giving out details that have come to them second hand. Generally, one or more public safety officers at the scene will provide essential information; that is rarely a reporter's role.

A good reporter also sets the stage for the interview.

The reporter's first questions will provide two kinds of information. The first kind—details of the other person's knowledge of the situation—will help the reporter begin to grasp what has happened. Asking a "when" or a "who" question will elicit this information: When did you hear the news? When did the police arrive? When did you arrive? Who has spoken to you? Who was here when you arrived? In a few seconds a reporter may learn the sequence of events that involved the other person. A question about an earlier interview may help a reporter determine whether and how to proceed with an interview. If the person has spoken with a public safety officer, the reporter might simply ask, "How did that conversation go for you?"

Good reporters also explain the ground rules.

This is the time to gain informed consent by identifying risks to the interview subject. It is also the time to help the source understand what the reporter intends to do. The reporter should explain why he is there, the kind of story he is expected to write or report, when it is likely to run, and why it is important for the person to speak to a reporter. Reporters should never promise anything that they cannot guarantee; the comments a reporter is about to write down or tape may never make it into print or on the air.

A good reporter also shares control with the interviewee.

Most seasoned reporters appear to be models of efficiency as they hurry among the police, emergency workers, and bystanders. They have a mission, know how to carry it out, and generally stay out of the way of others with urgent tasks. The person in trauma, on the other hand, has just lost control of his world. He doesn't fully understand what has happened, is subject to the orders and directions of others, and can do little to gain personal control over the chaotic situation.

An effective approach is to ask short open-ended questions. What have you learned? Who has spoken to you so far? How long have you been here? What happened? These questions carry no judgments and give the other person a chance to orient himself and the reporter to the event.

A person jolted by an event may need, and will certainly appreciate, a chance to decide some of the conditions of the interview. Would he like to sit or stand? Does he want to remain here or go somewhere away from the turmoil of the scene? Is there someone he would like to have present during the interview?

A good reporter anticipates emotional responses.

Frank Ochberg, the psychiatrist, offers this useful advice about dealing with emotional responses soon after a traumatic event:

As an interviewer, you can either elicit or avoid emotion. Most reporters would prefer to have their interviewees describe rather than display strong emotions (TV talk-show hosts excepted). So would I, in initial interviews with trauma survivors. It is not uncommon for tears to flow during the telling of an emotional event. Therapists offer tissues. Reporters should bring tissues if a tearful interview is anticipated. . . .

When survivors cry during interviews, they are not necessarily reluctant to continue. They may have difficulty communicating, but they often want to tell their stories. Interrupting them may be experienced as patronizing and denying an opportunity to testify. Remember, if you terminate an interview unilaterally, because you find it upsetting, or you incorrectly assume that your subject wants to stop, you may be re-victimizing the victim.

(1996:24, 25)

Listen.

In reporting, as in most other activities, people are not well trained to listen to the other person. People hear what they want or need to hear and often screen out signals that they do not expect or do not understand. Good listening requires hearing not only the words that are spoken and making sense of them but also noticing gestures, facial expressions, emotions, and body language. Thus it is important to take the other person fully into account and then remember and make sense of what that person heard and saw. Ken Metzler, a journalism teacher who is an authority on journalistic listening, compares the best listeners and the worst listeners. The best, he says, use the time to think about what is being said, anticipate what will be said next, and listen "between the lines for ideas and attitudes hinted at but not expressed directly." The worst listeners, he says, wait for facts, try to memorize them, are easily distracted or bored, and may jump on a single emotion-laden word (1989:87).

It may be helpful to think of conversation as a series of ideas (words) that are loosely linked in the structure of a sentence. When journalists write and edit carefully, those ideas are tightly packed, logical, and coherent. In conversations people space out their ideas, leaving unsaid much of what they might want to say. The interview with someone who has suffered a violent act is a good example of this. That person's account will hold conspicuous spaces. Damage to the emotions may make some thoughts unspeakable. A good interviewer will listen for those spaces and seek to understand what is missing and why.

A good reporter reviews with the interviewee what the reporter has learned.

A reporter may see the close of the interview as the end of a routine task, but the person with whom the reporter has been talking may see the closing quite differently. In a state of heightened awareness she has confided in someone who has appeared to be genuinely interested in the story. In those few moments she has worked with the reporter to reconstruct an event that has left her on terribly shaky ground. This is the time for the reporter to go back over the facts, to read back statements that she may want to quote, and to arrange to obtain photographs, continue the interview, or check back for other information. It is also the time to be frank about what the interview may yield in terms of a printed or broadcast story. Finally, the reporter should once again identify her publication or station and should leave a business card or telephone number. (This description is of a one-on-one interview when time permits such care. Obviously, chaotic disaster scenes and imminent deadlines will limit a reporter's options. And Coté and I are not advocating that a reporter read his story back to each person he interviewed. We think that the practices outlined here will prevent many postpublication complaints from people interviewed at the scene.)

An effective reporter thinks through what he has heard and seen.

The just-completed interview was not a routine one. What made it different? The person was enduring one of the most trying experiences in life. Such an interview can alter many of the assumptions that journalists make about the people they talk to. Issues of trust, harm, and responsibility to others emerge from such meetings to a degree unmatched in most news interviewing. This is a time for a few moments of reflection about what the reporter has just heard and seen.

Finally, the reporter should give some attention to herself. Whenever a reporter is near a scene of violence, or is talking to a trauma victim, the journalist may have an emotional response. Savvy reporters monitor how they feel and are responding to reminders of the event they have witnessed. Some reporters seek solitude and become almost fanatical about their privacy after doing difficult stories. It is important that reporters recognize their own response to the interview, talk about it with others, or give themselves a chance to reflect on it.

THE ANNIVERSARY INTERVIEW

Disasters and tragic stories invariably become subjects of news stories on their anniversaries. Anniversaries of such events as the Columbine High School shootings in 1999 and the attacks on the World Trade Center in 2001 still are marked with widespread news coverage. Shorter anniversaries—one month, six months—are excuses for revisiting the event and the people it affected. Editors love anniversary stories, which may serve as useful reminders of safety, criminal justice, or other issues. The good of such stories, though, is often exceeded by the harm done to trauma survivors when they are asked to again relive the event, either in an interview or when the story is broadcast or printed. Coté and I cannot repeat too often that such details may be painful to survivors and in some cases may set back their recovery from the initial trauma. But an anniversary interview that emphasizes how a survivor is living since the loss and trauma can be helpful to the survivor and informative to the public.

During the follow-up interview the reporter should observe all the guidelines for the interview at the scene. Let the other person decide when and where the interview will occur, whether a companion will be present for support, whether and how long a camera will run. Do not assume—as many producers, editors, and reporters do—that the person wants to be interviewed at home. A television reporter asked a rape survivor for an interview in her home; the woman agreed to the interview only if it were conducted in the reporter's home. When the survivor arrived, she was greeted by an exhausted reporter who had risen early and worked much of the morning to make her living room presentable for the television interview. "Now you know what it's like to be asked for interviews at your home," the survivor said.

The story also makes a good point about the timing of interviews. A morning interview might seem right for a reporter who likes to write in the afternoon. But a victim may find mornings difficult because of trauma-related illnesses or recovery from physical injuries. Our advice is to ask what time of the day the person would prefer to do an interview. Television reporters often are assigned to do live interviews for early evening news programs. Because that period often is reserved for meals or family gatherings, an interview can be disruptive.

The person being interviewed may appear much more composed and in control of his thoughts and emotions than when he was interviewed at the scene of the violent event. The journalist will be more relaxed, familiar with the original story, and (if the reporter has prepared for the interview) aware of much that has happened to this person since. It will be easy to expect that this interview will be a routine one. That is a dangerous assumption.

A university student proposed to do a story for the student newspaper on a young woman killed in a fatal accident whose corneas were donated for transplant. The woman's mother readily agreed to interviews, thinking the story would credit her daughter and encourage others to become organ donors. Yet as the interview progressed, the mother became more anxious and uncomfortable. Neither she nor the reporter had anticipated that the interview would revive painful memories and questions about the daughter's death. Although the reporter did not expect the woman to be troubled by the interview, she might have taken the early signs of anxiety as an opportunity to offer the mother the chance to end or postpone the interview. (If the reporter suddenly had decided to end the conversation, the mother might be troubled, reminded once again of how little control she has over traumatic symptoms.)

The reporter should focus on recovery, rather than the cause of the trauma, but even then runs the risk of evoking memories that will cause the other person pain. If the journalist's intention is to revisit the traumatic event, he has an obligation to explain that in advance and to be certain that the other person is willing to face those memories. Be explicit: say that the interview may cause the person unexpected stress, including sleeplessness, unwanted memories, and heightened anxiety. Reporters must remember that the trauma survivor may be vulnerable to troublesome memories, dreams, and fears even several years after an event. Think about the characteristic symptoms of post-traumatic stress disorder—unwanted memories, numbing, and heightened anxiety. Even six months later an interview is likely to be stressful.

Telling the survivor that the interview will focus on recovery and the aftermath of the event, rather than on the details of the event, is helpful to the interviewee. The survivor knows a great deal about recovery, after all, and is likely to value an opportunity to reflect on her capacity to regain old interests, revive old friendships, and to make decisions that reconnect her with the world. The journalist's interest in that process will be more welcome than a proposal to retell the details of an old and troubling story.

As the reporter asks a survivor to tell how he began to recover, she should keep these values in mind. Do not blame or judge the victim. Respect the courage of someone who tells such a private story. Do not ask questions that force the other person to revisit the traumatic experience.

Consider these words of E. K. Rynearson, a Seattle psychiatrist, about how the survivor uses a story over a long period to mend his injuries:

Rather than a brief chronicle, the narrative of someone traumatized will be intertwined with narrative identities from the past and will become a narrative theme of future identity as well. . . . To understand how and why this trauma happened to us or someone in our family begins a long inventory of actions and values. Are we responsible? How could we have avoided this? How could something so awful happen? How can I trust that anyone cares? Why should I risk caring for anyone else? Since there are no answers to this paradox-filled inquest, the tone of this long-term narrative is one of contrast and ambiguity. Unlike the reporter's story, this one has no answer and no ending.

(n.d.:6)

Although those who suffered violent events sometimes want and need to tell their story as a way of understanding what has happened to them, their stories are not necessarily going to provide the answers that reporters seek. In cases that are most troubling to survivors, reporters substitute a different story for the one the survivor told; all that the interviewee really contributes may be a fact or two or some quotable comments. The survivor saw the interview as an important event, even a step in the recovery process. Yet when the paper arrived or the news show came on, little from the interview survived.

In a very small number of cases reporters develop a continuing interest in, and a relationship with, a survivor. Reporters in Oklahoma City revisited survivors and family members of those who died, saw them at memorials and other community events, and in some cases talked to them during trials. Reporters learned to walk a delicate line between their feelings for other members of their community and keeping some professional distance. Reporters noticed that some survivors used their experience to speak out whenever possible on victim issues. Reporters recognized that they were being lobbied to promote the survivors' ideas and quickly became sensitive to conflicts between their duties and the demands of what some called "professional victims."

Some reporters eagerly identify with those who survive violence because of a personal history of abuse, sexual assault, or other traumas. That identification may be so strong that the reporter ignores professional boundaries in order to become a confidante and even advocate. A skilled reporter needs to concentrate on understanding and reporting events accurately; deep emotional connections to people in those stories can undermine those goals. Yet Coté and I would agree with those who say a reporter sometimes can be very helpful to a victim or family member. But we believe that the best result for everyone occurs when the reporter understands his own needs and is sensitive to signs of trauma and growing distress in others.

Constructive interviews result from self-awareness and knowledge of trauma's effects on others. Trauma stories need to be told if journalists are to support its victims as they travel the long road toward recovery.

Here are some tips for conducting good interviews with survivors of violence:

- Respect the other person's efforts to regain balance after a horrible experience.
- Be careful about conveying secondhand information in the interview—both to the inteviewee and to readers and viewers.
- Respect the other person's need to focus on his or her present circumstances.

- Set the stage for the interview by carefully informing the person about your identity, your reasons for doing the interview, and how the interview might be used.
- Explain the ground rules.
- Share as much control with the interviewee as possible.
- Anticipate emotional responses, and allow the subject to make decisions about stopping or temporarily halting the interview.
- Listen carefully.
- Review the salient points of the interview with the subject.
- Take time to assess any personal response to the interview and discuss that response with others.
- Keep these guidelines in mind when doing anniversary interviews.

ANH DO

Crossing Cultural Borders

A video-store owner displayed a communist flag and a portrait of Ho Chi Minh in his shop in Orange County, California's "Little Saigon" in 1999. Intended as a gesture of support for better relations with the Vietnamese government, the display sparked daily demonstrations by hundreds of Vietnamese Americans, and the shop owner was hospitalized after protesters attacked him.

The scope and fury of the response surprised many in Orange County, but Anh Do, a reporter for the *Orange County Register,* understood what lay behind it. An estimated one million Vietnamese, including Do's uncle, were imprisoned in "reeducation camps" after the Vietnam War, some for as long as seventeen years. "Reeducation camp" was the Vietnamese government's euphemism for concentration camp: 165,000 people died in the camps, and thousands more suffered torture and other forms of abuse. Among those protesting in Orange County in 1999 were survivors of the camps and their family members.

Anh Do.
Photo courtesy
Orange County Register

Do, who covers the Asian community for the *Register,* knew about the survivors of the camps, but she had never talked with them at length and delved into their trauma. The demonstrations at the video store prompted the paper to pursue the story of the camps in detail.

Do was joined on the story by reporter Hieu Tran Phan and photographer Eugene Garcia. That they'd be able to convince the survivors to recount their experiences required a leap of faith. It was not something the survivors talked about; many had never even told their family members about the camps. "When people have suffered something so physically unbearable," Do says, "they never want to suffer that again."

Do had experience in interviewing people who had suffered trauma. Her coverage of the Asian community included reporting on home-invasion robberies, murder-suicides, hostage situations, and gang warfare. One incident left an indelible mark on her. A mother shot to death her four-year-old mentally disabled daughter, drove with the body to a freeway off-ramp, and lay down on the pavement beside her dead daughter. A car ran over the two of them, killing the mother. The murder-suicide occurred too late for the night police reporter to cover it, and Do was put on the story in the morning. She and a photographer went to the father's home to talk with him. "I had rarely seen grown Vietnamese men cry," Do says. "He was crying the whole time, trying to make sense out of the craziness. I was shocked that he would even let us inside."

Do says courage takes over when she is covering breaking news. She knew this likely would be her only opportunity to talk with the father, and she says she tried to be delicate with him, as she always is in those situations. Do says she tries to visualize how people will feel when they pick up the newspaper the next morning and see themselves in print. She tells them the newspaper is going to do the story, and she explains that their voice is an important part of the story. She answers every question they ask and shares information with them. She'll say to the victim: "This is what the police told me; what did they tell you?"

"The individuals in that situation appreciate that," she says.

Interviewing the camp survivors presented different challenges. The project's team members decided early on to emphasize simplicity, clarity, and the uniqueness of each subject's experience. They decided that the best way to achieve that was by writing the stories in present tense. "You want to put readers at the scene and that's one of the easiest tools to use," Do says. "The idea was not to just provide information but to tell a story. In order to put these people in the prison, you paint a picture." Such an approach required intensive interviewing.

The reporters pointed out to survivors that their stories would teach younger Vietnamese Americans about the camps. They made appointments for interviews, and many survivors wanted to meet in a park or a coffee shop—away from their families. Some she wanted to interview canceled the appointment or simply failed to show up. "In many cases they were men," Do says. "They talked to their wives, and their wives said don't go there [to the memory] again." When survivors did agree to talk, they sometimes could not remember what had happened or, worse, became physically ill while reliving the horrors.

The interviews would stretch on for hours, with the reporters going over and over details. They asked their subjects to draw scenes, such as their prison cells. Many of the initial interviews took place at night after work hours and some lasted until midnight. Do says the lateness and the dark led to more intimacy. "You just get philosophical and personal, rather than at 8 A.M. on a Monday morning," she says.

Do says she's willing to cry with her subjects, to celebrate joyous memories with them, and to share her own experiences. Her father was a journalist in Vietnam during the war, and her family fled to the United States in 1975 when she was eight years old. "I think empathy is a natural tool, but the only way it works is if it's genuine," she says. "If you honestly feel some of their pain, I think the sentiments translate.

"It was very important for me to respect their experience," she adds, "but not to pretend to understand their experience. How could I?"

Do speaks Vietnamese, but she says sharing a language should not be a prerequisite for pursuing an important story. "Find a person you can trust—who can be at ease with your source—and have him be the guide," she says. She advises taping the interview for backup and for providing context. She suggests submitting written questions to the source and asking a son or daughter to relate what their parent told them about her or his experience. And, she adds, "Concentrate on the speaker in front of you, because that may be the first and last interview you have with him."

The *Register*'s final product was a twenty-page special section detailing the stories of a half-dozen camp survivors. Do says stories such as these can provide the reader with a better understanding of humanity while also serving as redemption for those who have experienced the trauma. Her point was articulated well by one of her subjects, a former lieutenant colonel in the South Vietnamese army who was imprisoned for nearly thirteen years. "You must not forget, because then you can make the future better," he told the reporters. "If you remember us, our souls will not die in vain."

Hope: Caring for Newborns Inspires an Inmate to Start a Family—Bribing a Guard at Her Husband's Prison So the Couple Can Be Together

ANH DO

This excerpt from "Camp Z30-D: The Survivors" shows Anh Do's ability to learn key details of Hong Nga's story through precise and persistent interview questions. The small facts of the story build a firm platform for an account of a woman's journey from a Vietnamese reeducation camp in the 1970s to her present life with her sons in Southern California. Her resilience and sacrifices are clearly described against the backdrop of the reeducation camps where at least 165,000 people died after the fall of Saigon in 1975. The complete project, which was cowritten with Hieu Tran Phan, was published in the Orange County Register on April 29, 2001.

All during that first summer in Camp Z30-D, the female prisoners smile at one another, silently acknowledging the wonderful things about to happen, even amid the horrors of building their own concentration camp.

When will the first one take place? How will they handle it? Is it possible to nurture fragile little lives in the confines of a bamboo jail?

Several of the women around Hong Nga, 24, are expecting—already pregnant when the summons ordering re-education confinement arrived months earlier.

"How do we nurse?" One wonders.

"Where can we find more food?" questions another.

"What names will we give them?" asks a third.

Despite their swelling stomachs, they dig trenches, raise pigs, plant corn under the harsh sun.

Hong Nga, a captain in the South Vietnamese army who anchored the official evening news, watches them in the quiet twilight, wishing for a child of her own. She offers to take on their heavy chores, carrying water buckets and hauling big loads.

Sometimes she thinks of her own childhood, when, born as Dong Nga Thi Ha, she would sit for hours by the radio or television, listening to her favorite stars, mimicking their speech and aspiring to be a face and a voice for her nation.

As the hot, long summer days grow shorter, the women start to have their babies. Accompanied by guards, they leave the camp overnight and give birth with the help of midwives. They return with their babies the next day.

New mothers are not given extra food, but other inmates readily offer theirs. They are allowed one to two months to nurse, and then they return to the fields either taking their babies with them or leaving them in a makeshift nursery.

Hong Nga, one day, gives up her bed slot to a tiny girl with a head of soft curls. She prepares warm vegetable broths, rocks crying babies back to sleep, changes thin cloth diapers. Sometimes, when there is nothing else, they cover the infants' bottoms with the tattered fabric of their own prisoner's stripes or the leaves of a banana tree.

One day in the spring, a boy falls ill as his mother carries him on her back in the fields. He can't stop vomiting.

"Oh Lord, please don't let him die," the woman wails. The other women start to weep. There is no formula.

Hong Nga's heart thumps wildly. Her chest feels warm and heavy. A devoted Catholic, she prays throughout the night.

The baby recovers the next evening. Hong Nga runs over and kisses his cheeks.

"I treated the children in prison as my own," she says. "The time at Z30-D showed me that I had a mother's unconditional love."

As the years pass, the Camp Z30-D babies grow into toddlers, then young children. Hong Nga feels her life slipping away.

Her husband, a once-strong army captain, has written her, saying he is weak and sick in a jail in the North. One day, Hong Nga hears from relatives that he has heart trouble. She fears he will die before she can have a baby to carry on his name, Ngot Van Le. She aches for someone to sing to. Then she would have a reason to go on living.

Finally in 1979, Hong Nga is released from Camp Z30-D. She immediately sets out to fulfill her dream of having a family. But she discovers there is nothing left of her old home. First, she sells scraps on the streets of Saigon to keep a roof over her head and her mother's. Then she pawns all her valuables. After nine months of struggling, she scrapes enough together to buy a ticket to the North to see her husband.

At last, she is on the train to Hanoi. The 40-hour trip gives her time to think. She wonders if her husband, Ngot, still has that broad smile and thick, jet-black hair.

In Hanoi, she boards a bus headed into the mountains. She clutches gifts of rice, medicine, dried fish, sugar—and crumpled bills.

Finally, they gaze at one another across a prison table. He can't stop coughing. She fights back tears.

"He looked like a ghost with his sunken eyes, missing teeth and gray hair," she says. "I had to reach out and touch him, to make sure he was still alive."

After five years of separation, they have 15 minutes to talk. A guard stands at their side. Ngot looks into his wife's face, eyes shimmering with tears.

As the visit ends, Hong Nga makes the move she has been thinking about for years. She slips 10,000 dong, the equivalent of 80 cents, into the hands of the man carrying the rifle. He closes his fist. Hong Nga and Ngot will spend the night in a "guest cottage" a few miles from the center of the camp.

The couple shut the door behind them. Hong Nga has carefully timed the trip so she is ovulating. She glances around: dirt floor, bamboo walls, a ceiling of thatched palm fronds. In the middle is a raised wooden platform. No pillows, sheets or blankets.

"I want to have a child," she blurts out.

"Are you crazy?" he asks. "Get your head together. Think of all the reasons not to."

Neighbors will accuse her of infidelity. Even if they believe her story, the baby will bear the stigma of having a prisoner for a father. And just how does she plan to raise a child when she has barely enough money to feed herself?

"Children need two parents," Ngot says. "I could very well die here in prison."

"But that's why we must take this chance. There might be no second chance. Please, don't you remember the dream on our wedding day? We were meant to be a family."

"But what will you do with them when I am gone?"

"I don't know," she replies.

"How can you bear the burden of being an only parent?"

"I don't know. But I don't want to think about that now. I am not changing my mind."

Her husband grows silent. She blows out the kerosene candle. They feel awkward and try to avoid seeing the worry, the pain in each other's faces.

Hong Nga's skin tightens as she feels the cold board. Husband and wife cry. Their bodies shake with nervousness.

"There was no passion," she says, "only prayers for a miracle."

Nine months pass, and Hong Nga gives birth to a baby boy. She names him Khanh. The following year, she returns to the prison. The couple conceive another son, Duc.

"When I look at my boys, I remember the irony of hope being conceived in prison, a hopeless place," Hong Nga says. "It reminds me of a poetry collection titled 'Flowers From Hell.'"

EPILOGUE

In 1993, Hong Nga, her sons—then 11 and 12—and her newly freed husband immigrate to Orange County through a program for former South Vietnamese military veterans.

She borrows money from friends, buys a sewing machine and sets up business in the dining room of their nearly empty apartment in Garden Grove. A statue of the Virgin Mary looks on as she mends old clothes and cuts patterns for new ones.

But the years in prison continue to take their toll. Her husband, Ngot, grows weaker by the month. Hong Nga holds his thinning, shivering body, whispering words of encouragement through dark nights. Eventually, he collapses from a heart attack and dies in the hospital six months after setting foot on U.S. soil.

"Khanh, Duc and I made a vow at his funeral," Hong Nga says. "We promised that his sons would take his place. They would be living memories to the hope that gave them life right in prison."

Two years ago, Hong Nga saved enough money to start her own business, T&N Super Discount, a variety store in Garden Grove. Almost every week, she visits her husband's remains at Westminster Memorial Cemetery. The glass case with his ashes is graced with yellow lilies and a rosary.

Her sons now are working to fulfill one of their father's dreams: that they graduate from college. Living with their mother and grandmother, they take classes at Orange Coast and Golden West colleges, both pursuing degrees in computer science.

CHAPTER 6

Writing the Trauma Story

Like any well-told story, a survivor's story has a beginning (lead), middle, and end. Unlike novels and fairy tales, it probably does not have a happily-ever-after ending; it may have a "kicker" in more than the usual journalistic sense of a news story climax with a twist or jolt. After all, it is a real person's story, with all the potential for toil and trouble, trauma and tragedy, and drama and inspiration that a real life can bring.

Reporters need to remember that the story is the victim's story—or should be. Trauma may leave a person feeling violated, angry, powerless. Many trauma victims feel their suffering has had some purpose if their story is told at the right time and in the right way. It can be a catharsis that releases some pain and gives their lives new dignity. That is a step in the process of progressing from victim to survivor.

ACCURACY COUNTS

Many things in the way a story is written may upset a person, but what that person finds to be upsetting sometimes is not what journalists would expect. Soon after the Victims and the Media Program began at Michigan State University, William Coté sat down with leaders of the Michigan Victim Alliance, people who had been raped or shot or were parents of murdered children. Asked what had bothered them most about print or broadcast reports about their experiences, they did not cite brutish interviewers or sensationalistic stories. Several of these survivors replied, "The mistakes! The mistakes!"

Survivors of violence often complain about stories with misspelled names, incorrect ages and addresses, wrong job descriptions, or a mangled chronology of events and dates.

Most survivors of trauma want their story told, and told accurately, because they desperately want to reenter their community, and they see the story as a potential passport. The journalist's role will be giver of help—the reporter will help an injured person tell a story. Mistakes in those all-important stories can shatter the trust and confidence the survivor craves.

Stories can further shatter the trust and confidence of survivors when errors or omissions leave the impression that people are partly responsible for the violence against them. A story noting what a raped woman was wearing when she was attacked might give the impression that she was "asking for it." A television tape showing a bar where a bystander was shot to death in the crossfire of a gun battle might be taken to imply, "Well, if he hadn't been in a place like that . . ."

Whether such impressions are intended or not, victims and their families and friends will be especially sensitive to every word, description, and fact. Reporters, photographers, and editors must try to think how the story, photo, or tape will look or sound from the perspective of those most affected by what happened. It is true that journalists cannot edit solely to please the subjects. Nonetheless, they can consider whether certain details and facts form an unintended tone or impression or are extraneous to the story.

When Dan Anderson was shot and nearly killed by a prowler in his yard, he was too sick for days to worry about how it was being reported. (His wife, Pat, had to cope with those earliest stories by herself.) As he recovered, though, and began reading the stories, the Lansing, Michigan, resident saw in one newspaper's first account that he was shot when he "went outside to investigate a prowler." That, he felt, made him appear to be stupid or reckless.

Actually, Anderson explains, he called the police about a prowler and the dispatcher asked him whether he could get a description of the man. Anderson then went outside to look—and was shot—only because he thought he was following the dispatcher's directions. Just a relatively minor difference? Not to Dan Anderson and his self-esteem.

It is true that mistakes that sources complain about sometimes do not originate with reporters. Mistakes can abound on the initial incident forms that harried police officers filled out. Witnesses and suspects often give conflicting and confusing statements at crime scenes. Other information that a reporter gets often is second or third hand, filtered through intermediaries such as police desk sergeants and public relations people. But who is likely to be blamed for any mistakes in print or on the air? The reporter, of course.

Reporters can do a lot to avoid these pitfalls by double-checking every fact, no matter how basic. If something is not certain or relevant, it should not be in the story. Should the story include a casual comment from a police officer that the driver in a fatal accident "may" have been drinking if the reporter does not know the result of blood alcohol tests or, indeed, whether any were taken? If mentioning alcohol seems necessary, it is often better simply to say something like, "Under routine procedures police will conduct blood tests to determine whether alcohol could have played any role in the accident."

Mistakes also can creep, or jump, into stories when the writer lumps too many people into one category without careful distinctions. Coverage that said both too much and not enough prompted a friend of a woman killed by a serial murderer in the Seattle area in the 1980s to write a letter to the *Seattle Times* to protest how the story had characterized her friend. Because several victims had been identified as prostitutes, coverage regularly used that identification. The letter reflects the hurt in such cases:

> She had three children and a man who loved her very much. She lived in a normal neighborhood, in a normal house with hardwood floors located on Crown Hill. She had training in Montessori school teaching and her hobbies were designing children's toys and studying religion. She was not and never had been a prostitute. . . .
>
> What the media did to that family was nearly as tragic as the circumstance of her death. . . . Some referred to her as a "Street Person," some said nothing at all about who or what she was, all they talked about was prostitution, one station even made the mistake of calling her a prostitute. The kids were returning home from school each day in tears. . . . I am sick to death of these being written off as "Justifiable Homicides." . . . Listen, folks, it's time that we all get real about this thing, and address the REAL problem, which is MURDER!!! NOT PROSTITUTION!!!
>
> (Guillen 1990:95–96)

Accuracy is the first step in discharging the professional journalist's duty in writing a story. It is not the journalist's job to heal, but it certainly is the journalist's obligation to do no harm.

THE DEVIL—AND PAIN—IN DETAILS

Even accurate facts that might appear to be harmless sometimes can wound someone who is already suffering. Hugh Leach, a veteran reporter and copy editor at the *Lansing (Mich.) State Journal,* learned that painfully. He has covered many violent events in his career, but he tells journalism students that he did not fully appreciate all the potential ramifications of what he and others reported until he found himself on the other side of the journalistic fence.

Leach's seventy-year-old mother was savagely beaten and left to bleed to death by two robbers who broke into her Arizona retirement home. Leach traveled to Arizona to help handle the funeral arrangements and to deal with media inquiries. He thought many of the newspaper and television reports in Arizona and Michigan about the murder were accurate and sensitive. He found, though, that three little words in one paragraph of an Arizona paper's feature profiling his mother offended him keenly: the description within the lead noted she "weighed 90 pounds, loved to smoke, took in stray cats and was sweet to her neighbors." It was the "loved to smoke" that offended him.

"It's true that she smoked cigarettes," Leach told us. "That was accurate, but why did they have to mention it in the story? Her smoking didn't have anything to do with someone breaking into her house and killing her. I was surprised it bothered me so much, but it did. I know they were just trying to do a personality profile of her. I understand that type of story. But is that one of the things to remember about her? It hurt. It hurt." Again, details that seem to add dimension to a story about someone's life might be received differently by sensitized readers.

Journalists would do well to remember what a reporter character in a movie said when intimate aspects of her own life were about to be published: "Yes, it's accurate—but is it true?"

Sometimes, sadly, it is impossible not to report critical details of a crime without adding to the grief of families and friends. Journalists often must be the bearers of bad news, like it or not. A California newspaper ran a powerful package of stories about murdered teenagers in the city, reporting how one youth was killed when he drove with friends into a high-crime neighborhood to buy drugs. Family members, suffering deeply, protested that mentioning why the young men were in the neighborhood was not necessary. Most of the paper's readers, though, probably would have guessed that drugs were involved or would have imagined even worse reasons. The reason he was there was an unavoidable link in the chain of events that led to the killing.

On the other hand, some details that unnecessarily provoke horror or repulsion do not have to be reported. That might seem to be a matter of ordinary taste and common sense, but reporters too often include such details in their stories.

Some facts that have to be reported need not be repeated in subsequent stories. That's a frequent complaint from upset families that do not need to be reminded of details of their loved ones' deaths, especially not weeks or months after the crimes. The hurt to families can be even worse when reporters repeatedly describe the cruelty responsible for the deaths. That was highlighted in a letter to *Time* magazine from the sister of a 1975 victim of the serial killer Theodore Bundy. From the time her body was discovered to the time of his execution in 1989, stories mentioned where her body was found. "We, her family, did not need to hear, see and read the same fact for 14 years," the sister wrote.

PLANNING THE PROJECT

Just as the reactions of victims tend to depend on how long ago the trauma happened—hours, months, or years—the best way to write a trauma story can hinge greatly on the time factor. One approach is appropriate when a man is still fighting for his life in a hospital burn unit after someone firebombed his apartment building. The reporter wants to tell readers when and where it happened, whether police have suspects, the condition of all survivors, and how the police investigation is proceeding.

A different approach is appropriate for an anniversary feature about how a particular man copes with his crippling and disfiguring injuries, as the *Austin American-Statesman* did in an inspiring word and photo feature. The two-part series by reporter Michele Stanush and photographer Lynne Dobson details the struggles of thirty-seven-year-old Emmett Jackson to deal with his devastating injuries and the death of his wife, Diathia, and child at the hands of an arsonist who was seeking revenge against someone in the building.

Stories right after the firebombing understandably focused on the crime and the attacker, but the *American-Statesman* two years later unsentimentally and vividly treated the lengthy and painful process of Jackson's recovery, with little and big successes and setbacks.

One way to examine the two different types of stories and their timing and approach is to consider them as acts in a real-life play or drama. Act I includes the reporting right after an event, telling readers, listeners, or viewers the traditional "5Ws"—who, what, when, where, and why. Act II, by contrast, portrays the longer-term effects of trauma, profiling the victims months or years later and describing how they cope in the continuing recovery process. Reporters usually are much more geared by instinct, tradition, the routines of their work, and competitive pressure to do Act I stories swiftly after a traumatic event. One of the defining criteria of *news*, after all, is the reporting for the first time of something that has happened very recently or has just been uncovered. Otherwise, it is old news or not news at all.

It definitely was an Act I situation, for example, when Dan Anderson was shot by the intruder in his yard. Hours after the shooting he was on a respirator and unable to communicate when a reporter tried to enter his intensive care room to interview him. Intercepted and removed by nurses, the reporter then tried to find Pat Anderson. She was in a nearby lounge but turned down the request. This was a situation in which no interview was appropriate.

Now, more than twenty-eight years and about thirty surgeries later for Dan, the Andersons tell their experiences to Michigan State journalism students, who are assigned to craft Act II stories that explore how trauma affects victims and their families. "I'm glad to talk about it and proud if maybe it helps these young people," Dan says.

PROFILES

Personality profiles are virtually indispensable in writing about people who have suffered trauma, so it is useful to review what this type of human-interest writing usually includes and how best to apply it in the context of trauma. As with any profile, the aim is to make the reader know the person vividly through the skillful blending of details, observations, word pictures, and creative writing.

The story should report what the person looks, sounds, and acts like, and it is appropriate to note the subject's age, hobbies, family, occupation, favorite foods, pets—in short, anything and everything that makes the person real for readers or viewers. Then the reporter must think carefully about whether any one thing or incident seems to capture the person's essence in a dramatic capsule. That should be the lead, told smoothly, quickly, and irresistibly.

Writing about victims varies from the more common profile of someone who has gained the spotlight through personal effort. In the victim profile the main character is not always alive, and the news peg may be all too obvious or painfully well known. Comments from people who know or knew the subject become doubly important. Also especially necessary—and effective—is putting the reader in the other person's shoes.

Some of the best profilers in journalism say they consciously use techniques traditionally attributed to good fiction writers: rich, colorful details and vivid narration that immediately drop the reader into the middle of the scene (action) and compel further reading.

THE CURTAIN RAISER

As with any story, the lead is the lure, hook, and showcase, the reporter's only opportunity to grab readers or viewers and make the story so enticing that they will not turn away until they have savored the last word. Leads are particularly challenging in stories about violence. Both Act I and Act II situations offer great opportunities to write dramatic, prize-winning stories or scripts. They also offer many opportunities to sensationalize and titillate the audience or to demean and injure victims and their families and friends. The difference between one and the other often can seem subtle—except to those who like or detest a tone, approach, or phrase in a story. Here are some examples of leads.

The first in the two-part series "The Test of Fire" in the *Austin American-Statesman* begins with this lead by Michele Stanush:

> April 1993—Emmett Jackson sits rod-straight in the front row of a federal courtroom, a Dallas Cowboys cap guarding his scarred scalp and a black patch covering his left eye.
>
> Metal claws have replaced Emmett's fingers. There are bare nasal cavities where he once had a nose and holes where there once were ears. His lips were rebuilt by doctors.
>
> (1994:G1)

Stanush goes on to relate that Jackson is in the courtroom to hear what will become of the arsonist who killed his wife and little girl and left him so disfigured. The lead does not draw a pretty picture, but the word image it conjures is so vivid and compelling that readers cannot resist the rest of the story.

Ralph De La Cruz powerfully presents similarly stark drama in his lead for "Path of a Bullet," from the Long Beach, California, *Press-Telegram*:

> Three hours short of his 17th birthday, Martine Perry is lying naked on a stainless steel hospital table, life seeping out of his body.
>
> A baby wails in a distant corner of the emergency room. An elderly woman pleads with a nurse to hold off putting a tube down her throat. And Martine

lies silent, motionless, blood oozing from his head, as eight people work frantically to revive him.

(1996:K1)

Again, the lead is dramatic and plunges the reader instantly into the middle of the action, blending background facts (name and age) and the sights and sounds of the hospital emergency room.

Consider this lead from a *Detroit Free Press* project that aimed to bring home to residents the cost of that city's high murder rate:

On a gray misty morning, Margeree Jefferson wakes up early to wash death off her front porch.

She lugs a bucket of hot water, puts it down with a splash and collects bottles of Ajax, Pine-Sol, bleach and all-purpose cleanser. She puts on blue rubber gloves and black winter boots with rubber soles, even though it's the second week of June. "It's just the thought of this, that this is somebody's blood," she says. "I'm not superstitious, but it might be a bad omen to walk inside your house and have somebody's blood at the front door."

Jefferson, 62, dips a mop into the bucket and slops the water onto the painted wooden porch. As she scrubs back and forth, swirling the mop, bloody suds collect at her feet. Her expression is blank. This is the reality of living inside a murder scene—a grandmother has to wake up early and clean up the blood of a stranger before it dries and leaves a deep stain that might never come out.

Some stains never do.

(Seidel 2004:1G)

Reporter Jeff Seidel used this woman's actions to step back a bit from violence but to show how violence continues to play on the emotions of Detroit residents.

Leads about trauma, however, do not always have to immediately focus on gore or physical descriptions. Sometimes a lead can set the scene for horrific narratives to come, using suspenseful wording to encourage the reader to read on and on. That is the approach chosen by Debra McKinney for "Malignant Memories" from the *Anchorage Daily News*, describing how three women dared to face their haunting recollections of childhood incest:

SEATTLE—Twenty-five years have come and gone since Margie last visited the old man's farm. She's not sure she can even find the place. She's not sure she even wants to.

The 51-year-old Anchorage travel agent has made a lot of progress lately confronting her fears. But she still has trouble talking about what happened in the barn.

(1993:A1)

The writer was physically right there with the people she described. Accompanying people as they relive traumatic scenes often is not possible, but when it is, the effort is well worth it. For that to happen, the writer and photographer must have the trust and confidence of the people involved. People who have been suffering post-traumatic stress for months or for decades are not going to open themselves up to journalists who seemingly might not give them respect and dignity. The survivors have been hurt enough. Why should they give reporters a chance to wound them more?

Only when the writer has proved in initial interviews and contacts that the survivor will be the focus and not the target of the story is the subject likely to say to the journalist, "Okay, come along with me."

MINE THE DETAILS

Once a reporter has the basic facts and the lead, the three most important things in writing a compelling story about trauma are details, details, and details—the appropriate ones, that is. Illuminating, flowing, and dramatic details make the story come, and stay, alive until the last word. Take, for example, this background detail in Stanush's story about burn victim Jackson: "In his old life, Emmett Jackson was an easy-going supermarket baker who loved the feel of raw dough between his fingers. *Texture is the key,* he'd say."

That's a poignant observation about a man who now has no fingers or hands. Stanush also broke a journalistic custom by using italics in that quote and in others, such as *"Why am I not dead?"* spotted strategically throughout the story. Newspapers seldom use italics in news stories because, among other reasons, they can be distracting and overwrought, but she did it deliberately—and effectively—to show readers when she was conveying something Jackson was thinking. How did she know that? One way, of course, was to interview him about what he was thinking at key points. She also loaned him a tape recorder so that he could relate his private thoughts when he was alone.

In addition, Stanush interviewed Jackson's family and friends, doctors, counselors, therapists, paramedics, and coworkers over a fifteen-month period. She told of his triumphs, such as getting a driver's license again and climbing a steep hill outside his rehabilitation center, inspiring therapists to name the mound Jackson Hill. Many quotes and observations tell of his love for his lost wife and baby, his regularly attending church services, and his hope of becoming a public speaker, talking to people about fire and crime.

The Jackson stories were unsentimental and frank. In addition to relating many inspiring and ennobling facets of Jackson's life, the accounts also note that he had served nearly three years in prison for forgery and burglary, and before he met Diathia, he "padded his pockets with big bills, drove a Lincoln Continental and hung out with fast-living women." Today, the stories reveal, he indulges in smoking, some drinking, and nightclubbing. "In the rehab hospital, he jokes to nurses: 'When I get outta here, all I want is a bottle of Bud and a babe.'"

A key factor here is that Jackson was willing to have such events and thoughts revealed. To him the reporting of his past and current lifestyles—good and not so good—was an important step in helping him feel he was rejoining the human race and his community. He wasn't nominating himself for sainthood. He simply wanted people to understand something of what he had been through and to know that he was trying to be a better person but still Emmett, still human. Such details, for better or worse, counted. Descriptions of people, places, and things are among the details that keep the audience moving along. Debra McKinney combined those three elements, along with quotes, in this passage as the three women searched for the house where one of them had been abused decades earlier:

Slowly the car headed down the gravel drive. At the bottom, Vivian stopped in front of a little yellow farm house, the kind you'd expect to have an apple pie cooling in the windowsill.

"Amazing," Margie said.

The place was just the way she remembered it. There was the chicken coop. And the old chopping block. And the big pear tree the guinea hens used to roost in. And there, behind the little house, beyond the gate with the "Keep Out" sign, was the barn.

"I don't want to get out," Margie said.

Vivian put an arm around her and hugged her. Ezzie gently rubbed her back.

They all got out of the car.

(1993:A8)

Doesn't that make a reader what to know what they find and how Margie reacts? Thousands of readers did want to know and kept reading as the story unfolded. A lot of it wasn't pretty, but it was compelling and, ultimately, inspiring.

Just as inspiring and riveting was the story of a sixteen-year-old Florida boy who was abducted one hot July morning and stuffed into the trunk of his father's car. He was dumped out and left for dead after being driven for five hours around the city while the heat of the day was magnified to 130 degrees in the tight, dark trunk. Reporter Craig Dezern's story, "The Miracle of Philip Chandler," in the *Orlando Sentinel* used powerful writing and moving narrative to tell what editor John Haile rightly labels "a gripping tale of terror, survival and hope." Again, the reporter wove telling details into the vivid story after the teenager's parents gave Dezern and photographer Angela Peterson access to Philip's hospital room, home, church, and school at each stage in his recovery.

Among the grabbing details is a section in which Philip's parents keep watch at his hospital bed as he tries to overcome the severe brain damage caused by heat stroke. The parents are no longer planning his funeral, but doctors warn them that Philip may never come out of his deep coma. After one day's vigil his parents are about to say good night to their son:

> Eve leans in, and one more time she asks, "Philip, can you give me a hug?"
>
> Slow and shaky, but with a purpose, Philip lifts his arms from the bed and drops them around his mother's neck.
>
> It is eerie, like being hugged by a dead man. Philip's face is still emotionless, his eyes fixed at something far away.
>
> "Jim, did you see that?"
>
> "Do it again."
>
> Eve asks for another hug. Philip responds the same.
>
> She is ecstatic, laughing and crying. This is the miracle she prayed for, but didn't dare hope for.
>
> (1993:7)

Anyone who contends that "a respectful story is a dull story" should reconsider after reading these stories. All the stories cited here focus on victims, all pretty ordinary people who had extraordinary things happen to them. Extraordinary bad things. The details of how they sought to cope and recover from the blows furnished the stuff of exciting journalism, illuminating not so much the evil visited on them but how courage, faith, love, and simple endurance often match and overcome evil.

THE KICKER

Reviewers of novels are harsh on writers who do not have an exciting denouement or at least wrap things up nicely and leave the reader with a sigh, gasp, or laugh. Readers of news stories and features should be just as demanding, yet many a promising story seems to end with hardly a whimper or fails to leave a feeling of any kind. That especially should not happen with stories about people who suffer trauma. By their very nature such chronicles are ready made for a concluding kicker. The problem may be deciding which of several tacks to take in ending the piece.

Act II stories give the writer more opportunity to tell the whole story and then end it with something that focuses on the person, whether a quote, observation, or fact. The point is to leave the reader with a certain impression, a certain feeling that will help sear the total message of the story into memory for a long time to come. It could be a near-perfect kicker if it magically manages to combine a sense of what the person both has lost and is now regaining in recovery.

Craig Dezern perhaps comes close to such a kicker in "The Miracle of Philip Chandler." The sixteen-year-old finally is home after four months in the hospital but still struggling to overcome the crippling physical and mental effects of the brain injury. The closing scene is in his den, where he is watching the movie *Aladdin* on television. Dezern asks Philip if, like Aladdin, he had three wishes, what would he ask for?

> Philip imagines this for a minute, one eyebrow cocked in speculation. He holds out one long finger to begin counting off his wishes.
>
> "To be normal again."
>
> He holds out two fingers and thinks some more, longer this time. Then he closes his hand.
>
> "That's really all I can think of."
>
> (1993:16)

It is impossible to fully appreciate a kicker without reading the whole story, but even in isolation the power and imagery of that writing shines through. Built on the crafted foundation of a skillful lead, smooth flow, and telling details, such an ending brings the reader and another person together for at least this one close look into the survivor's world.

ACT III?

While the concept of the two acts seems valuable, some trauma and media specialists have had a nagging feeling that something still is missing in describing and encouraging even longer-range and broader news coverage. They believe that journalists should pay greater attention to Act III. Act III can refer to coverage that places specific traumatic events within broader sociological, historical, or even economic contexts. Such coverage is sorely lacking in explaining events. If well done, it could even help newspapers regain lost numbers of readers by providing something rarely available in other media. Most important, a benefit to society might be that citizens, acting in their roles as voters and taxpayers, might gain a deeper and stronger knowledge base for making critical decisions about how to cope with violence in their communities, nation, and the world.

For a concrete and imaginative example of some aspects of Act III journalism, consider again the story from the *Press-Telegram* of Long Beach, California, "Path of a Bullet." It leads readers through the aftermath of the gang shooting death of a seventeen-year-old, as starkly noted in the lead that describes Martine Perry on an emergency room gurney. The twenty-two-cent handgun bullet that killed Perry caused devastating physical and emotional costs, but the report also traces the economic costs—$1.2 million for hospital expenses, police investigations, court proceedings against his killer, and dozens of other things.

"Path of a Bullet" (with the secondary head "We All Pay the Price") actually was not one story but a package. The central narrative by Ralph De La Cruz tells of Perry's death, life, and funeral. Other stories, photos, and charts explore such aspects as tracking down suspects, how tracing gun ownership often fails to produce suspects, the costs of prosecution, why youth kill, and ending gangs.

It might seem daunting for publications without the journalistic and financial resources of the *New York Times* or *Newsweek* to tackle such comprehensive ventures. The *Press-Telegram* demonstrates, however, that the midsize and smaller papers that serve most U.S. readers can marshal their staffs for worthy Act III stories. One key is to focus on what a paper knows best: its own community. Then choose a topic that deeply affects that community, whether gangs, domestic abuse, illegal drugs, or another subject that directly or indirectly victimizes many residents. Innovations worthy of duplication are the occasional collaborations between midsize newspapers in separate cities and between newspapers and television stations in one community.

Here are some tips for writing or producing stories about survivors of trauma:

- Bear in mind that accuracy is essential if the reporter on a story about a survivor is to retain his or her trust and that of the survivor's family and friends.
- Avoid repeating the details of an assault or other tragedy weeks or months later unless good reason exists for doing so.
- Avoid the shorthand words—*prostitute, homeless*—that stereotype and detract from the complexity of a person's life.
- Build the story on details carefully chosen to humanize and give dignity to the subject of the profile.
- Consider how graphic details will affect survivors when considering which ones to use. Is the detail essential to telling the story?
- Look for opportunities to tell Act II stories, the accounts of resilient individuals who have found ways to respond to traumatic injury.
- Look for ways to build social context into reporting about individuals.

SONIA NAZARIO

Writing from the Inside

"One of the things I do as a reporter is empathize," explains Sonia Nazario of the *Los Angeles Times*. "It helps me to get inside their heads." For her Pulitzer Prize series, "Enrique's Journey," her empathy went beyond sensitive questions, careful listening, and sharing control. In order to write about the dangerous journey made by thousands of Central American children desperate to enter the United States in order to reunite with their mothers, she joined them.

"Enrique's Journey," the result of years of work, reads like an adventure story: three-and-a-half months on the road, from Honduras through Mexico to the Rio Grande. Nazario rode buses, an eighteen-wheeler, and atop railcars, interviewing along the way those who risk their lives to reach the United States and those who help and harm them. She was observing and learning about the hardships, the violence, the setbacks, and small successes.

Sonia Nazario.
Photo courtesy *Los Angeles Times*

Nazario credits her family for the empathy and survival skills she needed for this project, particularly her ability to communicate across cultures. "I'm such a mutt," she explains proudly. Her father was a Syrian Christian, her mother a Polish-born Jew. Raised in Buenos Aires and Kansas City, Nazario is fluent in Spanish and English.

She also knows how to work under the press of fear. During Argentina's Dirty Wars (the 1976–83 government campaign against suspected dissidents and subversives, thousands of whom were "disappeared") she submitted to strip searches in order to visit an imprisoned relative—terrifying and degrading enough for an adult, let alone a girl of fifteen. "I know what it is to go up to the line of danger," she says of the terror and oppression her family experienced from the inside.

Armed with this knowledge, Nazario wove as wide and deep a safety net as she could before retracing Enrique's journey herself, interviewing jailed migrant kids to learn the points of danger along the way and building up sources in every city, "someone in power who could get me out of trouble." A letter she obtained from the assistant to the president of Mexico helped convince an armed immigrant rights group to accompany her and photographer Don Bartletti through Chiapas, the most dangerous area. That letter also helped her get on and off the trains when they *weren't* moving.

Nazario rode seven separate trains for a total of eight hundred miles (Bartletti was on the same trains, but they largely stayed apart to avoid interfering with each other's work). At the end of each day—the longest was sixteen hours—she was exhausted: "I'd find some horrible hotel and sleep." The full weight of the experience did not hit her until after she was home; she became ill and for six months had nightmares of "being chased by someone trying to rape me." Only a shadow, she realizes, of what immigrants on the trains experience.

And while she is grateful for the rest and therapy that restored her spirit at home, she still wonders about the people she wrote about. "I ask personal, probing questions. I stir the waters. How do they handle it afterwards?" she asks, reflecting on the tough interviews. "I worry about that, my noble purpose against their trauma."

"Enrique's Journey" has been highly praised as fly-on-the-wall journalism at its best. How Nazario translated the experience into words is no less daunting. The empathy she brought to the story and sharpened during the assignment carried over to her writing, bringing readers with her into the slums of Tegucigalpa, onto the train, and jumping from car to car.

She begins inside the head of Enrique's mother, Lourdes, in 1989 and writes in the present tense: "The boy does not understand." How does a mother leave her children? Only the clearest, simplest words can attempt an answer, words even five-year-old Enrique should be able to understand, though he never will.

Inside Lourdes's head, Nazario details what life will be if Lourdes does not leave Honduras: no money for school, barely enough for food. The description of children scavenging in the trash dump is unforgettable. Nazario contrasts this with what a job in the United States will provide them. "It is for them she is leaving."

From the moment Lourdes leaves, through six installments, Nazario plunges the reader into the middle of the action, weaving information from previous chapters briefly and deftly, rarely letting up on the pace. Suffering is individual and particular, and she offers plenty of detail: limbs mutilated by the trains, the gang rape of a young woman, beatings by police. Nazario is equally detailed in describing those who help. Stories like that of the impoverished one-hundred-year-old woman who fills bags with tortillas and beans to give to the migrants, and of the food throwers of Veracruz, are among the most touching in the series. Their compassion is as vivid as the violence.

Writing across language as well as culture, Nazario is nevertheless economical in her use of Spanish words and careful to translate in a way that advances the action. "'¿Donde esta mi mami?' Enrique cries, over and over. 'Where is my mom?'"

Periodically, she moves from the particular to the general, providing context: "one of 48,000 children"; "most are robbed, beaten or raped." This altered tone and tense allows the reader to escape from the suspense of the journey and at the same time understand more about it. Then it's back to the story and the present tense. The effect is like watching a video documentary, the voice of the narrator juxtaposed with the cinematic immediacy of film.

The present tense does more than maintain suspense. Writing in relatively short sentences and with few contractions, Nazario evokes the cadence of the Spanish language, implying genuine respect for those she is writing about. In her hands the present tense also captures the reality of fear and its long half-life after the violence is over. It also reinforces the underlying message that "Enrique's Journey" is happening now, again, today and every day.

With a story so personally written, credibility was important. Nazario provides extensive endnotes following each installment that thoroughly explain when and where she got the information. This was especially important, given the editorial decision to not use the full names of Enrique or his mother in order to protect them once the series was published. All corroborating sources, and all facts, needed to be thoroughly attributed.

A desire to see the truth and tell it first drew Nazario to journalism and has propelled her since the start of her career covering social issues for the *Wall Street Journal.* Her 1994 story "The Hunger Wars" exposed malnutrition in Southern California suburbs and schools, received a George Polk Award, and resulted in the speedy adoption of free breakfast programs. "Orphans of Addiction," a finalist for the 1998 Pulitzer, chronicled the lives of the children of addicts. In "Driven to Extremes: Life in the Antelope Valley" Nazario described how five-hour daily commutes fray the fabric of community and promote family violence.

Complex stories without easy endings. Chronic problems and dehumanizing conditions. By getting inside the lives of others and carefully writing about their experiences, Sonia Nazario reveals how violence can take root in the cracks of corrupt systems and broken lives, and how choices made for good reasons can have tragic consequences.

Enrique's journey does not end when he finds his mother in North Carolina or when he finds work. It ends with his girlfriend's decision to join him, leaving their baby daughter behind in Honduras.

It ends by beginning again.

Enrique's Journey: Defeated Seven Times, a Boy Again Faces "the Beast"

SONIA NAZARIO

This remarkable story covers thirty-two full-size newspaper pages in the Los Angeles Times reprint. Chapter 3, of which this brief excerpt is a part, describes the perils children face in traveling by rail in Central America. A photograph in the newspaper showed boys leaping for the ladders on a moving train, the danger clearly evident. In these paragraphs Nazario bests even a compelling photograph as she shows how Enrique, who was seventeen at the time, must leap toward that moving train if he wants to survive. The series was published in the Los Angeles Times from September 29 to October 7, 2002.

The cemetery is a way station for immigrants. At sunup on any given day, it seems as uninhabited as a country graveyard, with crosses and crypts painted periwinkle, neon green and purple. But then, at the first rumble of a departing train, it erupts with life. Dozens of migrants, children among them, emerge from the bushes, from behind the ceiba trees and from among the tombs.

They run on trails between the graves and dash headlong down the slope. A sewage canal, 20 feet wide, separates them from the rails. They jump across seven stones in the canal, from one to another, over a nauseating stream of black. They gather on the other side, shaking the water from their feet. Now they are only yards from the rail bed.

On this day, March 26, 2000, Enrique is among them. He sprints alongside rolling freight cars and focuses on his footing. The roadbed slants down at 45 degrees on both sides. It is scattered with rocks as big as his fist. He cannot maintain his balance and keep up, so he aims his tattered tennis shoes at the railroad ties. Spaced every few feet, the ties have been soaked with creosote, and they are slippery.

Here the locomotives accelerate. Sometimes they reach 25 mph. Enrique knows he must heave himself up onto a car before the train comes to a bridge just beyond the end of the cemetery. He has learned to make his move early, before the train gathers speed.

Most freight cars have two ladders on a side, each next to a set of wheels. Enrique always chooses a ladder at the front. If he misses and his feet land on the rails, he still has an instant to jerk them away before the back wheels arrive.

But if he runs too slowly, the ladder will yank him forward and send him sprawling. Then the front wheels, or the back ones, could take an arm, a leg, perhaps his life.

"*Se lo comio el tren,*" other immigrants will say. "The train ate him up."

The lowest rung of the ladder is waist-high. When the train leans away, it is higher. If it banks a curve, the wheels kick up hot white sparks, burning Enrique's skin.

He has learned that if he considers all of this too long, then he falls behind—and the train passes him by.

This time, he trots alongside a gray hopper car. He grabs one of its ladders, summons all of his strength and pulls himself up. One foot finds the bottom rung. Then the other.

He is aboard.

Enrique looks ahead on the train. Men and boys are hanging on to the sides of tank cars, trying to find a spot to sit or stand. Some of the youngsters could not land their feet on the ladders and have pulled themselves up rung by rung on their knees, which are bruised and bloodied.

Suddenly, Enrique hears screams.

Three cars away, a boy, 12 or 13 years old, has managed to grab the bottom rung of a ladder on a fuel tanker, but he cannot haul himself up. Air rushing beneath the train is sucking his legs under the car. It is tugging at him harder, drawing his feet toward the wheels.

"Don't let go!" a man shouts. He and others crawl along the top of the train to a nearby car. They shout again.

The boy dangles from the ladder. He struggles to keep his grip.

Carefully, the men crawl down and reach for him. Slowly, they lift him up. The rungs batter his legs, but he is alive. He still has his feet.

CHAPTER 7

Pictures and Sounds of Trauma

Can you remember offhand precisely where you were and what you were doing on September 11 last year? Probably not. Yet nearly all Americans older than a toddler on September 11, 2001, can remember exactly where they were and what they were doing when they heard the shocking news of the terrorist-piloted planes' crashing into the World Trade Center, the Pentagon, and a field in Pennsylvania.

This is a vivid example of flashbulb memories, historic events that are burned into the minds of individuals, communities, or whole nations. Television gave its audience powerful sights and sounds on 9/11, and in the days that followed as Americans struggled to respond.

Exactly why and how people are drawn to watch such moments of history, good and bad, again and again, has not been fully established, but these images are locked into viewers' individual and collective consciousness for better or worse.

Some photographs do have power to install themselves permanently in the viewer's memory where the viewer repeatedly tries to make sense of them in the context of each new reminder. Photojournalism is critical in this process as it contributes in two ways to people's understanding of the world: First, by providing the stunning, startling images that tell how violent humans or nature can be; second, by reprocessing the most compelling of those images through viewers' many cultural forms as they adjust the meanings they give to the pictures. The first kind of image keeps viewers in the moment of experience with survivors, witnesses, and those who respond. The second kind of image plays a valuable role of linking the historical moment captured in photographs to the present; through that linkage of then and now, people navigate their lives.

This chapter looks at news photography, the dilemmas facing those who provide it, and at the ethical issues that arise as news media process images of violence and trauma and incorporate them into their reporting.

Coté and I believe that the photographer's mission is to bear witness to events on the public's behalf. It's an exalted role in a society based on freedom of information, and it requires the sort of effort that often places the photographer in harm's way and in the presence of death, injury, and destruction. The best photojournalists pursue violence as a way to convey truths to the world about the horrors they see. Ron Haviv, a photographer with the agency VII, captured the wrenching violence of the breakup of Yugoslavia in the 1990s. Haviv later wrote: "The war progressed from barber against butcher to commando against civilian and finally evolved into tank against tank. And as it did, I photographed both sides, hoping to show the world what was happening." Haviv saw the war through to the end, lamenting the needless slaughter but providing an archive of overwhelming war imagery (2000:182–84). Peter Howe, who photographed conflicts in Northern Ireland and El Salvador, said of Haviv and his numerous counterparts—men and women—who capture the raw images of war: "Whatever their motivation, it is through their bravery and commitment that those of us who live safer and more normal lives can know the sinister side of our planet" (2002:13). The mission helps drive some photojournalists back into wars and disasters and, their accounts suggest, camaraderie with colleagues and competitors eases the difficulty. Still, the work is some of the most risky and emotionally demanding in journalism.

THE PHOTOGRAPHER'S DILEMMA

News photographers may be the first media people on the scene of a calamity and are working under intense deadline pressures. Because they often are the first to arrive, even before rescue personnel, photographers may become participants in the very news they are covering.

All those factors were part of the mix in Anniston, Alabama, in 1983 when a small television station's camera crew (no reporters were immediately available) taped a man setting himself on fire. The thirty-seven-year-old jobless roofer had telephoned the station earlier and asked it to cover the self-immolation, which he said was to be a protest against unemployment.

The two television videographers (one experienced and the other an intern) notified police, then went to the park. Police found the site and left before both the man and the television crew arrived. As the videographers approached, the man doused himself with lighter fluid and tried to ignite it. The first match went out after fifteen seconds. He lit a second match. This time the flames spread swiftly over his body. After the man was engulfed in flames, the eighteen-year-old college intern did try to put out the fire with his notebook. The man survived after he rushed across the park and a volunteer firefighter put out the flames with an extinguisher. The experienced videographer kept the camera rolling.

The case has been viewed from every ethical viewpoint. The photographers were callous—a view that a network news report later promoted; the camera operators tried to stop the victim but backed off because of his warnings; the photographers fully expected the police to stop the man and were doing their duty—concentrating on recording the event. It's a great case for an ethics discussion because it forces attention to the photographer's responsibility in the presence of the imminent death of another. How can a photojournalist help? The answer is not always to drop the camera and lend a hand.

As Ron Haviv captured the terrors of the war in Bosnia in the 1990s, he became a witness to executions of civilians by soldiers. Ordering Haviv to lower his camera, the soldiers shot one man and then another. Haviv turned the experience into a vow, as journalist Chuck Sudetic later wrote: "Haviv told his friends that if he had another opportunity, he would take the picture." The opportunity came later as Serb soldiers rousted Muslim civilians from their houses and killed them. To gain evidence of the killings Haviv stood far enough away to snap pictures. He later hid a crucial roll of film so he could hand over other rolls demanded by an officer. The surviving images contrast the mechanical "cleansing" by troops with the painful views of men and women injured, screaming in shock, dying and dead, and they constitute the evidence the world needed about the character of that war (Haviv 2000:16–19).

Men and women who show us famine, flight from war, natural disaster, and other forms of massive suffering must in some way address the question of what kind of help they can give. As observers, journalists should recognize the answers as singular efforts to address one of the profession's most difficult dilemmas. Where one photographer may answer, "There are too many victims," another may find ways to help one or more people. David Loyn, a BBC correspondent whose beat is the developing world, said after the December 2004 tsunami: "Now all of us as individuals want to help the individual in the place that we are, and all of us do occasionally take the wounded soldier to the hospital or help an individual. But if you've got a city where there is that much effect, then actually remaining disengaged is quite a good thing. It's unprofessional to help everybody" (Dart Center 2005).

Photographers always will face this question. In some cases guilt will enter into the decision as an emotional force that can overwhelm reason. At such times the journalist will need conversation and contact with other photographers, friends, or family. These are difficult choices, and photographers often must act on their own convictions, even as they face critical second-guessing from others. The profile of ABC News photographer Fletcher Johnson that follows this chapter details how he responded to the plight of refugees from the 1994 Rwandan genocide. His words bear on the ethical dilemma faced by many photographers: "You would not want to leave that kind of place and say all I did was make pictures."

THE PHOTOGRAPHER AS INTRUDER

Photography raises the issue of intrusion on people suffering unexpected and devastating events, whether in a living room in Dallas or near a beach in Indonesia. Use of camera equipment usually does not raise dilemmas of the sort that Haviv faced, but it does require photographers to plan carefully to make shoots as sensitive as possible. So often the trivial things are what can either upset or soothe someone. That became apparent in the taping of scenarios for instructional videotapes in the Victims and the Media Program of the Michigan State University School of Journalism. The tapes feature working reporters and editors who interview actors playing the parts of victims and relatives.

In the many critiques that followed the tapings, the actors, real victims, and their advocates often talked about the equipment. One frequent complaint was that a male television photographer and sound technician should not have placed a lapel microphone on a woman "rape victim" for the interview, even though he told her what he was about to do.

Another complaint was that the television reporter and camera operator had promised the rape survivor that they would hide her face so well that nobody could identify her, but viewers sometimes could make out her face. That should not happen in these days of electronic masking, which can blank out faces on tape. If masking is not available or desirable, the photographer can position the camera from the rear so that showing the person's face is simply impossible.

Reporting teams can avoid or diminish some objections about radio and photo coverage with a little forethought and by using specialized equipment. "Gun mikes" can pick up voices from far enough away that shoving a mike in someone's face is simply inexcusable. Modern strobe lights operate so briefly that, according to studies, subjects do not experience lingering physical effects.

Television floodlights are another matter. A battery of those powerful lights from the cameras of several stations at a scene still can heat up, literally and figuratively, already uncomfortable victims and families. Short deadlines and competitive pressure often make it tough to avoid that lighting excess. When possible, one option is for one station at a time to photograph the person, reducing the number of mounted camera lights and perhaps allowing for more careful indirect lighting. One station could provide the lighting while everyone else makes photographs.

Sometimes, though, the best step a photojournalist can take is to turn the camera off—or not turn it on in the first place. That may not earn praise from the boss, or even guarantee gratitude from the victim, but if a photographer or broadcast reporter really does not want to do harm, it may be necessary.

One style of journalism, encouraged by market competition, compels news teams with cameras to run after survivors of a disaster or make callous attempts to gain information and get an interview. Many viewers were outraged by the coverage of the bombing of Pan Am flight 103 over Lockerbie, Scotland, on December 21, 1988. Scores of reporters traveled first to New York's John F. Kennedy International Airport, where the Pan Am flight had been scheduled to arrive, to question stunned family members and friends, many of whom were just then learning the fate of the passengers. Journalists then hit Syracuse University, the intended destination of thirty-five students killed in the blast.

In subsequent days print and broadcast journalists overran the upstate New York campus looking to interview friends, relatives, and professors of the dead students. The depth and persistence of the outraged reaction to the Pan Am 103 coverage did not soon fade, either. Interviews by scholars several years after the bombing uncovered a strong undercurrent of persistent bitterness among relatives against all the media and especially television.

Probably the ultimate in accusations of harm resulting from media harassment by photographers came after Princess Diana's death in France in 1997. The paparazzi that pursued her everywhere to snap candid shots were accused not just of bothering her but perhaps of causing her death and that of her friend Dodi Al Fayed. Critics contended the high-speed crash in the Paris tunnel would not have occurred if her driver had not been trying to elude the superaggressive photographers who perpetually hounded Diana.

One reason that electronic journalists face so much criticism is the nature of the mechanical beast—the equipment. The very pieces of hardware that make it possible to hear and see so much also can intrude and frighten. Microphones and television cameras, complete with their bright lights, are necessary tools for broadcast reporters, but they can intimidate people. Even in happy situations more than a few normally talkative people suddenly are struck dumb when the mike or lens turns to them. When someone already is disturbed or grieving, the presence of in-your-face equipment can exacerbate the trauma.

In addition to criticizing the emotional distress such techniques cause, many citizens have complained when crushes of television and radio people have blocked driveways and streets with vans and equipment, trampled and littered their yards, or knocked over furniture inside their houses while taking pictures or "awaiting developments."

DILEMMAS FOR THE EDITOR

While photographers can err on the side of snapping everything in sight, editors face true and challenging dilemmas as they present both still and video images. In the photo department or at the editing suite, push comes to shove between all that photographers have captured and the organization's sense of its obligations to an immediate audience. Many editors have described how tough it can be to make those decisions.

The dilemmas that most demand editors' clear reasoning involve drawing lines between available images of horrible events and representations appropriate for the medium. This section looks at some issues that force editors to draw new lines. But first, why do the media show images of violence, injury, and death? Wouldn't everyone be better off if newspapers, magazines, and television refused to show such pictures?

Biology and Pictorial Horror

So why do blood and guts sell? A prime suspect is that a basic attraction to violence and horror is rooted somewhere deep in the human condition. Those who study children's literature find many examples of gory details in fairy tales. Just think of some of the murderous and savage scenes in "Little Red Riding Hood" (a wolf devours a grandmother and in due course is killed by a woodchopper) and "Hansel and Gretel" (children abandoned by their parents end up shoving a witch in an oven).

"There is an undeniable interest when one is very, very young in horror and terror," psychiatrist Frank Ochberg says. "My take on all this is we do need to have certain images in our minds, and certain pathways in our brains, that allow us to incorporate scenes of violence, of horrible human cruelty and destruction. The way we digest them is to coat these scenes with humor, with mystery, with detachment, with kinds of pleasant shock and relief. This is the way we swallow the pill." That "pill" may be necessary, he contends, because people are not born with every image in their minds that they fear—or should fear.

"If we put all this together," Ochberg continues, "we can see there is a biological attraction to images of horror and terror, and an emotional response to it, whether it's television news or television fiction, or movie fiction or books or whatever. Our usual response is curiosity, interest, and even a certain amount of pleasure. That doesn't mean we're callous or corrupt or sadistic. It just means we're participating in a biological reality. Eventually, with enough experience and book learning, you come to know some of these things in your head are to be greatly feared, and you develop good ideas of what should be avoided."

Ochberg, however, has counseled hundreds of victims of traumatic stress and emphasizes that he is not advocating bigger and more frightening doses of horror and terror on television and in photos. "There are times when a dose of violence imagery is important," he says. "Does that mean we shouldn't have self-censorship? No; there are times when the dosage is excessive and not an 'inoculation.'"

Some media analysts suggest that repetitious violence works on the audience's sense of the world, leading people to believe that their communities are more dangerous than they really are. That belief, it is argued, turns people capable of responding to most life challenges into "victims," fearful and passive, rather than confident and careful. A related effect of watching excessive amounts of violent television may be desensitization. "As the violence levels depicted increase in intensity and graphic detail, we adapt, we adjust, we get used to it," writes Arnold Goldstein, who goes on to suggest that our desensitization only prods entertainment producers to reach for more shocking material (1996:40). Walter Jacobson of WFLD-TV in Chicago and Howard Kurtz, media critic for the *Washington Post*, argue that the growth in tabloid-style journalism on television and the decline of standards trace to the belief that "junk journalism" is easier, quicker, and cheaper to air than stories of more weight. Besides, they note, "dull news" often lacks exciting video. News coverage marked by violence contributes both to people's fears and their loss of empathy. Journalists also fear that the violence that should be prominent in news reports—the wars, the natural disasters that leave people and nations in dire need—gets lost in a flood of relatively meaningless violent images.

The local evening newscast highlights how television wields that power. Nearly every viewer probably can predict exactly when during the newscast that heart-wrenching or bloody story of a violent event will air. Many stations have the practice, if not policy, that "if it bleeds, it leads." Few television viewers or newspaper readers have not seen and reacted viscerally to such images as rescuers pulling a limp body from a river, grieving mothers writhing on an airport floor, or the blood-splattered interior of a wrecked car.

Some people suspect that newscasts go out with little discussion about ethical issues, but in many cases they would be wrong. Here, Coté and I want to examine a handful of news judgments that required editors to carefully examine their policies and their assumptions about audience reaction.

These cases show editors deciding that some images of death and injury should be shared with their audiences. The decisions challenged conventional industry thinking about the showing of bodies, whether graphic images from distant places are used more frequently than those taken in the community or nation, how image choices may promote the nation's war effort, and how novelty and prominence may override concern for those in the audience. The line between acceptable and not acceptable in U.S. media is shifting steadily, as these cases illustrate.

Harrisburg Horror

R. Budd Dwyer, the Pennsylvania state treasurer who killed himself before reporters and photographers at a news conference in the state capitol in Harrisburg in 1987, gave no advance warning of his intentions. Dwyer was facing prison after convictions for bribery, mail fraud, and racketeering. He presumably was going to make a statement about the matter and, many reporters thought, resign. Apparently, nobody but Dwyer knew what he really intended. Cameras were rolling and clicking when he pulled a .357-caliber Magnum out of an envelope, put the long-barreled pistol in his mouth, and pulled the trigger.

The question after the shooting became how much to show on air and in print. Many editors and news directors in Pennsylvania and across the nation agonized about how much of Dwyer's press conference they should show. The Associated Press moved a series of photos that included the gun in Dwyer's mouth and another at the moment of death. Taken together, who used what often depended on how close a station or paper was to the event. In general, the farther from Harrisburg, the more likely it was that a station or paper would show the most graphic photos. The *Patriot,* Harrisburg's hometown daily, used a large front-page photo showing Dwyer with the gun in one hand and warding off the observers with his other hand. Hundreds of miles away, the New York

Daily News ran four large photos on inside pages, showing Dwyer warding off observers, the gun in Dwyer's mouth, the instant of death, and Dwyer's bloody body slumped on the floor.

The proximity principle reared its head in the Dwyer case: Although folks are most interested in local events, editors will carefully screen images of death and suffering for the home audience. Death in distant places will be shown more realistically. The same evening that the networks declined to run the Dwyer tapes, they showed soldiers shooting down demonstrators in the Philippines. Similarly, the next day several prominent papers that withheld the Harrisburg photos ran gory pictures, often on the front page and in color, of the dead or wounded Filipinos.

In recent years editors have defied the proximity principle in ways that both support ethical journalism and undermine the public's confidence in news. Deciding what sounds and images to broadcast or print when journalists have only minutes or hours to make decisions can be extraordinarily difficult. The stakes are even higher when the broadcast is live. Although the benefit of the live shot is immediacy, a drawback is the meager time for editorial judgment to gauge how live footage of an event or interview will come across to viewers. The shock can be overwhelmingly personal if a family member or friend hears about a loved one's death over the air—or even sees it on a television screen as it happens.

Actually, considering the proliferation and competitive pressures of television news coverage, it may be surprising that more live televised killings have not occurred. U.S. television watchers witnessed an actual killing for the first time in 1963, when Jack Ruby shot Lee Harvey Oswald, the accused assassin of John F. Kennedy.

It was not, however, until April 1998 that the first suicide on live television actually happened. A disturbed man stopped his vehicle on a Los Angeles overpass, got out, and at one point unfurled a banner that read, "HMOs are in it for the money! Live free, love safe, or die!" After setting his clothes, his pickup, and his dog on fire, the man placed a shotgun under his chin and pulled the trigger. Seven local stations and MSNBC were showing the scene live. Two local stations interrupted children's programs for the occasion.

Now, the stations did not know that the man intended to kill himself. The live coverage started after police reported a sniper was driving along the freeway and stopping at various points. That certainly was a newsworthy event at afternoon rush hour on one of the most crowded thoroughfares in the United States, but did it have to be televised live? Even if the likelihood he would commit suicide was not immediately obvious, the knowledge that he was armed and apparently a sniper should have alerted news directors to the possibility that live coverage might show him committing violence.

Tom Goldstein, dean of the Columbia University School of Journalism, noted in a commentary for *TV Guide* shortly after the suicide that the stations had an alternative to live coverage: "Every live event is not newsworthy, and journalists are being asked to make quick editing judgments of what is important. It was easy not to show the suicide last month. Some stations demonstrated commendable strength by cutting away from the scene—or, better still, not going live" (1998:41).

An incident in the Iraq war turned the issue around. Present with his video camera rolling when a marine killed a wounded Iraqi insurgent, a scene later shown by NBC News and other television services, freelancer Kevin Sites took pains on his Web site to explain to the marine unit he was covering why the incident went to broadcast. He noted a number of mitigating circumstances, mentioned the cooperation of commanders, and noted that the marine who had fired the shot had himself been wounded.

> So here, ultimately, is how it all plays out: when the Iraqi man in the mosque posed a threat, he was your enemy; when he was subdued he was your responsibility; when he was killed in front of my eyes and my camera—the story of his death became my responsibility.
>
> The burdens of war, as you so well know, are unforgiving for all of us.
>
> I pray for your soon and safe return.
>
> (Sites 2004)

Showing Bodies

One of the most variable ethical lines involves showing bodies in still photographs or video. Until a few years ago the proximity rule applied generally across media. Newspapers and television, if they showed bodies, usually did so in international contexts and rarely in domestic settings. Bodies of American victims or military personnel photographed abroad were rarely shown. But that rule is changing.

In 1999 the *Rocky Mountain News* in Denver published a photograph of the body of a boy killed at Columbine High School, published it in fact before the boy's parents had official confirmation that their son had died. Janet Reeves, the director of photography, studied an image taken from a helicopter showing, in its lower lefthand corner, students and a police officer crouched behind a parked car, marked the picture, and passed it on. Another editor pointed to the top of the picture where a boy's body lay sprawled on the sidewalk. The paper had already issued an extra edition at 3 P.M.; at 4, Reeves, editor John Temple, and managing editor Jack McElroy decided to run the picture inside the next morning's edition. For four more hours staffers discussed whether to run the picture of a body that had not been identified. Although the parents of the boy, Dan Rohrbough, gained confirmation of their son's death after they recognized their son in the picture, the photograph violated the newspaper's policy about showing bodies and provoked other questions about the rush to publication. For the documentary *Covering Columbine* (2001), Temple told an interviewer, "We needed to show people. We could not soften what had happened to the point where people didn't realize how terrifying this event was. We didn't put it on Page One. . . . If you'd made it to [page] twelve or thirteen, you knew where you were."

With the Iraq invasion by U.S. forces in 2003, media editors once again addressed the question of showing Americans wounded or killed in combat or as a result of the storm of bombings aimed at both occupying troops and civilians. In April 2004, a year after the invasion, Barry Fitzsimmons, the *Seattle Times*'s photo editor, was invited by a caller to look at a picture a friend had sent to her. On Sunday, April 18, the paper published on its front page the picture that the caller wanted Fitzsimmons to see. Taken inside an aircraft in Kuwait, it shows rows of military coffins, each draped in the red, white, and blue of the U.S. flag. Publication of such images had violated Pentagon policy since 1991, a policy still in force at the start of the 2003 invasion. Taken by Tami Silicio, a cargo worker at the U.S. military area of Kuwait International Airport, and e-mailed to a friend in the States, the image stirred readers to voice both strong support and anger. Some applauded use of the picture as a step toward candor about the war's casualties, while others argued that the families of the dead deserved to be spared such images at a time of grief. Executive Editor Michael Fancher denied that publication of the image constituted a statement against the war. "Silicio says she believes the soldiers' families would be proud to see how their loved ones are treated, and we have tried to be true to her intent" (Fancher 2004:2).

Silicio, who was fired for giving the *Times* access to the photos, later told a Seattle newspaper: "When you look at the photo, you fill with compassion. You can feel the grief. That's how I was feeling in my heart when I took the picture. I was thinking about the overwhelming sadness of those irreplaceable lives lost, the true cost of this war. It's about the dignity and respect and care that they are given going home" (Pliego 2004:1).

Events of the war have forced media editors to reevaluate policies about images of dead or wounded Americans. In May 2005 the *Los Angeles Times* studied six major newspapers and two newsmagazines during a six-month period when 559 Americans and Western allies died. The newspaper "found almost no pictures from the war zone of Americans killed in action" and only forty-four pictures of Westerners wounded in Iraq. Photographers in Iraq said they were rarely at the scene of an attack or bombing and they sometimes were prevented from taking pictures by military personnel. Photographers embedded with a military unit are not permitted to take photos that show identifiable dead or wounded people, and the military can block release of pictures until family members are notified, a process that sometimes takes so long that the news value of the pictures is lost (Rainey 2005).

But editors confront another kind of obstacle when they choose to picture a wounded or dead American. When an Associated Press photographer photographed a dying young soldier being rushed to a field hospital after an ambush, a number of newspapers used the image. Some readers reacted angrily, accusing the publications of being "cruel, insensitive and unpatriotic" (Rainey 2005:1).

U.S. media remain influenced by the proximity rule, especially in times of war, when sentiments about the rightness of the military action are divided and often intense. Since the first Gulf war in 1991, however, sensitivity to media timidity about images has sometimes played a role in the decision to show more realistic photographs. When four American contractors were killed in Fallujah, Iraq, and their charred bodies were hung from a bridge over the Euphrates River, the American media used the images widely but did not publish or broadcast the most disturbing images of the killings, which had been transmitted to media outlets. Editors often appear deeply conflicted between the obligation to show some photographic evidence of the reality of war and the fear of reader or viewer anger when the images appear to undermine the national cause (Robertson 2004).

When editors place graphic images in a framework of explanation about an event or a pattern of events, they are more likely to be serving the goal of truthful reporting to their readers or viewers. When the images are placed within a page or article layout, or within a visual program in ways that minimize their emotional impact while contributing to public understanding, the realistic nature of the photographs is defensible. One trend is clear. At a time when the most troubling images—beheadings of captives by terrorist groups, for example—are available visually on Web sites and other sources, and international media are pushing the envelope of graphic detail, editors will continue to face difficult decisions about what to show, and how to show death and injury constructively.

GUIDELINES

Given all the conflicting advice and situations, it may seem impossible to conclude there's any one "right" way to handle visuals when it comes to broadcasting death. Some of the most practical and blunt proposals come from professional organizations. For example, The Radio-Television News Directors Association has been a leader in exploring the topic in newsletters, meetings, and seminars. Similarly, *News Photographer* magazine for years has published vigorous internal debates and soul searching about who should be pictured, and how, in violent situations. Other intensive explorations have come from organizations with a teaching mission, among them the Poynter Institute for Media Studies and the Dart Center for Journalism and Trauma.

Here is a list of guidelines that come from the recommendations of these various organizations:

- Do not knowingly allow a live broadcast of a killing, whether homicide or suicide, especially in close-up and showing wounds and blood.
- Build in a delay of several seconds during live transmissions to allow managers to make a decision about whether to show something.
- Insist that photographers and photo and graphics editors join other editors or news directors in deciding which photos to publish or tapes to air.
- Be sure relatives have been notified before announcing or showing the identity of a person who has been killed.
- Give viewers of television news reports enough advance warning of what they are about to see so that someone can leave the room, remove children, or change the channel.
- Remember that children may be able to see a photo in a newspaper left lying around or may watch a television report when adults have left the television on.
- Think about the relative effects of photos published on the front page and inside pages of a newspaper, as well as of images in color versus black-and-white. Something that might be too graphic for someone (especially a child) glancing at a front page could be less troublesome inside.

- Tell the whole story—before, during, and after—of what happened to the human being involved, not just the death, no matter what photos or footage are used.
- Show tape of a death or other traumatic event once if it meets standards, but do not use file tape in subsequent telecasts.
- Discuss the decision, how it affected survivors and the public, and whether the staff should have handled anything differently as soon as deadline pressures ease. The more discussion there is of these experiences, the more likely a news organization is to avoid thoughtless miscues in the future.
- Do not assume that these, or any other guidelines or policies, will save anyone from agonizing about what to show and not show. They will not and perhaps should not.

It behooves photojournalists and broadcasters alike to celebrate the power for good under their command and to respect the harm that same power can do, unchained, to aggravate human suffering. Dramatic and compassionate visual and audio journalism does and will draw listeners and viewers, sell papers, and win honors. Photos and voices that vividly tell the whole story of ordinary people under extraordinary circumstances will have even more important roles in this new century. Coverage that ignores or debases the human factor will increasingly draw the contempt it deserves.

News organizations also must recognize that their photographers are vulnerable to traumatic injury and that editors are vulnerable to emotional distress when they view a stream of graphic, troubling images, most, if not all, of which, will not reach the public. Teams and their managers can agree that it is alright to switch monitors off, or at least to look away, when a particularly graphic feed is coming in. That sensitivity should apply to sound, which can be heard throughout an editing room, as well as to images. Those who must view or hear troubling images should be encouraged to take frequent breaks outside the workroom. Finally, managers and coworkers must recognize the emotional burden of viewing troubling images as a work assignment and provide both rotation opportunities and respect for the sacrifices the job requires.

FLETCHER JOHNSON

Eyewitness to Hell

Fletcher Johnson has seen his share of violence and trauma in twenty years as a news photographer for ABC News. He covered the second intifada in the Middle East, the war in Kosovo, and the war in Iraq. He points to two assignments early in his career that left an indelible impression on him and helped prepare him for the stories he later would cover.

A child stands alone on a road, brush receding to mountains behind him. The boy clutches a red rag tied around his middle and peers back over his shoulder. He is going nowhere and has nowhere to go. But he's not alone. He is one of more than a million Rwandan refugees stranded in a rocky corner of eastern Zaire.

Fletcher Johnson.
Photo by Charles
Breiterman

It's 1994. Ethnic genocide has killed a half million of Rwanda's 7.9 million citizens. Many of the survivors, including this little boy, have fled from Rwanda to Goma, Zaire. They have left behind the probability of being murdered to die in Zaire from starvation and disease. Bodies litter the side of the road, awaiting burial in mass graves.

Fletcher Johnson trains his lens on the boy, a child not much older than his own son back home in suburban Washington, D.C. After making the shot, Johnson heads up the road to the child. A translator explains that the boy's parents died here in Zaire, and Johnson loads him into a van and takes him to an orphanage. It's one bit of help he can offer, one drop of water he can throw on this Dante's inferno. "You would not want to leave that kind of place and say, 'All I did was make pictures,'" Johnson explains.

The road to Goma was a flood of what Johnson describes as "death scenarios." "You would shoot someone and go down the road, and by the time you came back, they were dead," he says.

He saw a dying woman giving birth, photographers hovering over her. He told them to stop shooting. At six feet, six inches and 275 pounds, he literally carried the weight of authority. "I just felt it was exploitive," he says. "At that level, dignity supercedes the image."

Johnson made his share of tough images. His job was to expose the horrors of the genocide but, he says, "Everyone has a threshold."

He came upon two children lying in debris by the side of the road. A few yards away orphans like them took shelter from the sun and heat under a French military jeep. These two, however, lacked the strength to pull themselves to the shade. Johnson squatted down beside them. One boy rested his head on his arm and peered at the camera; the other—a little brother?—couldn't lift his eyes for more than a few seconds. "They can't make it," reporter Jim Wooten intoned in the voice-over that accompanied the televised image. "They won't make it. They're beyond help."

Goma, Zaire, pages 157-158

Top: Boy on a hill. "This young boy walked alone and turned as I was shooting him. He stopped, stood frozen, and just stared. His stare went right through me and I was struck by his solitude in that madness. He was the first of two children Trevor Barker [sound man] and I took to an orphanage."   Photo by Fletcher Johnson; ABC News

Bottom: Fearless Angel. "The doctors in Medecins Sans Frontières/Doctors Without Borders are fearless, tireless, and selfless."   Photo by Fletcher Johnson; ABC News

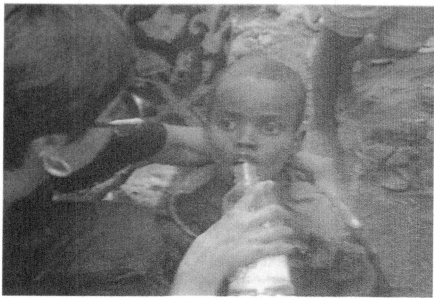

Death. "When we first drove past this woman and child, she was desperately flailing away on the pavement. When I returned an hour later she was dead. Truth be told, it became an easier picture to make." Photo by Fletcher Johnson; ABC News

Orphans. "Countless children had been left orphaned; these three were in relatively good condition. I found that the children [who were] moments from death were impossible for me to photograph." Photo by Fletcher Johnson; ABC News

Everyone had a breaking point in Goma, Johnson says. This was his.

"I hadn't been exposed to that much death. I don't know that I'd seen a dead body, maybe at a crime scene," he says.

"How do you deal with that and keep working? How do you find ways to cope with that, the feeling of helplessness?"

He retreated to a nearby airport where he and other journalists were staying in tents. He needed to remove himself from the images of death; he needed to fix his eyes on something else, *anything*. And then he headed back out. For ten days he walked the road of death with his camera perched on his shoulder. "If you're running and gunning and the action is moving, you can make any image," he says. "But Rwanda was different, because it was one scene after another of death playing itself out.

"You could be judicious: 'How am I going to shoot this death scenario? I'm going to move the camera a bit so I can see the face better.'"

He adds, "The imagery kind of stays with you."

As emotionally overwhelming as the Rwanda story was, it was relatively easy to shoot in a surreal way. The dead and dying proved willing subjects. Mostly, they just gawked at Johnson. He didn't have to worry about gaining access or establishing rapport. It was a matter of applying his skills as a news photographer to serve as an eyewitness to hell.

Two years earlier he'd faced a different kind of challenge, this one much closer to home: a section of North Philadelphia known as "the Badlands."

The neighborhood had long been surrounded by heavy industry that provided a steady stream of jobs, but nothing remained in the way of an economy—nothing legal. It had become an open-air drug market. Dealers shouted out the product of the day, while others openly hawked "works": syringes, spoons, and other implements used by addicts. Houses—some abandoned, some still occupied—served as shooting galleries. Johnson had done documentary work before, but he had never tackled anything like this. How could he make people trust him? How could he trust that he would be able to enter this world and leave it at the end of the day with his Betacam, and in one piece?

He carried his camera on his first day in the Badlands, but he didn't shoot much. Instead, he worked the perimeter, seeing and being seen. He wanted to get a feel for the place, gauge how people would react to him. "Just kind of show that you could walk through there without too much trepidation and fear," he says. "Kind of make a presence."

He knew he had to include images of drug dealing and people shooting up, but he didn't want to work surreptitiously. "I wanted to get closer," he says. "I wanted to meet the people who were there. I wanted to hear what people had to say. I wanted to get closer to the truth, and I don't think you can do that from the back of a van with smoked windows."

Most people scattered when they saw Johnson and his producer, soundman, and production assistant. The journalists persisted, though, and eventually ingratiated themselves with the older residents, "the elders," Johnson calls them. They tended not to be as paranoid, and the others in the neighborhood trusted their judgment. "If you get the blessing of the elders," Johnson says, "it tends to make things easier."

He talked with anyone and everyone, even people he knew wouldn't be part of the story. It was important to show that he was willing to listen, to hear the stories, *all* the stories.

"The drug world engulfs all kinds of people, but at the core they're like everybody else," he says. "They're very open, once you get to know them, because not many people spend time talking to them.

"They live in a very raw state. They're very vulnerable in a way; they're a living, open sore. If someone takes the time to act humane with them, as opposed to locking them up or calling them a junkie, they are very receptive to that: 'This is someone who asks me a question and actually cares what I say.'"

Johnson spent a few weeks over two summers in the Badlands, making all kinds of images, including one of a man holding a mirror up to his face so he could inject heroin into a vein in his neck. The story was slated for a news show called *Day One,* but the executives at ABC decided it was too grim and killed it.

A couple of years later producer Leroy Sievers of *Nightline* was discussing possible stories with Johnson, and the Badlands came up. Johnson took Sievers to the neighborhood, and they immediately encountered a man hawking works in the middle of the street. Sievers's jaw dropped at the Kafkaesque scene.

The story clearly was about the drug trade, but they wanted to show more. How did the neighborhood evolve to this point? What about the residents who wanted a better life for themselves and their children?

The groundwork that Johnson had laid in his earlier visits enabled the *Nightline* crew to go beyond the sensational and provide a well-rounded portrait of the neighborhood. They showed addicts shooting up but also profiled a man who made sure people used clean needles; they showed drug deals going down while children cavorted nearby but also gave voice to a woman struggling to provide a relatively normal life for her six-year-old daughter.

The story aired in 1995, but it was not over. In the spring of 2004 *Nightline* returned to the neighborhood in a segment titled "The Doctor and the Reverend: Getting Well in the Badlands." Johnson had stayed in touch with Merryl

Philadelphia "Badlands," pages 162-163

Top: Lost home. "This woman cries as she watches her house being demolished. It was targeted by the city and her neighbors as a place for the drug trade, and it had long been abandoned. To her it was home."   Photo by Fletcher Johnson; ABC News

Bottom: "No shame in my game." "Kids were exposed to the drug trade early. This drug dealer explained how it was just a basic way of survival; a sense of shame had no place in the game. In fact, dealers carried respect."   Photo by Fletcher Johnson; ABC News

Top: Drug trash. "It was difficult to accept how things could get so bad; sometimes I felt I had to be in another country. The kids lived in this drug debris and it was just normal."   Photo by Fletcher Johnson; ABC News

Bottom: Protecting turf. "Every day parents closed off parts of Percy Street to stop the drive-by drug buying and to allow the kids to play in the streets."   Photo by Fletcher Johnson; ABC News

Jackson, a heroin addict for more than thirty years who had been shown briefly in the 1995 report. Now, Johnson had heard that Jackson had emerged as a survivor and had been drug free for more than eighteen months.

"It's one of these stories that kind of sticks with you," Johnson says of the Badlands. "You see people in very difficult conditions, and you find you can learn from everybody. They have interesting insights into human nature."

The report labeled Jackson "the doctor" because of his skill at finding collapsed veins and shooting drugs into addicts. "The reverend" was a white suburban housewife and ordained minister named Joanne Muller. In her unceasing visits to the Badlands, the minister turned her energy toward Jackson. In a 2005 e-mail Fletcher Johnson continues the story:

> Finally, it was a bullet to the groin and jail that slammed Jackson onto the road of recovery. After six months out of rehab he reaches out to reconnect with Joanne. The reunion is a great value for both of them. As he heals, Joanne is there to keep him grounded spiritually. He is bolstered in knowing their bond goes without judgment or conditions. As for Joanne, he represents a reaffirmation of her faith. He is a symbol of hope and redemption and, in her view, who else but God could salvage the worst of the Badlands?

The insights that Johnson has gained about the evil of humanity and the dignity of human beings are not his alone. His viewers learn the same lessons, thanks to his patience, his determination, and the images he makes with his camera.

CHAPTER 8

Reporting About Children

"They're okay!" shouts the rescuer. "She's okay," says the doctor after the accident. "Kids Okay," says the headline after a shooter menaces a school playground. Until the 1970s Americans tried hard to believe that children who were not injured physically suffered only brief and minimal emotional harm in disasters and violent events. Not much was known about how children react to tragedies except what parents reported. And parents, caring and loving as they were, often turned out to be unreliable observers of their children's emotional states. Over a few months, parents typically said, trauma symptoms rapidly disappeared.

Researchers rarely questioned the children, and their parents' hopeful observations lent support to both a government and therapeutic view that children truly were lucky survivors of disasters and violent events. Research on the resiliency of children in stressful situations, such as extended illnesses and their parents' marriage breakups, fed the assumption that youngsters could handle anything, including trauma. So "they're okay" seemed the right thing to say after disasters, so long as no one suffered bleeding wounds or broken bones.

Today researchers know that the phrase, hopeful as it is, is misleading. Promoting the error through news stories is a disservice to the children whose emotions are under siege and to those in the community who are trying to help children.

Getting the story about children right is difficult, in part because Americans have so many complicated ideas about them. Cute and appealing as news subjects, they also call up a lot of assumptions about what a child is and how a child is to be valued. Why the notion of the resilient child eased the consciences of adults during the Great Depression of the 1930s, World War II, and the Korean War is understandable. Adults were preoccupied with the demands of the time; it helped to think that once the crisis was over, everyone would return to normal. War and depression had separated children and parents and made children witnesses to the horrors of war. Yet as recently as the 1940s it was still widely believed that children were not much affected.

Images of children encode many of society's hopes and fears. During a war or famine and after a natural disaster or act of violence, journalists find children to photograph or interview. Reporters and photographers know intuitively that a child's plight rivets the attention of readers and viewers. If they can see the physical harm to the most vulnerable, they will take note of the crisis. Starved frightened children, bones etching deep lines in stretched skin, repeatedly remind the audience of the horrors of famine, genocide, brutal civil war, and the AIDS plague. Stunning images of American children linger in the memory after people have forgotten most other news pictures. Indelible are the pictures of a dead child in a firefighter's arms in Oklahoma City and the aerial view of the ghostly naked body of a boy lying on the bed of a pickup after the searing blast of the eruption of Mount Saint Helens in Washington State. But the living, cherubic child is an equally powerful image. The face of Jessica McClure, the baby freed from a well in Midland, Texas, in 1987, lifted spirits across the country.

Americans dote on messages that say that innocent and helpless children can confront terror and recover readily. The "okay" boy or girl reassures people. The child in obvious distress is troubling and for good reason. People's concern for their own children helps them to identify with any child's plight. Journalists are as vulnerable to those feelings as anyone.

The emphasis on child victims in news coverage is universal, if not often acknowledged, by journalists. Children are important bearers of the values of society. That is why newspeople seek them out and why everyone pays attention to stories about them. And that may help to explain the desire to say that apparently whole children are "okay" after they have confronted some form of violence.

New knowledge about the emotional damage that children suffer contradicts the cliché. A thoughtful physician is not likely to dismiss the possibility that the child is suffering from trauma; a reporter should be as careful. Since the early 1970s new ways of studying trauma in children argue that regardless of age, they are likely to suffer long-term trauma symptoms from a variety of violent events. These newer studies place a greater value on children's reports about what they feel. Many of these studies conclude that children who have survived hurricanes, earthquakes, and tornadoes; have witnessed school shootings; or suffered other acts of human violence such as sexual or physical abuse will have traumatic symptoms long after. School-age children and adolescents may experience all the traumatic reactions seen in adults and satisfy the diagnostic criteria for post-traumatic stress disorder, according to the National Child Traumatic Stress Network, a resource center funded by the U.S. government. The youngest children—those in the first five years of their lives—are most likely to be deeply affected by trauma, although their symptoms may differ from those of older children and adults. According to the network's Web site, "It is extremely difficult for very young children to experience the failure of being protected when something traumatic happens... . Because a child's brain does not yet have the ability to quiet down fears, the preschool child may have very strong startle reactions, night terrors, and aggressive outbursts." Thus evolving knowledge about trauma gives a better understanding of the sweet, wise, and photogenic children who may be the first candidates for interviews and pictures as journalists arrive at the scene. A series of horrifying, violent episodes endured by American children since the early 1970s has taught this lesson, as have the natural calamities and countless wars that other children around the globe have survived.

HOW DOES TRAUMA AFFECT CHILDREN?

Small children may be traumatized by a sudden unexpected event that injures or kills their classmates, parents, or other relatives and robs the children of all sense of security. In 1984 a sniper opened fire on a crowded Los Angeles elementary school playground from his home across the street, killing a child and a passerby and wounding a staff member and several children. Children who had been at play watched friends cut down, sensed the danger to their own lives, and saw human bodies mangled. A bullet cut through the side of one girl, taking out lung and heart tissue. As the passerby was killed, children saw his intestines burst from his abdomen. Inside the school, as teachers hastily taped paper over windows and told children to hide in closets or under desks, many children thought gang members were attacking the school and would kill them. Bullets shattered the windows of some classrooms. Although many children had already gone home, others were separated from their families, and for a time police denied parents access to their children.

Therapists who treated the children found devastating effects. Kathleen Nader, one of the therapists, later wrote: "One month after the sniper attack, 77% of children present on the playground under direct attack and 67% of children in the school had moderate to severe post-traumatic stress disorder (PTSD)." Children who knew the girl who was killed had significantly more trauma symptoms. Fourteen months later children exposed to the shootings still had significantly more symptoms and more severe reactions than the children who had left the school early, were told by teachers to hide under their desks, or were on vacation at the time.

The children, of course, suffered the same trauma symptoms as adults: unwanted memories of the shootings, heightened anxiety, and, over time, decreased interest in people, some aspects of their lives, and the future. For some, such symptoms as bad dreams and fears faded quickly. Other children received help for as long as two years after the shootings. A loss of interest in life may have endured much longer.

The children who are nearest to people who are killed or injured or who are directly threatened with loss of life themselves are most likely to show extreme trauma symptoms. They are most likely to suffer anxiety, depression, and PTSD, including symptoms of avoidance. Even mild levels of exposure will lead some children to experience intrusive reminders of the event.

The journalist might keep this commonsense scale in mind when children are involved in newsworthy events: If the child suffers directly in the traumatic event, the degree of trauma is likely to be high. If the child only witnesses injury, death, or terror as it affects others, the child witness will suffer. The more the child cares about those who are most affected, the more likely the child is to show symptoms of trauma. After the explosion of the space shuttle *Challenger* killed Christa McAuliffe, a schoolteacher, and six other astronauts in 1986, researchers interviewed children in McAuliffe's hometown who did not know her and children in a city three thousand miles away. The study found that because children were likely to care about her, youngsters in both groups were likely to develop such trauma symptoms as new or exaggerated fears of flying or of death and dying or dreams about McAuliffe or the deaths of others in their lives (Terr 1990:327).

Danger is a constant in children's development. A small child may fear water or electric outlets, an older child a lonely walk to school. The awareness of danger stimulates emotional and physical reactions. Growing up, in part, is the process of learning to manage those fears. Sudden violence blocks that path to maturity and the result often is traumatic injury. A feeling of helplessness may foster physical reactions, such as rapid heartbeat and trembling. The cry for help may not bring a response from an adult. Feeling unable to cope, children will fantasize later about what they could have done and blame themselves for not stopping the violence. They may become passive and nervous, dwell on the event in their mind, fearing it will recur, and in play repeatedly act out their role in the violence. Both objects and people will easily remind children of the violence.

In such single-event traumas children place more of their trust than usual in the adults around them—teachers, parents, and administrators. Those same adults also may be reeling from what happened, less able than usual to give emotional support to the young. Children often wait, while school staffs, emergency workers, and others find ways to regain control of their chaotic situation. The parent's role is especially critical, particularly for infants and preschoolers. The mother or father often serves as the protector in whose care the child can try to understand the event. Children deprived of contact with parents during and after disasters later fear being separated from their parents even in routine ways.

Some experts on children's trauma believe that long-term symptoms may be related to such social factors as whether the community or school organized quickly to deal with the emotional damage, whether and how long the child was separated from parents, and how each adult responded. Communities that prepare for a natural disaster are likely to reduce the incidence of lasting emotional disorders among the children. Normal routines, even in wartime, and open, frank discussions of risks, ways to deal with them, and the possibility of death and injury may reduce stress enough to limit long-term effects among children.

A different emotional response may occur in children who are victimized by another person, rather than by a natural disaster. Trauma specialists note a variety of forms of anger and rage that may follow an event in which a human blocks the child's innate ability to resist or escape injury. The adrenaline that encourages survival may lead to a buildup of both fear and aggression if the child cannot take action. If these horrors are repeated, anger may overwhelm the fear. Over time, the anger may evolve into one of three behavior forms: identification with the aggressor, retreat into victimization, or general control marked by occasional outbursts or wild rages (Terr 1990:63).

When relatives or other children die in violent circumstances, trauma often confounds the natural and lengthy process of grieving. Unable to work through the process of grieving, a child may become locked into protest or despair for several years.

It is not unusual, though, for a child caught in a single event to already be suffering from some type of prolonged trauma, such as homelessness following a parent's death, a disability or disfigurement, sexual or physical abuse, survival of a war, refugee status, or the aftermath of a car crash. Responding to the combination of traumatic experiences, the child may take on other emotional traits. One kind of response is to disappear into a cocoon and stay there. This kind of self-protection may be labeled denial, dissociation, or repression, and it may take such emotional forms as a lack of feelings, rage, and unbroken sadness. (Some research shows that children caught in a disaster are less likely than adults to pass through the emotional phase called denial; that is, they are more realistic about what has happened to them.)

Dissociation occurs when someone wraps his emotions in a cast, to use psychiatrist Sandra Bloom's description, to keep from suffering. Adults, including reporters and photographers, may do this when they confront troubling scenes. Most adults, though, know rationally what happened to them even as they shut off their emotions. They have clear memories of the event and can recount its details with a fair degree of accuracy.

Those who treat trauma in children say that dissociation is a much more powerful response in them, one that may completely eclipse the child's memory of the reality of the event. "Given the powerlessness and defenselessness of children, dissociation is often the only thing they can do to protect themselves," Bloom writes (1997:37). The result of locking up the emotional stress of an event may be, in some cases, a complete inability to contend with or understand reality.

A shooting at a high school may not be as traumatizing as it would be at an elementary school, but traumatic symptoms will occur nevertheless. Columbine High School students interviewed on television after the April 1999 shootings in Littleton, Colorado, showed signs of the confusion, agitation, and numbness that come with acute stress. In general, even at high school age, symptoms of trauma are likely to be more severe than for adults. Some children exposed to violence or its effects may simply find it hard to communicate or may communicate incoherently, child psychologist Donna Gaffney told us.

When the trauma is prolonged, as in repetitive physical and sexual abuse, the child's identity may be so affected that it exists only in fragments that have no integration with each other. Memories and emotions tied to one event may exist entirely separate from those of another event.

Like victims of single events, such as shootings, tornadoes, and fires, children caught in warfare suffer emotional injury. Researchers studied a group of Kuwaiti children after the occupying military forces of Iraq were expelled in 1991. These children showed levels of traumatic reaction similar to those of survivors of the 1989 earthquake that leveled Armenia and those who witnessed or were under fire from the school sniper in Los Angeles. Most of the Kuwaiti children knew someone who had been captured, injured, or killed; a majority had seen dead or injured people in the streets; and a third had witnessed the killing of humans.

LESSONS FOR THE JOURNALIST: AT THE SCENE

Journalists should consider ahead of time which of their actions at the scene may be harmful and which may help children. Strange adults—reporters—and unfamiliar gear—cameras—may add extra stress for children who are trying to deal with the frightening images of the event as well as their own troubling emotional responses. Caught in a frenzy of media attention, children may find that reporters are frightening. A reporter who covered a sniper attack on children in a Stockton, California, schoolyard remembered that the children, already frightened by blood and bullets, were "being chased by a mob, microphone poles extended like weapons, cameras trained on them, people shouting at them to stop. Some reporters even tried to interview them as they fled, yelling, 'Did you see it? Did you see it?'" (Libow 1992:380).

News personnel at the scene risk being part of the contagion of fear and trauma that will affect children. Emotional stress is contagious. The reactions of people whom the child trusts—teachers, parents, and siblings—can heighten the fear that the child feels, and small children are especially vulnerable to the effects of contagion. How is it communicated? A look of panic or fear on a mother's face as she arrives at a congested school site may become one of the images that a child captures as part of the trauma. The anger of a parent who does not know whether a child has been harmed will affect the child who is watching. A reporter or camera operator, shouting in the tumult of a chaotic scene, also contributes to this confusion and contagion. When administrators have time to follow their disaster plan after a violent event at a school, teachers and others greet the parents and help them calm down before they see their children.

After a murderous shooting spree in a Fort Worth, Texas, church in September 1999, police acted quickly to isolate the child witnesses and relatives from the media as crisis counselors rushed to the scene. Yet when reporters finally were allowed to conduct interviews, aggressive individuals still intimidated some children with their lights, cameras, and intense questioning.

In the years since, parents, hospital staff, police, and school officials often ask for or insist on isolation of traumatized children from the media. Coté and I think that such actions serve the needs of the children. After a school shooting in 1998 in Springfield, Oregon, hospitals set up media centers where reporters could interview wounded children but only as they were being discharged and then only if the children wished to talk to the media.

INTERVIEWS AND PHOTOGRAPHS

As a general rule, Coté and I believe that journalists should not interview or photograph children aged ten or younger in connection with devastation, disaster, homicide, and accidents. We base this argument on our knowledge that trauma is likely to affect most the young children who are victims or witnesses. The possibility of traumatic harm is sufficiently great with young children that few interviews are defensible. The child who is the only eyewitness may give important information, but most children will have little to add to accounts that are available from older witnesses. Traumatized children need to recall the event but in ways that pay attention to their emotional responses to memories. The typical journalist's interview will not help the child do that; indeed, it may make it harder for the child to deal with the trauma.

Journalists who decide that their reporting requires the child's words or picture should discuss this need openly with both the child and a parent. Parents provide critical emotional support when the child is frightened. In general, without a parent's permission and assistance, reporters and photographers should not approach children of any age who may be traumatized. Do not leave the decision about talking to the child solely to the parents, though. Parents may be under stress too and may find it difficult to decide whether to expose a child to media attention. They may think the child is fine, may not know what harm has been done, have a sense of whether a press conference or interview would be helpful or harmful, or understand that the media event may actually have adverse effects. Some parents grant interviews to show gratitude for public support or to encourage financial donations. The author of a textbook on interviewing wrote that journalists should not interview children without a parent's consent "except at a news event." If the "news event" has affected the child, we believe that journalists have a responsibility to participate in protecting the child from unnecessary stress. In other words, journalists are not justified in talking to children or photographing them simply because the confusion of the scene makes them accessible.

Finally, the reporter should ask the child if she or he wants the attention. Elsewhere, we have endorsed the recommendation of some editors that interview subjects be given the equivalent of an informed consent form, a detailed statement about what the reporter or photographer wants and what might actually appear in the newspaper or on television. The needs of a child make this negotiation much more difficult but no less ethically necessary. The child is trying to gain control of a confusing world. Deciding whether and how to participate in news coverage can be a part of regaining control. Some children want and will enjoy the experience, while others will be upset by it. Still others will have delayed negative reactions. Neither the reporter nor the children will know how they will respond to the interview.

The reporter should make a point of telling the child and parents that even talking about the event may cause unpleasant feelings and a belated sense of a loss of privacy. Attention that the child receives may be appealing at first, but the family may not anticipate that classmates may scold or tease the child. Judith Libow, who treated traumatized children in a California hospital, warns that personal disasters and publicity—even media attention that exalts the child as a hero—may turn out to be harmful. "Many children react to personal disaster with intense pessimism about their future, expecting their lives to be shortened and new disasters to befall them," she says (1992:382). Children, then, have a hard time reconciling the upbeat news approach with their internal sense of the traumatic aftermath. It is a mistake, though, to think that a child, especially one younger than ten, cannot be part of a decision about talking to a reporter. The dilemma that a reporter or photographer faces with a child at a disaster scene has no ready response. No one can say with certainty that some or any of the consequences will occur. We are arguing for calm, thoughtful negotiation with the child and adults, one that restores some degree of control to the child and lets everyone know that troublesome consequences may arise.

Reporters and photographers must be realistic when talking to the child and parents about whether the news organization will use photographs and how much of the interview the story might use. Children whose trust in adults has been undermined may not understand why a thirty-minute interview turns into a thirty-second story or why a distracting photo session never yields a picture in the newspaper or on television. Libow describes the disappointment of a boy taped for a story on a local news program about his fight against leukemia. "He was ready on the designated night, his hospital room filled with friends and family to watch his story," she says. "He was seriously depressed for days afterwards when his story was bumped, without warning, to make way for a more pressing news item. His story was never televised" (383). Some reporters make a point of repeating several times during an interview that a picture or story may not be used.

The end of chapter 5 lists ways that journalists can reduce stress for an adult who is being interviewed. These ideas apply as well to interviews of children or teenagers. The reporter should find someone to give youngsters support during the interview; locate a calm place to talk that is away from the sights and sounds of rescues, medical aid, destruction, and firefighting; and sit with the children, keeping at their eye level.

If the interview takes place some hours or days after the event, the reporter should consider seeking the help of someone trained in interviewing trauma victims. That person may be able to help the journalist gain useful information.

The reporter should anticipate that the child's version of the event may differ from that of an adult observer. An adult might think of a tornado's strike as a single event, but small children sometimes remember several different traumatic events, each distinct and not necessarily linked in the child's mind. A reporter might interview a parent who is grateful for a child's safety and in denial about the child's losses, such as friends' deaths. The child, needing and wanting to grieve for those losses, may be bewildered by the parent's responses. Children also may feel extraordinary guilt about their role in the event, and that guilt may be reinforced by questions or references to details of what happened. Guilt can be based on a failure to act, being safe when others were hurt, or acting in ways that endangered others. Some experts have noted that small children may be confused about times and physical characteristics (particularly of strangers). On the other hand, they may remember details peripheral to the center of the action better than some adults because the children are not as adept at focusing on the salient details of what happened.

Few reporting textbooks say anything about interviewing children, implying that all interviewees are pretty much alike. One of the few writers who makes a distinction between adults and children, Shirley Biagi, makes these suggestions about interviewing children:

- Ask open-ended questions. A reporter is more likely to obtain information by asking what happened, rather than "Did you see the car hit the boy?"
- Ask the same question several times. "Information that remains the same through several sessions is more likely to be accurate," she adds.
- Independently verify what children say.
- Interview each child privately.

(adapted from Biagi 1992:83)

Journalists also should think about how the things they take for granted in their work may affect a newly traumatized child. Flashes and cameras may be reminders of what happened. Journalists need to be aware that the child may fear a violent adult and so may shrink from rapidly approaching strangers and loud voices. Journalists have learned to act quickly and assertively at work. But that loud bang, quick pace, and assertive voice that work so well around adults may trigger fears and memories in the child. Some children, in contrast, will be pleased by the attention and want the reporter to be pleased by their responses. This may result in comments the child thinks the reporter wants to hear, rather than the child's actual thoughts.

WRITING AND EDITING THE STORY

Avoid the "poster child" trap. Appealing, photogenic children invite a journalist's attention and too often they are quite willing to cooperate. Some children, though, do not understand why they attracted the attention, and many of their peers may be hurt or confused by being ignored in favor of the chosen one. The "poster child" represents only one identity, one gender, and a unique part of the event; using only this child ignores all others.

When shots were fired in a Seattle high school, wounding a boy and a girl, television reporters were able to interview the girl in her hospital room in time for evening newscasts; police kept the media away from the boy while they questioned him. The media coverage, which emphasized extensive interviews with and photographs of the white girl and completely ignored the African American boy, angered other students. In the balanced attention that student reporters paid the two victims in their school paper, they asked why journalists did not interview the boy after the police finally finished questioning him. The answer most likely was that it was too late that day to do an interview, and by the next day more current stories had eclipsed the shooting. A familiar variation on the poster child report is a focus on the gifts, money, and attention from the public. Reporters need to ask themselves whether barraging a child with such attention really is a helpful act at that stage.

Reporting sometimes places too much emphasis on a single traumatic symptom, such as attempted or completed suicides. When these examples receive extensive news coverage, or are translated into fictional dramatic treatments in movies or on television, copy cats often follow. If the copy cat case is newsworthy, journalists should place it in a broader context by calling on experts, examining trends, and looking at prevention efforts.

Respect the child's need for privacy. Being shown on television or in news photographs in pajamas or hospital gowns bothers some children. A boy who was injured in a drive-by shooting was afraid to return to school because he had to wear an eye patch. A boy whose picture appeared in a Seattle newspaper was identified in the caption as a resident of a homeless shelter, which the accompanying story said he did not want classmates to know. Children's fears sometimes disappear with careful help from trauma specialists, teachers, parents, and journalists. When a girl about to begin school was badly burned in a campfire, such intervention, aided by a local newspaper's effective stories and photographs, enabled her to prepare to go back to school.

So is it really necessary to name children described or quoted in the story? Traditional news practice argues for full and accurate identification. An awareness of what a child might endure from public knowledge of his or her experience suggests a compromise. Alex Kotlowitz, who has reported about children for the *Wall Street Journal* and in several books, asks the child or a parent for permission to use a true first or last name. "You need to consider the well-being of that child you are writing about," he argued in a meeting with other reporters at the Casey Journalism Center on Children and Families. Other reporters have regretted using real names for children.

Do not assume that children are in denial about a traumatic event because they do not talk much about it. Denial, as we have noted, is more likely to be an adult symptom after a devastating event. Children often act quite thoughtfully and selflessly in threatening circumstances. In some cases, though, they may find themselves helpless to do anything, and that very knowledge may affect their later recovery. In contrast to the few children who can be heroic in a threatening situation—the student who wrestles a weapon out of the hands of a shooter, for example—most children can do little to affect the crisis that surrounds them. But it is often misleading to say that the children, individually or as a group, behaved helplessly. When a woman shot herself in front of a fifth-grade class, she did so after the children, at their teacher's urging, had begged her not to take her life, then prayed for her. Kathleen Nader, a child trauma expert, tells of an eight-year-old boy who watched as a woman killed several of his classmates in a schoolroom, then noticed and shot the boy's friend Bobby. "When she had turned her focus to Bobby, he [the other boy] had promptly run for cover and slid like a baseball player behind the file cabinet, effectively saving himself." The boy's self-image was shattered until he began to accept "the competence with which he had saved his own life" (1997:166).

Educate readers and viewers about the long-term character of trauma. "Only one child came out of the Dunblane school gym physically unharmed," read a newspaper dispatch about the killing of a teacher and sixteen kindergarten pupils in a Scottish school in 1996. This variation on the "okay" cliché harmfully separates physical from emotional injuries. The reporter should have recognized the likelihood of severe traumatic injury to that child whose "clothes were drenched in the blood of his classmates" and explained it in stories soon after the event.

Do not include vivid and startling images in the coverage. We do not know exactly where to draw the line between acceptable coverage of a death scene, for example, and coverage that goes too far. But reporters and editors need to expect that many children who were at the scene will later become glued to the television set, watching replays of their own traumatic experiences or connecting the latest event to one they have experienced. That coverage will remind them, above all, that the world is an unsafe place. The images that appear in newspapers and on television will trigger the troubling images in their memories, adding to the difficulty they have in dealing with the trauma. Images mentioned but not shown can be harmful as well. In a television report about a train wreck the reporter mentioned that one of the last acts of rescuers was to pull the body of a very young child from the water. Children who knew the victim might imagine the victim's death and appearance, might ask whether she had died instantly or how long she had been alive in the water, whether she was scared or in pain, and why no adult helped her in time to save her life. A mother complained bitterly when a newspaper story included an eyewitness's description of her son's last futile struggle to break out of a car as it sank into a lake. While the mother will continue to struggle with that horrible image, classmates of the boy also may be plagued by those few printed words.

Finally, think seriously about the tone of the report. Most news is about bad things, and some media, especially television news shows, actually go to the extreme of banning good news. In doing so, they often work at odds with school officials, health experts, and parents who are trying to restore a sense of safety for traumatized children. Even after children appear to be out of the way of direct harm, their sense of danger will persist. If media reporting continues to focus on the death, injury, and danger without taking into account the efforts to restore safety, children will be supported only in their fears. Some Seattle mental health experts responded angrily when a local television station that had covered a devastating fire refused to send a news team to cover the firefighters who returned to the neighborhood to reassure the children about their safety. News reports should provide information not only about how bad things have been but also about how to respond in case of another such event. A television weather reporter calmed small children in a school that had been struck by a tornado when he visited them to explain what causes a tornado and what protective actions to take during a storm.

Coté and I have argued that children should be protected from media attention, especially if they are ten or younger. They also need protection at any age if a devastating event has affected them directly. What we have suggested contradicts the values of many journalists who believe that their first obligation is to tell all they could learn about an event, even if it means using children to do so and naming those children. Children are traumatized by violent events. The closer they are to danger, the more likely it is that they will have post-traumatic stress disorder or many of its symptoms. A major event may leave a neighborhood or community with a long-term problem of recovery because of the suffering of its children. Journalists need to sacrifice images of and quotes from the cherubic faces they find at disaster scenes and, in the interest of supporting the long-term health of those children and their communities, rethink the ways they present news of violence.

Most journalists sense the risks in media coverage of children but must respond to their profession's interest in detailed coverage of violent events. The Casey Journalism Center on Children and Families at the University of Maryland has honored constructive reporting about children for many years and regularly brings journalists together to share ways to make reporting on children better. Gabrielle Crist exemplifies an extraordinary commitment both to respect the needs of child victims of violence and to inform the public about child trauma. Crist's 2000 series, "Eric's Blessing," told readers of the *Fort Worth Star-Telegram* about ten-year-old Eric Watkins, who had seen his father murder his mother. After months of cautious contact Crist gained Eric's trust. Her series, printed over six days, recounted the murder, Eric's actions to try to save his mother, and the aftermath, including the trial of his father, which resulted in a probation sentence. Crist understood the impact of trauma on the boy and helped readers understand the long-term effects of the trauma that Eric had suffered. In one installment she wrote about the distance Eric had yet to travel in facing his own emotional injury:

> In therapy, he hasn't worked through the trauma of seeing his mother lying in a pool of blood. Eric can recite the events of the shooting as if it were a report on what he did over the summer break, but he doesn't yet connect to the terror he felt when it happened.
>
> He hasn't dealt with his anger toward his father, or with the prospect that his father might someday want to see him. And although somewhere in his

mind he realizes that his mother is dead, Eric fantasizes about her return, looking forward to the day she shows up and takes him home.

(October 6, 2000:1A)

THE CHILD ABUSE STORY: A NEED FOR BETTER REPORTING

When children are in danger, and the danger—the fire, the earthquake, the shooter—is readily apparent, journalists quickly report the story. The child endangered in the home by parents or other relatives through physical or emotional abuse or neglect is far less likely to gain the attention of journalists. As a result, the public hears less about abuse and neglect, common experiences in any community, and learns little about how to stop the abuse and help the victims. Stories about domestic violence often focus on the adult perpetrator and victim and ignore or pay scant attention to the children in the home, who usually are both victims of and witnesses to the violence. A study published by the Casey Journalism Center showed that news accounts of youth crime and violence and child abuse and neglect rarely included context that helps the reader or viewer connect the particular event to trends or resources. In contrast, reports on child care and teen childbearing usually included that information. (2002:9).

It's not surprising that journalists struggle to help people understand how common sexual abuse of children is. Experts say authorities, ranging from police to family court officials, often disbelieve women who accuse spouses or partners of abuse, although very few such claims have been proved false. Journalists confront strong social resistance to treating child abuse with the same candor that they might use in reporting an accident or natural disaster involving children. Collectively, everyone wants to believe the cultural assumptions about safety in the home, school, or church and the trustworthiness and integrity of parents, teachers, coaches, ministers, and priests. A journalist who challenges those assumptions may face community and institutional hostility, as well as resistance among newsroom colleagues. Some forms of child abuse that are being reported with some degree of candor and clarity—sexual abuse of children by priests and other clergy, assaults on teen athletes by coaches, incest—were systematically excluded from news coverage for much of the twentieth century.

Secrecy is essential to the violation of the child in the initial act, and journalists have found that secrecy by the offending institutions often blocks the journalist's best efforts at getting to the truth. Those who study the perpetrators of sexual violence against children note that offenders often are appealing people, earning admiration in their communities for public-spirited actions, having roles that the public assumes indicate integrity and trustworthiness, and possessing the communication skills needed both to seduce the child and to plant fear should the child disclose anything about the assaults.

These conditions were critically important to continuation for far too long of a pattern of child abuse by priests in the Roman Catholic Church. A few priests exploited children, usually boys, with whom they had contact in the course of church rituals or activities. Although some children reported sexual abuse and some parents complained to church authorities, in many cases the offending priest was either reassigned or required to undergo brief, and often ineffectual, therapy. Although the media, usually a local newspaper, reported on a few such offenses, until recently Americans had no national sense of what some have called an epidemic. The media often failed to attack the institutional secrecy that protected abusers from being identified to the public. As a consequence, the child victim often grew into adulthood without finding support for his suffering or for identification and punishment of the offenders.

In 2001 the "priest scandal" became a national issue in the United States, leading the church hierarchy to undertake significant changes in its handling of priests accused of sexual abuse of children. Journalists moved the issue from the local stage to a national level that for a time preoccupied newsmagazines, national newspapers, and network and television news services. Coincidentally, the pattern for national public awareness was being set at about the same time in Ireland. There, Mary Raftery, a producer for RTE, the Irish national television service, used a powerful documentary, *States of Fear,* to enable adult victims—men and women—to tell about abuses they endured until the end of the 1960s in the industrial schools that various Catholic orders had run since 1868. The 1999 documentary led the Irish government, which had subsidized the schools, to offer a public apology. Raftery and two associates reviewed the history in a book, *Suffer the Little Children: The Inside Story of Ireland's Industrial Schools* (2001).

Much of the credit for gaining national attention for the abuses in the United States goes to enterprising journalists in Boston. Kristen Lombardi, then a reporter for the *Boston Phoenix,* an alternative weekly newspaper, learned in January 2001 about a large number of negligence lawsuits against the Archdiocese of Boston and began to seek out some of the eighty-six victims associated with the cases. "The victims were almost completely underground," she has said, but five of them spoke to the reporter. Lombardi's story in the edition of March 23–29, 2001, brought a flood of calls and messages from other victims, and interest in the disclosures in other media increased, especially after Bernard Cardinal Law responded that the children and their parents bore blame for the assaults. Meanwhile, a team of reporters at the *Boston Globe,* the region's leading metro daily, began working in August 2001 to gain access to court records of the cases, many of which had been filed as early as 1996. In January 2002 the *Globe*'s investigation lifted the story into the national media spotlight, enabling victims and journalists in other cities to press local church authorities for both greater disclosure and reform. The *Globe* reporters received thousands of calls and messages from victims and from others who had information about abusive priests.

The Boston case showed what keys enabled reporters to make the public aware of a pattern of institutional abuse of children. The victims' lawsuits produced both details about their accounts of abuse and documentation of church responses. Once the court records laid the groundwork for investigations, journalists could begin to talk to survivors. That process required reporters to develop a special ethical code for interviewing survivors who had been abused as children but now were adults (see second bulleted list at the end of the chapter).

A NEW RESOURCE ON CHILD TRAUMA

In 2002 the federal government created the National Child Traumatic Stress Network to coordinate the work of both university and grassroots treatment centers. The network provides accurate information about children's trauma for parents, caregivers, and police and other first responders. It also serves journalists who cover violence against children, both through its website—www.nctsnet.org—and by direct help from staff members.

In closing, we offer these suggestions to journalists who report about children and violent situations:

- Do not assume that children are emotionally well after a traumatic event, even though they may appear to be responding normally.
- Avoid actions at the scene that may frighten children. Cameras and microphones can be intimidating. Even a journalist's scowl may communicate fear to a watching child.

- Avoid making an attractive or available child witness or survivor into a "poster child."
- Involve the child and her or his parents in your discussion about what you are reporting and how you are doing it.

Reporters who covered abuse cases have offered suggestions for interviewing survivors. They point out that most victims find it empowering to tell a reporter about their experience. They may find disclosure uncomfortable in the short term but over time will value being interviewed.

- Decide on a policy about naming victims and apply it fairly. In the priest sexual abuse scandal, the *Boston Globe* promised anonymity to any victim who requested it.
- Approach survivors carefully, looking for evidence of ability to cope with the emotional pain of disclosure. Doing interviews will not help some survivors. Indeed, the interview may do more harm than good.
- Begin the interview with a careful explanation of ground rules, including such matters as whether the person will be named and how the interview will be used.
- Allow the survivor to stipulate the rules for his or her participation, including having a therapist or other representative present during the interview.
- Do not revisit courtroom testimony that may cause the survivor more pain.
- Focus the interview on the survivor's efforts to recover from the abuse, rather than on the abuses.
- Provide information about support groups and agencies that assist survivors, because reports of abuse of children move other victims to speak out. Provide lists of books, articles, Web sites, and videos that can help a person find help or decide how and whether to speak about such a personal experience.

A *Globe* reporter told the Dart Center for Journalism and Trauma, "The experience of having been shunned made many victims and their families even more willing to speak with us, because they were so angry and disappointed and disillusioned as a result of their poor treatment by the church. Then, after our stories began to run, many victims grew even angrier, because they realized that the betrayal they had experienced was not an isolated event" (Cox 2003:2).

JANE O. HANSEN

Moving Readers to Protect Children

In January 2001 readers of the *Atlanta Journal-Constitution* opened their Sunday paper to the front-page story written by Jane O. Hansen, "Selling Atlanta's Children." As the deck bluntly explained, "Runaway girls lured into the sex trade are being jailed for crimes while their adult pimps go free." The photo, placed prominently above the fold, was stunning and unforgettable: the shackled ankles of a ten-year old girl.

The series continued through Monday and Tuesday. The response was immediate. "I will be writing my representatives to plead with them to change this situation," wrote one of the many readers who were shocked at the child sexual exploitation that Hansen exposed.

Jane O. Hansen.

By March the Georgia legislature had passed two laws, one making it a felony to pimp any child eighteen or younger (until then it had been a misdemeanor "no more serious than a parking ticket") and another that gave courts the authority to seize assets used in the business of pimping children. The Atlanta Women's Foundation received a generous donation to purchase a home for the young victims, and a special fund was created to treat and protect them.

For Hansen, catalyzing reader action like this is one of the rewards of reporting. "If you do your job right, you can have an effect." "Right" meant balancing the victims' stories and descriptions of social and legal systems accurately, with all their complexity, heartbreak, and viciousness. From the first paragraph she put a human face on child sexual exploitation. By the eighth paragraph (still on the front page) she had tied the crime to other cases. Experts in juvenile court and federal and local laws, police and social workers, information and statistics on prostitution and pimps—the series included them all—but the story never let the reader forget that ten-year-old girl or stop caring about her and her eleven-year-old sister. Nor were they the only young victims Hansen described. One article explored how and why girls become prostitutes. The final story was about mothers whose daughters had been lured into prostitution through chat lines and included advice for parents, as well as specific ways for readers to help through volunteering, contributing, and lobbying.

Throughout, most of the girls were not named, nor were their faces shown (the most notable exceptions were girls who were missing and whose guardians wanted them identified). But the reality of their lives and the violence of sexual slavery made people sit up and take notice.

Behind the series was Hansen's considerable experience and tenacity. She began writing for the *Journal-Constitution* in 1982, covering education issues. In 1990 she was a Pulitzer finalist and won SPJ and Selden Ring investigative journalism awards for "Suffer the Children." This seven-part series uncovered the suffering of abused and neglected children and showed how the abuse occurred in foster as well as natural homes. The *Journal-Constitution* sued to get the records she needed—of children killed while under the "protection" of Georgia's child welfare system—and asserted that confidentiality should not apply to protect the privacy of children who were already dead.

By the time Hansen began the work that would become "Selling Atlanta's Children," she was a veteran at scaling obstacles put in her way by state agencies and the courts, and at questioning policies. In her experience "confidentiality laws have done more to protect tormenters and harm children." She also was clear about her motives. "As a journalist, I am often driven by the public's need to know about people who lack a voice," she wrote in a guest article for Georgia's forensic science newsletter (Hansen 2001).

The idea of covering child sexual exploitation in Atlanta came to her indirectly, through a column she had written in 1991 about a private Christian school that would not hire Jews. The mother of one of the students Hansen had interviewed called to compliment her. Nine years later the same mother became familiar with the problem of child prostitution in Atlanta through her volunteer work in the courts and called Hansen again. Would she be interested in hearing more?

Hansen knew the story was important. She also knew there would be resistance, both within the newspaper and among readers. The stories of child sexual exploitation had been written before, about immigrant children or kids in other countries, making it, from the perspective of editors, an "old story." That these were local girls in Atlanta made it "new" enough, but even juvenile judges had trouble getting the district attorney to prosecute because prostitution was considered a "victimless crime." The public generally assumed that teenage prostitutes were not victims—that they chose to sell their bodies.

To overcome reader bias Hansen needed a very, very young girl. Reporting about a child prostitute would frame the story more powerfully than quotes from agency officials and experts alone could provide. "When talking about child sexual abuse, we have many statistics and research, but numbers make people *numb*," she explains. "If I can write about one child behind those numbers, and if the story is compelling enough, then it will have impact. Then it will move people."

Learning about a ten-year-old girl's case (and that of her eleven-year-old sister) was only the beginning. Juvenile hearings are closed by law, and it took months of reassurance on Hansen's part before Judge Nina Hickson would let her inside the courtroom or, for that matter, be introduced to the girl. Hansen talked to other judges who knew her reporting on previous cases and could recommend her to Hickson. She offered past news stories that showed she was protective of confidentiality and photos that showed they could be taken without identifying the girl; she even agreed to let the judge see photos before they ran. At the same time, Hansen worked to win the confidence of the child advocate and probation officer in the case.

The resistance did not end with Hickson's permission. When Hansen showed up with photographer Kimberly Smith, the bailiff stopped them; after Hickson upheld the permission in chambers, the Department of Child and Family Services objected. It took another hearing that day before the photographer was allowed to take the picture that so riveted readers. "You have to really believe a story needs to be told," says Hansen, looking back on the effort behind that front page and what kept her going.

When strangers kidnap or kill children in a school shooting, the violence is explosive. Police, emergency medical technicians, and news media rush in, and the public rallies to help and prevent the crime from happening again. When violence takes the form of child abuse or childhood sexual exploitation, the explosion is muffled, as though it were taking place far underground. Jane Hansen succeeds in reporting these hidden stories in ways that make the public aware, outraged, and demanding of changes to make children safer.

Selling Atlanta's Children

JANE O. HANSEN

Hansen's clear, compelling descriptions link the reader to the two small girls in this story. Their plight, as children forced into prostitution, is framed credibly by the reporter's attention to the social system that created the abuse and the legal system that tries to respond to it. In this first installment of a three-part series, Hansen provides a careful melding of small human details with a well-researched discussion of the Georgia criminal justice system. This article appeared on the front page of the Atlanta Journal and Constitution on January 7, 2001.

The courtroom door opened, and a guard led the defendant inside. She was dressed in standard jailhouse garb—navy jumpsuit, orange T-shirt, orange socks and orange plastic flip-flops. Metal shackles around her ankles forced her to shuffle. "All rise," the bailiff said. The judge entered and took her seat on the birchwood bench while the defendant sat down at a table and chewed her finger.

At issue was what to do with her.

She had been in and out of an Atlanta jail since August. It was now November. Her sister was in another jail. As lawyers and officials debated whether she should remain behind bars, probation officer Gail Johnson asked if the defendant could address the court.

A little girl, her hair pulled into a tiny pigtail and her head bowed, rose from the defendant's table. She was 10 years old, a runaway and an alleged prostitute.

"I think I have been locked up long enough," the girl said in a small, high-pitched voice. She began to cry and rubbed her eyes with balled-up fists. "If you would just let me go home . . ."

But for children like her and her 11-year-old sister, also an alleged prostitute, it's not that simple.

In Atlanta, prostituted children often go to jail while the adults who exploit them go free, court records show. Attitudes toward prostitution are partly to blame, say Juvenile Court judges and others. But a lack of children's programs in Georgia, particularly for girls, has left some judges no choice but to place exploited children, such as these, in detention for their own safety.

"The last thing I want to do is detain her, because it comes across as punitive," said Fulton County Juvenile Court Judge Nina Hickson. "But I've got to make sure that she's safe."

In Georgia, pimps are rarely arrested, even when the prostitute is a child. When pimps are charged, their cases often are dismissed or result in a small fine, court records show.

There are no reliable statistics on the number of prostituted children, although Atlanta judges say they are seeing an alarming growth in their courtrooms. But statistics for adults show a clear disparity in the system's treatment of pimps and prostitutes. Since 1972, 401 adults—nearly all women—went to prison in Georgia for prostitution; no one went to prison for just pimping.

"I think there was an unwitting bias that the woman was the perpetrator," said Mike Light, Department of Corrections spokesman and a former parole officer. "She was the one out having sex. . . . The pimp was just collecting the money."

Atlanta police say it's harder to arrest pimps than prostitutes. And prosecutors say it's difficult to build a case against pimps because prostitutes often are reluctant or scared to testify against them.

"We need evidence," said Carmen Smith, solicitor general for Fulton County State Court. "We need witnesses."

But critics say too often, police and prosecutors fail to distinguish between prostitutes who are adults and those who are children, such as the 10- and 11-year-old sisters. Many child prostitutes are runaways who are often escaping physical or sexual abuse at home and then are exploited on the streets.

Yet in the eyes of law enforcement, said Judge Hickson, "these girls aren't seen as victims. They're seen as consenting participants."

Juvenile Court judges and others have begun pressing for change in Georgia to bring harsher penalties against those who exploit children. They want the Georgia Legislature to make the pimping of children a felony punishable by up to 20 years in prison. They want authorities to become more aggressive in arresting and prosecuting men who pay to have sex with underage prostitutes, as well as the adults who sell them. And they want some alternative for helping these girls other than putting them behind bars.

In recent months, local and federal prosecutors have begun to respond. The Fulton district attorney's office has brought felony charges against about a dozen alleged pimps believed to have prostituted children. The U.S. attorney's office hopes to bring federal charges against pimps under the nation's racketeering laws.

Still, says DeKalb County Juvenile Court Judge Nikki Marr, not enough is being done for children whose lives may already have been destroyed.

"It's not a priority," she said. "That's what it comes down to."

YOUTH CENTER LIKE AN ADULT PRISON

In the waiting room at Metro Regional Youth Detention Center of Atlanta, the state's largest youth jail, the public telephones are only 4 feet off the ground—about the right height for a child. But everything else about Metro looks and feels like an adult prison—with razor wire outside and electronic doors inside. Children are often taken to court in shackles.

"Whoever had her on the streets should be behind bars," said Johnson, the probation officer for the 10- and 11-year-old sisters.

This particular day, she had come to pick up the older sister and transfer her to Girls and Boys Town in DeKalb County, the only emergency shelter in Georgia designed especially for girls. Finally, a bed had opened up for the child.

Girls and Boys Town offers up to 30 days of counseling and education in an unlocked residential facility. Judges from as far away as South Georgia have sent girls there. But with only 16 beds, there is sometimes a waiting list.

The 11-year-old had been waiting in jail for three weeks, since she had been picked up as a runaway and charged with lying to police about her age.

The day Johnson retrieved her from Metro, the child emerged in the hot July sun hugging a teddy bear. "I love him because he's pretty, soft, he has all kinds of decorations on him," she said. Even the guards were upbeat to see her leave.

"Look what she got on," Johnson muttered. "She's a baby herself."

The girl was dressed in high-heeled sandals and a skimpy sundress, her peach-colored bra peeking out from the low-cut top. As she walked toward the car, she teetered on the heels, like a child playing dress-up. But she worried that if her brothers saw her, "they'll tell me I'm too grown."

On the way to Girls and Boys Town, Johnson stopped at McDonald's to buy the girl lunch. Over a Happy Meal, the girl said her older stepsister, who had given her the shoes, and a cousin had introduced her and her younger sister to prostitution after taking them to a hotel on Fulton Industrial Boulevard.

"They told us to stay on the streets," the girl said. "If anybody tries to talk to us, talk to 'em."

Atlanta police had picked her up on Bankhead Highway after a man flagged down officers, saying he had found a runaway child. She told the officer what she was doing and said she and her 10-year-old sister were staying in a hotel, but she insisted she was 14.

According to the police report, the patrol officer called the youth squad and explained that two girls were working as prostitutes. The officer asked how to handle it, thinking the youth squad would want to investigate. Instead, the officer was told to drop the child off at the county shelter.

"I found this odd," the officer wrote in the report. "I was concerned that someone was prostituting these girls out of a hotel, and I could not even get an investigator to give advice."

Eventually, the officer charged the child with false information and obstruction. A spokesman for Atlanta police said officers did subsequently investigate but found no evidence of prostitution.

In a separate interview, the 10-year-old said the boyfriend of a relative had made the children prostitute.

"He forced me. He wouldn't let me go," the 10-year-old said, sitting in Hickson's chambers. Speaking softly, the child sat hunched over with one hand partially covering her left eye, the other holding her right cheek. She never smiled.

"He told me he'd kill me if I left," she said.

At first he "was buying us stuff." She realized something was wrong, she said, "because of what he wanted in return." He wanted money "by me prostituting."

"I was really scared," she said. "He'd pull my hair, and he punched me."

The child said if she could, she would "change back the hand of time. I would change all this. It's not worth seeing your life taken by prostitution stuff."

But she also didn't think it was right that she and her sister had sat so long behind bars.

NO MORE CHILDHOOD

Georgia judges no longer send adult prostitutes to prison. Adult prison beds are increasingly reserved for violent offenders.

But the opposite trend is occurring in Georgia's youth jails and prisons, where the beds are increasingly used by nonviolent offenders, including child prostitutes. In 1999, four of five admissions to Georgia's youth jails were for nonserious offenses; girls are the fastest-growing population.

Many child prostitutes enter the Juvenile Court system charged with something other than prostitution, primarily running away. The number of runaway girls arrested in Georgia skyrocketed between 1988 and 1998 from 312 to 1,645 a year. Not all runaways become prostitutes, but national studies say up to a third of runaway and homeless youths exchange sex for shelter, clothes and money—what experts call "survival sex."

The 10- and 11-year-old sisters wound up behind bars because they kept running away from home in violation of their probation. But both girls were also in jail because there was no other safe place for them.

"They need treatment," said Alesia Adams of Victims of Prostitution, a new program in Fulton County to help child prostitutes. "These two break my heart. There's just no place to put them."

Atlanta vice Detective Herman Glass says many of the underage prostitutes he has arrested need years of therapy. Without it, he sees the same faces recycling through the criminal justice system.

When he recently arrested a 19-year-old girl prostituting on Metropolitan Parkway, he realized she was the same girl he had arrested six years earlier, when she was 13.

"The system has failed her," Glass said with emphasis. "She still is out there prostituting. There is nothing for these girls."

Glenda Hatchett, a former Fulton Juvenile Court judge, said putting prostituted children in the state's youth jails was the wrong solution, but she sometimes had no choice.

"There were times I was concerned about her getting back with her pimp and disappearing," Hatchett said. "I have put girls in Metro until I could figure out where else to put them." But it was a Catch-22, she said, in which the victims were further victimized and exposed to hard-core criminals.

Judge Hickson is similarly frustrated. She said she looks into the eyes of children who have been prostituted and she sees nothing. No hope. No dreams. No more childhood.

"Now that I have a daughter of my own, it affects me emotionally," she said. "Seeing the despair and no life really affects me."

FRUSTRATED WITH THE CASE

By fall, Hickson had become particularly frustrated with the case involving the 10- and 11-year-old sisters. Both girls were back in jail.

At the November court hearing, the judge accused child welfare officials of dragging their feet in finding an alternative placement. She had never intended to keep the girls at Metro more than a few days, she said, and she was angry she had to convene court to force them [the child welfare officials] to act.

Everyone in court agreed the girls needed residential treatment. But nothing had worked. Girls and Boys Town had kicked out the 11-year-old for disruptive behavior. A group home in Griffin had made the girls leave after they locked themselves in a bathroom and yelled obscenities. A mental health program had rejected the girls, in part because of their history in prostitution.

Officials with the Fulton County Department of Family and Children Services said in court that the girls' mother had been uncooperative, and they were worried about sending the children home. Because of the girls' history of running away, the officials asked the judge to keep them in jail until they could find a suitable placement.

At a minimum, they asked that the girls be sent home with electronic monitors.

But Johnson, the probation officer, argued the child welfare agency had done nothing to help the mother or find an alternative.

The judge had heard enough. She addressed the 10-year-old.

"I don't want you locked up either," Hickson said to the girl. "But I'm also concerned about your safety and whether you're going to stay with your mom. Are you going to stay at your mother's?"

"Yes, ma'am," the girl said, and she put her face in her hands.

The judge announced her decision. Custody would remain with DFCS, but both girls were going home that day, and they were going home without electronic monitors.

After the hearing, the child said she was sorry for what she had done. "I was just following my sister, and I got in some trouble," she said, her eyes red from crying.

She said she would like to tell other girls her age, "Don't get yourself caught up in something like this. Don't be around the wrong people. Stay in school. Don't waste your life on something like this. Some people have caught HIV and AIDS."

She said she wanted to go back to school. Her elementary school has a mentor's program and more than anything, the child said, she wanted a mentor.

"It would help me be better off in life," she said. "Much better than I am."

That day, both girls went home.

"NO PLACE FOR THESE KIDS"

Today, the 11-year-old seems to be doing well at home, officials say.

But less than three weeks after the 10-year-old went home, she ran away again. In early December, police picked her up and returned her to Metro. Judge Hickson says officials will try once again to find a place to rebuild her life.

In the meantime, the child remains in jail.

"It's not the judge's fault. It's not anybody's fault," said Adams of Victims of Prostitution. "There's just no place for these kids to go."

CHAPTER 9

Columbine: A Story That Won't Let Go

"To walk through Columbine High School today is to be struck by the apparent normality of it all," Frank M. Ochberg, a psychiatrist, wrote for the *Washington Post* eighteen months after the shootings at the Littleton, Colorado, school that left fourteen teenagers (including the two killers) and a teacher dead. "But the cheerful ordinariness that prevails on the surface masks a painful paradox: Though the school and the community are gradually returning to normal, they will never, on one level, be 'normal' in people's minds again."

Ochberg, in writing about the school and community, offered a way for journalists there to think about the event: long after the day of the shootings— April 20, 1999—the community struggled against the powerful influences of shame and blame. Columbine required far more of journalists than the ability to report the violence that killed some and wounded many others; in the years since 1999 the Columbine story has forced journalists in Denver to become expert in the complicated dynamic of community recovery from trauma. Personal losses reverberate painfully, Ochberg wrote, "in the echo chamber Columbine has become—and may very likely remain—in these people's lives" (2000:B1, B4).

Schools and colleges have been sites of gun violence repeatedly since the early years of the twentieth century. Adults often choose children and teachers as targets for revenge to gain attention or express frustration. In 1996 sixteen children and a teacher died in a Dunblane, Scotland, elementary school before the forty-three-year-old killer shot himself. Adolescents also have used their schools as places to act out violent feelings. In recent decades students have taken guns more often into schools to threaten, injure, or kill classmates and teachers, but the violence often stayed part of the community's story and problem and rarely earned more than back-page interest in the national media. That changed in the mid-1990s as a series of shootings in widely separated cities shaped a story in ways the news media found impossible to minimize.

When a high-school shooter wounded two classmates in Seattle in 1995, newspapers outside the area barely took notice. When a fourteen-year-old boy killed a teacher and two students in a junior high school in central Washington State a year later, it was a regional story, as was the killing of a principal and student by a sixteen-year-old boy in Bethel, Alaska. In 1997 Pearl, Mississippi, witnessed the killing of two students and wounding of seven others by a six-teen-year-old boy who had just killed his mother. Two months later, in West Paducah, Kentucky, two students died and five were wounded in the shooting spree of a fourteen-year-old boy. By 1998 the national media were rushing in growing numbers to school shooting sites, especially to Springfield, Oregon, where a fifteen-year-old killed his parents, then opened fire in a high school caf-eteria, killing two students and wounding many others. Journalists also rushed to Jonesboro, Arkansas, where two boys, aged thirteen and eleven, used a false fire alarm to draw students and teachers out of a middle school building and into their line of fire; four students and a teacher were killed, and ten students were wounded.

After Jonesboro the organizations and publications that monitor media practices tried to summarize the lessons learned: Resist the rush to answer the question of why this happened (theories about satanic cults or the regional gun culture eventually collapsed). Don't separate parents from children. Don't in-trude on grieving families. Get the facts right. The Freedom Forum studied the Jonesboro coverage carefully and included this advice in "lessons for the me-dia": "Avoid drawing quick conclusions, making unsubstantiated assumptions or creating stereotypes" (1998:37).

Less than a month after the Jonesboro first-anniversary memorial, all thoughts and ideas about what the press should do in a school shooting were tested in the crucible of the violence in Littleton, a Denver suburb. Journalists, public safety experts, school administrators, students, parents, and the public came to learn that the list of lessons learned in previous shootings was shock-ingly incomplete.

On April 20, 1999, two heavily armed young men stormed into the Colum-bine High School in Littleton determined to blow up a good part of the sprawl-ing building. Unable to carry out that plan, Eric Harris and Dylan Klebold opened fire, first outside the building, then in the school library. They killed twelve students and a teacher, fired at police, then used 9 mm semiautomatic weapons to kill themselves.

THE FIRST HOURS

That Tuesday morning Denver-area newsroom scanners carried these words at 11:25: "Attention south units. Possible shots fired at Columbine High School . . . one female is down." The rampage of Harris and Klebold had begun ten minutes earlier when their pipe bombs exploded three miles from the school to distract police. Six minutes earlier the two young men had begun shooting students randomly. Immediately, newsrooms dispatched reporters, photographers, and equipment as television and radio stations began to report the few facts available to them. News teams and reporters headed for the triage site quickly established near the high school, while news helicopters hovered over the area. News organizations around the world besieged Denver-area newspaper and television editors with requests for images. Later in the day many journalists would go to an elementary school where Columbine students and their parents waited to be reunited. Ann Schrader, the medical and science writer for the *Denver Post,* was diverted from a nearby hospital to the school triage site. Schrader parked her car and ran. She told the *American Journalism Review:* "Dozens of kids were being brought out. Some were more seriously wounded. Guys were taking off their T-shirts and using them as tourniquets to stop the blood. I had to borrow a cell phone to call the desk. When I finally found a phone, it was difficult to call out, virtually impossible, because there were so many cell phones being used" (Shepard 1999:22).

Interviews of students and others who had fled the building began at once, and news cameras caught the shock, confusion, and pain in the faces of teenagers. George Kochaniec Jr., a photographer for the *Rocky Mountain News* of Denver, steered away from the school's main entrance and found instead the triage site, occupied by three dozen students who had just escaped from the library. There Kochaniec, shooting with a long-distance lens, saw and photographed Jessica Holliday, eighteen, her hands clutching her face, her head back and mouth open in a cry of pain, with Diwana Perez, her eyes closed in that moment of shock. The photograph was published widely on front pages of newspapers the next morning and in the weekly newsmagazines, an image almost iconic for capturing the emotions of two teenagers who had fled the school only moments earlier. (The image was part of a portfolio of first-day photo coverage that won a Pulitzer Prize for the newspaper.)

Meanwhile, as photo teams and reporters from around the country drove in satellite vans or flew toward Denver, local journalists moved rapidly to take control of the story, churning out both fact and error. The headline on the extra put out by the *Rocky Mountain News* said the death toll "Could Reach 25," a number repeated in the next day's edition and based on erroneous information from police. Two days later the paper was able to provide an accurate count of dead and wounded. The *Rocky's* extra had mentioned "gunmen in black overcoats" in a Page One picture caption. The next morning the paper declared the shooters "were members of the Trench Coat Mafia, a loose-knit group of current and former Columbine students fascinated with computers and drama." The statement was wrong, but the phrase "Trench Coat Mafia" appealed to journalists and editors grasping for the quick fix of an explanation for the killings. Its publication coincided with the arrival of hundreds of national and international journalists, who linked the student group—to which Harris and Klebold did not belong—to their rampage. The linkage took on a life of its own that continues as news references to Columbine circulate the false explanation. Also in the early hours a television station broadcast the words of a person claiming falsely to be a student hiding in the school, then fed the hoax call to CNN, which also broadcast the attention seeker's claim. A newspaper listed a funeral service for a boy who was not killed.

Mistakes may dog every news organization caught in a similar frenzied search for information. Indeed, even in reflection, some journalists argue that the story was so important that errors could be expected and excused, although too few corrections were printed or broadcast. Many journalists were uneasy about the spate of bad information and believed that the media could have exercised greater care. But the concern for accuracy suffered as competitive pressures rose, with national and international media flooding into a community already numbed by the shootings. It wasn't just the tents, platforms, satellite trucks, celebrity anchors, and demands for information that angered Denver journalists—it was the focus on individuals in an effort to personify a story, but the story was so complex that Denver reporters would be challenged for years to address all its issues. For their part, the local journalists held their own emotional reactions at bay as they struggled to pull the story together. When President Bill Clinton spoke live on the networks at 5:54 P.M., Denver time, more than one local journalist was stunned to realize that Columbine was a national story.

National television news teams camped in a park adjacent to the high school, which by Thursday evening—two days after the shootings—had been cleared of thirty explosive devices. (Bodies had been removed from the school on Wednesday evening.) As police lines were moved closer to the school, television teams jockeyed for positions that lent the best backdrop; NBC gained a clear view of the school's front entrance sign. Then the network teams built the Columbine story on the first efforts of the local journalists, bringing survivors and family members into the national spotlight. The magazine *Brill's Content* told of NBC's *Today* interview with a female student who first was threatened by one of the shooters, then witnessed his killing of another girl. The girl's hysterical story, first broadcast in Denver, then fed to both CNN and NBC, was played once again as the *Today* segment opened. Then Katie Couric, speaking from Washington, D.C., asked the girl to describe in graphic detail what she had seen and heard. As the girl spoke, viewers could not miss the lack of emotion in her voice and face, a contrast to her frenzied, gasping effort to communicate immediately after she had escaped from the school. Although the segment appeared to be giving eyewitness information, it failed to help viewers understand the emotional crisis that the young woman was facing. As she left the *Today* camp, the girl was besieged by reporters from other media. "Same questions. Same answers. Her tone grew increasingly remote and rehearsed," the *Brill's Content* writer noted (Siegel 1999:82). (Local reporters grew increasingly irritated as national journalists pressed them for details, interview leads, and directions.) The outsiders, the "parachuters," stayed through the week, then decamped, leaving the local media to untangle the story. National reporters returned when President Bill Clinton visited Littleton a few days after the shootings, on the six-month anniversary, and on the one-year anniversary. National media also forced Denver journalists to react to special reports on Columbine. For example, a December 1999 issue of *Time* described five secret videos the killers had made, and the newsmagazine provided a comprehensive update on the Columbine story. This forced local journalists to cover *Time's* coverage.

Some of the parachuters left Denver deeply affected by what they had seen at the school and at the funerals and memorials. For David Handschuh, a photographer for the *Daily News* in New York and father of three children, the rush trip to Littleton left a long-lasting emotional injury. "I cried at Columbine," he said. "A lot of photographers stood outside the church that day and did a lot of self-reflection. We asked ourselves why we do what we do and how we do it." Handschuh said he had experienced flashbacks of Columbine scenes for months after the shootings (2000).

THE WEEKS AFTER: THE STRESS INCREASES

Denver reporters, like their colleagues in New York City and Oklahoma City, have never escaped from their big story. Since April 1999 local journalists have produced thousands of newspaper, television, and radio reports on aspects of the Columbine story. The *Denver Post* and *Rocky Mountain News* were fighting for circulation in a head-to-head competition at the time of the shootings; since combining some of their operations in a joint operating agreement in 2001, the flood of stories about Columbine has continued: legal issues, evidence, investigations, personal stories, the suicide of a victim's mother.

A Denver television reporter, speaking from the school on April 20, 1999, suddenly broke her report and turned away from the camera to recover. Station anchors urged her to take some time before continuing. It was an early sign that the Columbine story would draw from the emotional depths of journalists and leave a few too wounded to continue news work. Some journalists later withdrew from the craft in response to the memories and stresses of their assignments. Others continued the work but found ways to let coworkers and managers know when they were asking too much or had crossed a line. Ann Schrader, the *Denver Post*'s medicine and science writer, balked when an editor asked her to interview neighbors of a Columbine victim's mother who had killed herself. Schrader and other reporters talked inside and outside the newsroom, searching both for understanding of their own discomfort and keys to the community's recovery. Every development sparked media attention and encouraged community resentment of the media. "There was just a lot of anger," Mike Patty, a *Rocky Mountain News* reporter said. "There was no healthy place for it to go" (*Covering Columbine* 2001). A *Rocky Mountain News* staff meeting, held a week or so after the shootings, began with journalists' stolidly maintaining their emotional detachment. When one person said she was not handling her emotions very well, "the floodgates opened for emotions everybody had been holding back," Patty said (*Covering Columbine* 2001).

Other local tragedies followed, and the media and the community found it impossible to untangle them from the continuing Columbine trauma. The mother of the shooting victim killed herself, two students were killed in a convenience store, and a popular basketball player hanged himself. Reporters readily linked the deaths to the Columbine shootings, whether that connection was actually justified or not, which forced those in Littleton to revisit the trauma. "Several people told me how newspaper and television attention to these more recent events recalled images of that April 20, even though the shootings were never mentioned," Frank Ochberg wrote (2000:B1, B4).

Community recovery was hampered by a common response among those with responsibility for Columbine, especially members of the school staff and the journalists who continued to mine the story. Distress at what had happened on their watch troubled school officials and kept them from responding to their trauma by seeking new jobs elsewhere. Not until a year after the shootings did a key person decide to leave the school district administration. "Until then, most of the administrators had felt they couldn't leave 'before the job is done,' referring to their mission of restoring confidence to Columbine," Ochberg wrote. Most journalists also remained in place, doggedly keeping the Columbine story alive and daily facing more evidence of resentment, not just from school officials but from others in the community. As school officers blamed the press for keeping the Columbine trauma alive, journalists grew resentful of school administrators' efforts to control information.

Some of the anger and resentment in Littleton and Denver have abated with time. Students have graduated and moved on, and officials in the school district and other public agencies have left for other jobs. Journalists also have turned their efforts toward covering other issues in the expanding Denver metropolitan area. The transition included a series of meetings of journalists and school officials hosted by the University of Colorado's Department of Journalism. At one of the sessions with Frank Ochberg journalists engaged in a lively session, candidly disclosing their thoughts and feelings, and energetically discussing ways to ease the stress. The meetings, though helpful, could not compensate for the lingering guilt and resentment.

Parent Sue Petrone wrote editor John Temple four years later about the photograph that the *Rocky Mountain News* had run that showed the body of her son, Danny, lying outside the school. The photo gave Petrone and her husband clear knowledge that their son was dead; officials apparently had not notified them before the paper came out. In a column Temple quoted from the private note: "Sometimes the reality of life is hard to understand and accept. As a person who was deeply impacted by a photograph you chose to print in your paper, I'm asking you to please continue to have the courage to print the difficult pictures and the fortitude to take the criticism of your readers for doing so. While you may not always or never hear a word from them, remember that there may be someone out there just like me who will be eternally grateful" (Temple 2004:2A).

Columbine students showed their resilience. To prepare for the first anniversary of the shootings, a number of students met with local and national journalists to share their thoughts and feelings about the previous year. Honest disclosures about grieving and losses led to tears and mutual support and, more than anything, reminded the listening reporters that the students, for all the terrible memories, were supporting each other in the present.

By all accounts, the national media coverage of the anniversary recognized the pain of revisiting that troubled event and, for the most part, avoided re-showing the most graphic images from 1999. However, as you read this, it is very likely that Denver readers and viewers are being reminded once again of that bloody day in Littleton.

CHAPTER 10

Reporting on Rape Trauma

On a Sunday morning in February 1990, an emotional and extraordinary story gripped readers of the *Des Moines Register.* The first of a five-part series told the story of a twenty-nine-year-old woman who had been raped by a stranger. He had entered her car as she was studying for a licensing test early in the morning in a college parking lot. The story spared few details as it conveyed some of the horror of the attacker's words and actions. Even more to its credit, the newspaper gave Iowa readers a clear sense of the emotional aftermath of a rape and the cycles of traumatic symptoms. They learned how waiting for the trial, delayed for months, and having to testify about the attack as the defendant looked on made the woman's trauma more painful. Although it was not the first newspaper profile of a rape survivor, it drew bags of supportive letters from readers and attracted national media attention. It underscored why so many who suffer rape do not go to the police in the first place. Countless rape survivors understood the woman's ordeal.

And readers of the newspaper also learned her name. Then and now newspapers regularly report rapes, but the usual practice is to withhold the name of the person who was attacked.

The *Register* had invited a rape survivor to tell her story. Its editorial judgment appeared to be that candor about rape and sensitivity to the woman's needs are compatible. The *Register* and its editor, Geneva Overholser, wanted to address the stigma of rape. "I understand," she had written in an open letter to readers the previous summer, "why newspapers tend not to use rape victims' names. No crime is more horribly invasive, more brutally intimate. In no crime does the victim risk being blamed, and in so insidious a way: She asked for it, she wanted it. Perhaps worst of all, there's the judgment: She's damaged goods, less desirable, less marriageable" (1989:6A). The stigma was "enormously unfair," Overholser said, adding that her newspaper would continue to follow a policy of not naming rape victims. But, she added, the stigma will persist unless women speak publicly about their experience and identify themselves.

Nancy Ziegenmeyer responded to Overholser's call. A reporter, Jane Schorer, and a photographer, David Peterson, began a long collaboration with Ziegenmeyer that resulted in a series that won a Pulitzer Prize the next year. The story (Schorer 1990) was an important addition to the literature of the rape experience, which had been growing steadily in books, magazines, and newspapers since the 1960s. The Ziegenmeyer-Schorer report gave a realistic account of the rape survivor's first year of recovery and showed repeatedly how even minor incidents set off those painful trauma symptoms of anxiety, avoidance, and unwanted recollections. In its details, then, it truly helped Iowa readers understand what a person goes through in the months and years after a rape.

But the series raised other issues that show what difficult choices reporters and editors face when they cover the rape experience. Those other issues, rooted in centuries of U.S. social history, have confounded journalism's efforts to come to terms with the realities of rape.

The first point that the critics made was that an African American man had raped a white woman, an assault that is most likely to get press attention because it involves a stranger rape and plays into racist stereotypes. Critics wanted the public to know that kind of rape case is rare despite the media's fascination with it and the hold it has on popular culture.

Only one rape in five is committed by a stranger. Four out of five rapists are relatives or acquaintances of the victim. This powerful statistic appears to hold across a wide variety of national and local studies. Its import is that by far the most common rape experience is one in which a betrayal of trust accompanies physical violence and the shattering of the victim's emotional stability.

The Iowa story also was about interracial rape, a kind of assault that is even rarer than stranger rape. One study shows that men raping women of the same race account for 93 percent of all rapes. The newspaper had helped a rape survivor tell a rare and important story, but its telling had invoked race as an important factor in rape. Although Overholser answered the criticism directly, the reporting still reinforced harmful myths about rape fostered by the history of race relations in this country. Overholser wrote, "One of the sad facts of this rape case is that the woman is white, the man black. This, unhappily, perpetuates a stereotype that is utterly contrary to fact. . . . Nationally, only 4 percent of rapes involve a black man and a white woman. While race was an issue in this particular crime, as some parts of the story show, there is no truth to the cruel stereotype" (1990:1C). Still, the series had inadvertently emphasized race over trauma.

Public discussion of the Des Moines series unearthed other contradictory assumptions about people who are raped. Although the newspaper wanted to weaken the stigma of rape by allowing one survivor to tell her story, a critic argued that social stigma is less of an issue if the woman has all the "right" attributes. The Iowa woman was an easy choice, writes Helen Benedict in *Virgin or Vamp: How the Press Covers Sex Crimes* (1992). Ziegenmeyer was middle class, white, respectable, and raped by a black stranger. "I do not wish to detract from the courage she showed in coming forth to tell her story," Benedict writes, "but had she been black, poor, in a bar, or attacked by a man of her own race or higher class, she would not have received such sympathy from readers and the press; she may not, with reason, have even wanted to take the risk of exposing her story" (1992). Rejection and blame by others because of a rape certainly play a part in worsening trauma symptoms or in delaying recovery.

Even in reporting on the Iowa story, other media fostered the fiction that it was the first or one of the first voluntary accounts of the rape experience. They made little or no mention of the many women who, since the early 1960s, had turned rape into a public issue through testimony at "speak-outs," sharing their stories in support groups, and creating rape counseling centers. Rape survivors themselves had found mutual support and raised important public safety, legal, and policy issues in the process, leaving journalists to catch up with both the social and mental health knowledge. Feminists working to support rape survivors had joined hands with women in mental health professions to put trauma at the core of the struggle to recover from a rape.

The Des Moines series showed that the most careful reporting may run afoul of biases against the survivor and foster rape myths based in U.S. social history. News conventions will emphasize some victims while ignoring others, and journalists will run into barriers to reporting realistically what a rape survivor endures in the months and years after an attack. It is essential that care be given to the task. Readers and viewers need to understand the realities of rape trauma—one in every eight adult women in the United States has been raped—and the disabling aftermath: eight in ten will suffer post-traumatic stress disorder (PTSD).

ISSUES FOR JOURNALISTS

Reporting on rape differs so greatly from documented patterns of sexual assault that the public is often ill informed about frequencies, circumstances, and most likely victims. Some of this disparity results from a news tradition of writing less about rape than about other serious crimes. To some extent it reflects social values and attitudes rooted deeply in American history and race and gender relations. It also reflects the preoccupation of the news media with the issue of naming rape victims. A consensus that the news media not identify rape survivors—a policy that Coté and I support—has inadvertently contributed to a dearth of information about the trauma that survivors endure and struggle to recover from.

This chapter describes rape trauma, from its immediate effects to those that still may intrude in the survivor's life months and years later. This knowledge frames our support for more reporting about rape so long as it satisfies three ethical considerations outlined in this chapter: it should place rape in a realistic context for the news outlet's community or region; it should name survivors only so long as they give fully informed consent to the use of their names, and it should give due attention to survivors' recovery and report accurately about the traumatic effects of the assault.

First, it is important to understand what rape is and what it is not.

Rape refers to the forced violation of another person's body. Rape can occur between women and between men, as well as between a man and a woman. However, it is a striking marker of U.S. society that men raping women is by far the more common pattern. Strangers, acquaintances, friends and spouses, adults, and children rape and are raped. The act of rape may involve physical force, including the use of weapons, or psychological coercion, or both. This use of *rape* differs from the variety of definitions provided by state laws that define the crime and set the penalties. In many laws rape is sexual intercourse that is forced or coerced. Sexual intercourse is sometimes defined as "penetration with a penis or object (such as a finger or pencil), either orally, vaginally, or anally, and includes oral sex." Laws sometimes invoke greater penalties when the rape involves threat or harm with a deadly weapon, a kidnapping, or felonious entrance to a building or vehicle. Under such laws physical or mental incapacity of a victim may be an element in the degree or level of rape that is charged. These differences in laws affect the conduct of police investigations and the trials and punishments for rapists, but they do not help to predict the severity of rape trauma—the sudden extreme helplessness and loss of meaning that follow a coercive use of force. The injury in rape is instant and long lasting and may or may not be aggravated by the particular circumstances that some of these laws address.

Rape is not about sex in any usual sense of the word. The rapist uses and violates sexual organs and body openings used in sex, but the violent traumatic effects are alien to the feelings of consenting sexual relations. The behaviors characteristic of rapists—anger, violence, intimidation, use of force, and abuse of power—and the trauma suffered by the victim distinguish rape from a conventional sexual act. Still, whatever is reported about a rape is filtered through some readers' or viewers' assumptions that sexual gratification played a role in the assault or what led up to it. Victim advocates struggle to put such notions to rest. In the view of Judith Lewis Herman, a professor of psychiatry at the Harvard Medical School, literature from pornography to academic texts advanced the erroneously harmful view for much of the twentieth century that rape "fulfilled women's deepest desires" (1992:30). The trauma of a rape destroys that argument. The defining element of rape is the choice of one human being to destroy another's autonomy over her body, initiating an interminable, painful struggle to regain control of her life. The words apply as well to men who rape men. The act appears to validate their power only when they use it to control another man, an obsessive desire for many male rapists.

Herman describes rape as a calculated "physical, psychological, and moral violation of the person" (57). The rapist uses power "to terrorize, dominate, and humiliate" a victim, she writes. "Thus rape, by its nature, is intentionally designed to produce psychological trauma" (58).

WHAT IS RAPE TRAUMA?

What happens to the victim during the assault? The initial attack surprises the victim, often includes physical injury and use of physical force or a weapon, and imposes the threat of death. The victim, a captive, then endures the violation of her or his body. Self-defense often becomes or appears to be useless, even life threatening; the brain and nervous system are overwhelmed. The foundation is set for a lasting injury. Herman writes: "Each component of the ordinary response to danger, having lost its utility, tends to persist in an altered and exaggerated state long after the actual danger is over. Traumatic events produce profound and lasting changes in physiological arousal, emotion, cognition, and memory" (1992:34).

In her book Nancy Ziegenmeyer describes her assault: "It was as though someone had hit a switch, and my body had shut off. Only my mind was working, part of it insisting this isn't happening, this isn't happening, the other part oddly focused" (1992:16). Nancy Venable Raine, a poet and essayist whose memoir of rape recovery, *After Silence: Rape and My Journey Back*, was published in

1998, describes her shock and terror. Assaulted by a man who had slipped into her apartment unnoticed, she suffered rape and torment for three hours:

> During the attack my terror seemed to implode and compress until it was like a hard dry seed. Once I was free of this devouring fear, a cold, even calculating awareness took its place, illuminating everything all at once and destroying all capacity for emotion. . . . He decided what was and wasn't possible. His world was, by my former measures, insane. A universe of ferocity that was sustained by fear and pain. I had no emotional reaction to this universe and observed it with the detachment of a yogi.
>
> (13)

In wrenching language she describes what happened in the first minutes after the rapist fled. "Terror overwhelmed me. My body shook uncontrollably. My thoughts were flawed in structure, like cups without bottoms. Words fell through them. Words no longer referred to anything, even themselves. My shock was so great I could not walk" (15).

Herman calls the emotional detachment felt by some rape victims "one of nature's small mercies, a protection against unbearable pain" (1992:43). People who tell of being raped sometimes place themselves in the position of an observer who stands away from the assault. The victim knows what is happening but does not interpret or judge actions in the usual way. The person's sense of what is happening may be somewhat distorted.

Along with the shock and dissociation, accounts of rape survivors testify to the will to survive. Raine involuntarily "withdrew all reaction," although she sensed that the rapist wanted an emotional response from her. Narratives from other women reveal intuitively smart answers and reactions, life saving in many cases. In her book *Still Loved by the Sun: A Rape Survivor's Journal*, Migael Scherer describes how, within the first minutes of her attack, survival instincts took over:

> With the sound of that closing door several things happened inside me simultaneously. I remembered, all in a single piece, a rape-prevention video seen while teaching high school twelve years ago. I remembered how I had broken up a fight between two boys in my classroom. I remembered a friend's escape from a rapist in Jamaica, when she distracted him with greed for her gold ring. Two messages sprang up: Stay calm. And: Use your wits; be clever. I forced myself to breathe more slowly. I forced my body to sag a bit against his.
>
> (1992:61)

The rape ended, the person who survives may face immediate contact with strangers, police, family, friends, and medical personnel. This occurs as she begins a lifetime of what Herman calls "the oscillating rhythm" of intrusive memories of the assault and the numbing constriction that follows the trauma. Balance, confidence, and control over reality disappear. In other sad outcomes the victim chooses to be silent about the assault, suffering the trauma without any help. Children raped or molested by parents or neighbors often endure the trauma in silence for all or much of a lifetime, cloaking their pain in ways that block recovery. Children raped by a teacher or clergy often have been silenced not only by threats from the abuser but by fear of being dismissed by adults convinced of the respectability of the attacker.

Trauma effects continue for years. Even as they subside or become less frequent, the rape survivor faces the possibility that reminders of the assault will revive the trauma symptoms. Individuals vary greatly in their response to rape, but studies suggest that although some trauma symptoms may fade after several months, fear and anxiety persist much longer, leading in some survivors to nervous breakdowns, suicidal thoughts, and suicide attempts.

Women who tell of their recovery from rape show how their need for privacy is heightened. Besieged by fears for their personal safety and a sense that even the smallest matters are out of control, survivors begin to rebuild that essential sense of control by making choices, sometimes about things that appear trivial to anyone else. Every relationship poses new stresses, every encounter may set off new fears; even friends and family now respond with blank stares and faltering conversation. The process is a turbulent one, marked by feelings of guilt, then of hatred, then of fear. Nothing in the day is predictable, nothing in life is certain. For most people privacy is simply a passive claim to keep things much as they are. Violations of privacy are, at most, minor irritations. For the rape survivor privacy is an essential condition for taking steps toward recovery. Choosing to give personal information to police, friends, and reporters often is a step forward. Choosing to give their name or to withhold it has proved profoundly important to survivors. The journalist who denies or invades the privacy of a rape survivor interferes with that person's right to try to recover from the assault.

THE IMPORTANCE OF CONTEXT IN RAPE REPORTING

Rape recovery involves struggling against a raging current of misperceptions about the assault and its victims. The survivor finds her suffering "edited" in the words and responses of others, then confronts distorted representations of rape in the media. No amount of clarity or accuracy in news reporting will end the trauma of someone who has been raped, but care in reporting may avoid the infliction of fresh wounds through stories that ignore or misrepresent the survivor.

Reporters should begin by trying to provide a realistic idea of the extent and frequency of rape in the United States and in their community. Infrequent mention of rape in the news media contradicts the troubling statistics about the numbers of Americans who have been raped. The cumulative national effect of rape, according to the Bureau of Justice Statistics (1998), is that 18 percent of women in the United States have been victims of rape or attempted rape. Rape of males is less frequent yet still accounts for one victim in thirteen, according to one study. Adult rape is mentioned most often in the news, yet teenagers, male and female, are more likely to be raped than are older people. Judith Lewis Herman notes that half of all rape victims are twenty or younger when they are raped (1992:61). The rate of rapes of women is far higher in the United States than in other industrialized countries, excluding nations involved in civil war or international conflict. The high rate of rape coincides with the evidence that only one-third of rapes are reported to police and only half of those result in arrests (Greenfeld 1997).

Margaret Gordon and Stephanie Riger assembled a useful picture of rape patterns by comparing the statistics in the U.S. Justice Department's Uniform Crime Reports with interviews of crime victims nationally and stories about rapes in daily newspapers in several major cities. In their book, *The Female Fear,* they report that interviews with crime victims yield the most accurate information but still understate the number of rapes (1989:35). The victim interviews, conducted by the National Crime Survey in conjunction with the U.S. Census, showed a rate of rape twice that which appeared in the Uniform Crime Reports, which are based on statistics from local police departments that regularly underrepresent rapes. Based on the number of rapes disclosed to interviewers, about 140 women in 100,000 are raped each year in the United States. Rates of rape of women are substantially higher—in some cases three times as high—in the nation's biggest cities, according to the National Crime Survey.

It is easy to see why those who collect data on rape are uncertain about the true extent of the problem. Consider just two reasons for the misleading statistics. First, people raped by relatives and acquaintances are not likely to call police or even acknowledge their rape to the people who do the interviews. Second, survivors often choose to list rapes as assaults, even in surveys. Further questioning does not necessarily bring out that the assault was a rape. Gordon and Riger comment, "There is general agreement that all official or publicly ascertained rates are underestimates, but no one yet knows how much higher the true rate is" (1989:37).

As incomplete as the government data may be, newspaper reporting distorts the reality of rape even more, Gordon and Riger found. When they analyzed rape stories in leading newspapers, they concluded that readers who wanted to know about the risk of being raped in their own communities were likely to be misinformed. For example:

- Newspapers do not report most rapes reported to the police. (Remember that most rapes are not reported to the police, and how hard it is to gain a clear idea of the frequency of rape in a particular community becomes apparent.)
- Newspapers rarely report attempted rapes. The national survey of victims shows that in every four attacks, three people escape without being raped. A content analysis by Gordon and Riger of newspapers in San Francisco, Chicago, and Philadelphia showed that in every fourteen reports about rape, thirteen stories were about completed rapes and only one about an attempted rape. Gordon and Riger comment, "This may be why women believe most rapes are completed, and that women have very little chance of getting away. The consequences of presenting such an inexorable view need to be considered" (1989:69–70).
- Newspaper reporting of rape tends to focus on older women, according to Gordon and Riger. As a result, the relatively high rate of rape among young women, especially teenagers, goes unreported.
- Victims report to census takers that 50 percent of rapes occur in the evening, between 6 P.M. and midnight. Only 5 percent of the newspaper stories studied by Gordon and Riger assigned a rape to that time period. The authors argue that rapes in that time period are more likely to be committed by dates and acquaintances and that those rapes "are also quite likely to be underreported or declared unfounded" (1989:70).
- Rape stories are less likely to include details than are stories about murders or assaults. Thus readers may not learn the victim's age, occupation, or condition, whether the rapist used a weapon, or even where the attack occurred. Stories rarely mention strategies that victims use to avert or lessen violence. Moreover, few stories provide statistics about rape patterns in the neighborhood, city, metropolitan region, or state. And news accounts too rarely emphasize strategies that might prevent rape, such as demanding identification documents from door-to-door salespersons or people coming to do repairs.

• News accounts often provide a distorted explanation of how the victim came to be raped. Reporters sometimes are misinformed or make wrong assumptions about the victim, the place, or other details. A rape that began with a meeting in a neighborhood bar may be reported in ways that imply that the victim was taking needless risks. Sometimes such details fit preconceptions held by a police officer or a reporter that no one questions until much later, if at all. They may also readily fit ill-informed ideas about rape held by many readers and viewers. Without care, reporting about rape can stigmatize the victim, making recovery more difficult, and misinform the public. News reporting that makes the victim seem responsible for the assault may simply foster more silence about the horror of rape.

THE ISSUE OF NAMING RAPE SURVIVORS

Although it may seem that issues of reporting about rape have been raised only in recent years, the struggle of journalists to come to terms with rape is at least a century old. That history may illuminate why naming survivors—the ethical issue most often raised in connection with rape coverage—remains so controversial.

Reports of rapes "are not wanted" by newspapers, the Associated Press told its correspondents, according to John Palmer Gavit in the 1903 *Reporter's Manual,* except when the perpetrator "is pursued and lynched by a mob or is rescued by authorities" (80). This brief statement conceals cruel assumptions about rape in the national past. Men accused of rape who were pursued and lynched by mobs usually were African Americans (Collins 1991), and the murderous exercise of vigilante justice often involved some action that white men interpreted as an affront against a white woman. Actual rapes need not have taken place for lynching—typically, the capture, torture, humiliation, and killing of the targeted person by a mob—to follow. The reporting mentioned the accused perpetrator, dead by that time and beyond fair justice, and the nature of his alleged actions but rarely named the woman who was said to have suffered the assault.

Journalists need to understand the racial dynamic of lynching and reporting about it. Historian Patricia Hill Collins writes, "Lynching emerged as the specific form of sexual violence visited on Black men, with the myth of the Black rapist as its ideological justification" (1991:177). The vengeance brought down on black men obscured another form of racist "social control"—rapes of African American women by white men as an element of slavery before the Civil War and one that continued afterward.

Through much of the first half of the twentieth century, the news media paid little attention to allegations of rape or to those who were raped, except in cases involving well-known people. By the 1950s debates about what drove men to rape had completely eclipsed any discussion of survivors' needs. Debates in law enforcement, courts, and mental health circles, as well as the news business, invariably were about offenders. Victims were rarely mentioned until the 1960s and then, in the words of Elizabeth Koehler, "only in the most derogatory, condescending and dismissive of terms" (1995:53). The near absolute omission of concern for survivors reflected the common prejudice that the woman who was raped invited the assault in some way.

Beginning in the 1950s, the press, the legal system, and medical experts began to question some of those assumptions. A few judges and some journalists asked whether rape victims needed special protection in legal proceedings.

In the 1960s and 1970s feminists did the most to convince the public and journalists about the trauma of rape. They made the case for the victims' suffering and challenged stigmatization, then framed the argument that rape was part of a system of violent behavior, generally carried out by men against women. Feminists argued that the way sexual violence was reported inscribed myths about rape, women, and male power and contributed to the stigmatizing of victims while helping to lessen the legal and social penalties for perpetrators. The myths were so pervasive that they were as likely to influence the thinking and writing of a female reporter as of a male reporter, feminists argued. Susan Brownmiller's important 1975 book, *Against Our Will: Men, Women, and Rape*, shaped public understanding that rape was a crime of violence. The book followed more than a decade of feminist efforts to call attention to the rape crisis through self-education, speak-outs, and victim-assistance centers. "Rape, after all, was one of the biggest causes of the 1960s women's movement," Helen Benedict told us.

Feminist teaching about rape gained credibility as it was linked to the evidence of the first clinical studies of rape survivors. These researchers described the trauma of rape and the lasting grip it had on the confidence and capacity of women. In 1972 Ann Burgess and Lynda Holmstrom began to study the women who came to the emergency room of Boston City Hospital. In time Burgess and Holmstrom proposed a model of rape trauma that includes a first phase of acute disruption in one's life and a second, long-term, process of recovery (see Burgess and Holmstrom 1979). The victims' symptoms, they note, resemble those seen in Vietnam combat veterans. In the same decade hundreds of rape crisis centers opened around the country, offering legal and emotional support. Judith Lewis Herman notes that early attention focused on rape committed by strangers, then was followed by growing concern for rape in relationships and marriage. She also credits the women's movement for the subsequent concern about domestic violence and sexual abuse of children (1992:29–31).

The news media inevitably reflected the new thinking about violence against women. As "lifestyle sections" of newspapers became forums for such topics, journalism began to seriously examine its own assumptions about rape and did so in open debate. The most significant result was the nearly universal acceptance of the idea that news stories should not name survivors of rape. The rule, though, usually was not linked to the trauma of rape. Indeed, the standard on names often appeared to reflect the convention of the early part of the century, that women who were "involuntarily involved" in the loss of chastity would face great difficulty regaining their reputations. In other words, the woman wasn't named because of the assumption that she would encounter hostility from the public if she were named; stigma rather than trauma supported the convention of not printing names.

Several highly publicized rape cases in the 1980s and early 1990s shattered the news media's consensus about not naming rape victims. Each of these cases— including the accusations against William Kennedy Smith, the Rideout marital rape case, the Preppy Murder story, and the Central Park jogger—was national news and attracted hordes of reporters spurred by the increasingly competitive character of news, especially about sensational occurrences or famous people. Each case, like that of Nancy Ziegenmeyer in Iowa, raised myriad ethical issues and forced some news organizations to confront opposition from their staff and their audience to the way the stories were handled. Rape changed from a local crime covered with some care by local media to one with the potential to set off frantic international media coverage. In the rush, conventions about publishing or broadcasting names fell by the wayside.

In her book *Virgin or Vamp* (1992) Helen Benedict isolates the details that helped spin coverage well beyond the routine. In one of those cases, the rape of a woman by four men in a bar in New Bedford, Massachusetts, in 1983, Benedict found these characteristics of newspaper coverage:

- Men wrote most of the stories that appeared in newspapers and magazines.
- Media attention to the ethnicity of the defendants distracted attention from the brutal assault against the woman. The concerted reaction of the community under attack prolonged the focus on ethnicity.

- The initial stories emphasized the victim's innocence, in part because the rapists "fit all the worst stereotypes." In time, though, defendants, reporters, and others helped to frame coverage to imply that the woman invited the assault.
- A near consensus to withhold the name of the victim held until the trial. Even then, some media respected the rule, although several newspapers and a local television station named her. The decisions stirred public and media debate about using survivors' names in news accounts.
- The trial, in which the woman testified standing up for fifteen hours over three days because no chair was provided for her, brought sympathetic coverage at first, followed by stories reporting testimony about graphic details of the rapes that, Benedict argues, "invaded her privacy, humiliated, and stigmatized her" (1992:124).
- By the time of the first verdicts against the defendants, community opinion had turned with fury against the victim. The press did little to change the hostility that hounded the woman out of the city.

Benedict, who remains emphatically opposed to naming victims without their consent, concludes that community and press fury turned against the woman because of several biasing characteristics—details that essentially ignored her trauma and what she had suffered and instead served to feed a prejudice that she too should be punished. "She knew the assailants . . . ; no weapon was used . . . ; she was of the same race, class, and ethnic group as the assailants; she was young; she was attractive, and, above all, she deviated from the norm of a 'good woman' by being alone in a bar full of men, drinking, when the attack occurred" (1992:142). In this and other cases, Benedict has argued, suspicion of the victim is latent in people's thinking, awaiting only certain details in news coverage to bring it to life.

Two more recent cases have shown that media coverage of rape remains bound to such social factors as race and class. In 1989 a young woman who was running in Manhattan's Central Park at night was raped and beaten. The woman lost much of her blood while she lay unnoticed in the park for several hours. Then she lay in a coma in a hospital for weeks afterward. The national media covered every detail of the horrific crime, yet most carefully omitted her name from every story. To the world she was "the Central Park jogger." The journalists' sensitivity to her right to privacy appeared to say that they would continue to respect the convention of withholding the identity of rape victims. A few criticisms of the reporting surfaced. The woman was white and fairly affluent— a stockbroker. Critics said her identity played a part in both the extraordinary attention and the refusal to report her name. Police and the media responded to the assault as they likely would have a hundred years earlier. Five young men were charged with the assault and convicted. Only after an imprisoned convict confessed to the rape in 2002 were the convictions vacated. Then, in 2003, Trisha Meili, the rape survivor, told all that she could recall of the assault in a book whose jacket not only named her but provided a photograph of her.

Two years after the Central Park assault, to the month, a member of the Kennedy family was accused of rape, and the consensus about withholding the victim's name came apart. Because the Kennedy family was involved, the story got saturation coverage around the world. The naming began in the British "scandal sheet," the *Globe*, a tabloid sold in U.S. supermarkets, then moved quickly to NBC News and finally to the *New York Times*. The *Times* not only named the woman but profiled her in ways that horrified many readers. The story mentioned her traffic violations, her mediocre school record, the illegitimacy of her child, her divorce, and other personal matters (Butterfield and Tabor 1991: A17). Some staff members, among them columnist Anna Quindlen, reacted so angrily that *Times* editors were forced to answer their objections in a meeting covered by the newspaper and widely reported elsewhere (Glaberson 1991:A14). Fox Butterfield, one of the five reporters for the profile, later said the story was done, in part, because the woman had hired attorneys who appeared to be trying to "court publicity" (Butterfield 1991:5). Also, the reporters were intrigued by the story of a woman who was not like the Central Park jogger. Almost as an aside, though, Butterfield framed the dilemma that faces journalists assigned to report on rape: What story does the reporter tell about the victim? "None of this behavior, of course, is relevant to whether or not she was raped. Our story was not intended to prove or disprove the rape" (1991:5). Quindlen wrote in her column for the *Times*, "I imagined one of the editors for whom I have worked asking, 'How does all this [the personal details] advance the story?' The answer is that it does not. It is the minutiae of skepticism" (1991:E17).

A third case in 2003 kept the debate alive and further polarized survivors and journalists but failed to provide a convincing case for changing the consensus about not naming rape survivors. When a woman accused a professional basketball player of sexual assault, some media reports named her. Poynter.org, the Web site of the prestigious journalism ethics organization the Poynter Institute, showed that the consensus to withhold a rape victim's name was under new pressure. The Web site did not name the woman, but it offered an argument for doing so from Geneva Overholser, the former Iowa editor who had invited Nancy Ziegenmeyer to tell her story in the *Des Moines Register* in

1990. Overholser warned that withholding names amounts to an ethical evasion by journalists. "Selecting certain categories of information and seeking to do social work by acting against this principle is dangerous territory," she said. She doubted, she wrote, that the protection of victims by the media had produced humane consequences. The leading reason to change the policy, she argued, is that the media culture has changed dramatically. The accuser's name is no longer the possession of a few journalists who might be expected to make an ethical choice about disclosure; in sensational rape cases the name is now available to, and being announced widely, on radio talk shows and on the Internet, two media affected little by prevailing ethical standards. "The responsible course for responsible media today is this: Treat the woman who charges rape as we would any other adult victim of crime. Name her and deal with her respectfully. And leave the trial to the courtroom" (Overholser 2003).

NAMING SURVIVORS: PRO AND CON

Coté and I believe that journalists may harm women, men, and children who are raped if their names appear in news reports without their consent. Before we make this argument, let us consider the arguments made by those who support using the names of survivors.

First, they assert that information that is central to the reporting of a crime and is on the public record should be disclosed. Journalists always have preferred disclosure to suppression of information. Second, not naming reinforces the stigma against those who are raped. They need to be noticed and respected in their communities. Third, the media routinely name other victims—victims of auto accidents, muggers, burglars, and murderers. One category of victims should not be made an exception. Finally, some people make false accusations of rape. A person who makes false charges does not deserve the special privilege of anonymity. (Rapes are falsely reported. A careful study by the *Columbia Journalism Review* shows that no credible estimate of that percentage exists—it may be 8 to 10 percent, about the same as for other major crimes except murder. Police agencies vary greatly in how they identify and report false and credible rapes [Haws 1997:16]).

We are persuaded that naming victims against their will can intensify the trauma of rape, a point that Overholser did not address. Strangely, most debates about rape today rarely mention trauma; people talk about the press's duty to disclose information and inconsistencies in protecting some victims and not others but not about trauma. Yet we are convinced by the knowledge gained about trauma since the 1970s.

The trauma following a rape is severely disorienting and likely to last for a long time. The victim loses the sense of control so necessary to survival and will regain it only after many setbacks, false gains, and unbelievable emotional pain. We know men and women who have been raped, and we have watched their long fights to regain control over their lives. We have seen the devastation in the personalities of students who have been raped while they were in our universities. And we have watched dear friends suffer deeply when, years later, they were forced to review in some ways the terror of the attack. We are fully persuaded by Judith Lewis Herman's conclusion that rape is intended "to produce psychological trauma." Of course, the degree and severity of trauma vary from crime to crime and person to person, but in general clinical evidence suggests that the victim of rape endures a degree of suffering deserving of special treatment. In writing this we know that victims of other crimes also feel violated and anxious; indeed, they may suffer severe traumatic symptoms.

People in the media ought to be giving support to survivors of rape by honoring their efforts at recovery. Survivors tell of the hurt and anger they experience from seeing news reports containing their names and personal information stated inaccurately or their experiences framed in ways that make the victim into a villain. "No wonder most rapes are never reported," writes Migael Scherer of the news coverage of her attack. "The unpredictable public scrutiny, the implication of blame, the focus on the suspect that shifts attention away from his victims—all add to our private anguish. And the realization that it is not the rape that is newsworthy, but the rapist and the investigation, is deeply disturbing" (1992:123).

As Nancy Ziegenmeyer and many other women have done, survivors are gaining the strength and confidence to tell their stories publicly (Ziegenmeyer, however, came to regret the way her story was told). Some, like Scherer, our colleague in the writing of this book, Raine, and Meili have told their stories in books. Others, like Kathy Sitarski (1996), have used magazines or newspapers as their forum for disclosure. These women have shown a way of talking about rape that serves them and the public well. Each such speaking out demands the same extraordinary degree of courage and commitment shown by the women who first told their stories in small support groups back in the 1960s. But each story also conveys a truth about rape that the public needs to understand. As Sitarski writes, "One reason violence isolates is because personal violence makes us ashamed. . . . The result is often painful isolation and patterns of quietness, invisibility, shyness, and other hiding behaviors. The very thing we need to talk about in order to heal instead gets buried deeper and deeper" (1996:23). The memoirs of survivors pull those thoughts of shame and guilt out of their hiding places, aiding the authors' recovery and offering models for others. In her 2003 book, *Back under Sail: Recovering the Spirit of Adventure,* Migael Scherer describes a five-day sailboat race she joined as a test—one she passed successfully—of her capacity to regain her enthusiasm and passion for life.

Helen Benedict makes a different argument for not naming victims and for protecting their privacy in the aftermath of a rape. It may not be shame that underlies the need of a victim for privacy and protection. "I believe that, because rapists use victims' sexual organs as the targets of their attacks, rape is a more intimate violation than any other type of crime. A victim should have the right to protect herself or himself from being publicly described in the act of being sexually tortured because of this violation of their private bodies," Benedict told us.

We believe that this country is coming to honor those survivors of rape who choose to speak publicly; their examples offer support for others. Because the public has these models of disclosure, based as they are on personal decisions anchored in the recovery process, journalists can afford to protect other rape survivors until they too are ready to speak out. (Discovery of a false rape accusation, of course, changes the journalist's obligation.)

THE REPORTER, THE SURVIVOR, AND THE TRIAL

Long after the rape the trial of the accused forces the survivor to relive and recount the details of the assault, often in view of the attacker and an audience of observers, reporters, and court personnel. For most, the emotional burden is like a second assault and has been called that often. Although the survivor may receive support from prosecutors and the police in a trial, she will not be represented by an attorney, may find that things she said to investigators will be used to discredit her testimony, and she will not benefit from the same presumption of innocence given the defendant. The risk of an acquittal or plea bargain is high (conviction rates for rapes are low), and retaliation by the rapist is a real fear.

In the Seattle trial of an accused rapist, a newspaper reporter played up the survivor's misidentification of the color of her attacker's eyes. Indeed, even after a jury convicted the man, the reporter persisted in saying the jury had done so although the victim had the color of his eyes wrong in her statements to the police. The news stories deeply troubled the woman because they implied that the jury's conviction of the man was not warranted. Moreover, it misinformed readers by leaving the impression that a rape victim knows every detail about an attacker. Although memory experts disagree about how the brain records the details of a traumatic experience, they seem to agree that the level of emotional stress affects the reliability of the memories. In other words, although defense attorneys may persist in playing up discrepancies in a victim's account to try to influence jurors, reporters ought to be aware that the story can be authentic, if not accurate in every detail.

We offer these suggestions for reporters who are covering trials of accused rapists:

1. Respect that the survivor faces an emotional relapse because of having to testify against and be in the presence of the person whom she believes committed the rape. "For days after the trial, I wandered around the house in a fog," Ziegenmeyer says, suggesting the effects of the trial experience (Ziegenmeyer and Warren 1992:124). It makes no sense to try to add to courtroom testimony by interviewing at the trial or even soon after.

2. Consider whether the graphic and invasive details of a rape—which are likely to occupy a good deal of the court's attention—should be part of the story. Will they help a reader or viewer understand the horror of rape or would including such information encourage a bias against the victim?

3. Think long and carefully about whether to use the name of a woman once she has testified in open court about a rape. A reporter may conclude, as some journalists do, that the story should use her name along with her words. We believe that in many cases trial reports should not name the person who testifies about being raped for the reasons we have discussed in this chapter.

"RECOVERED MEMORIES" OF CHILDHOOD RAPE AND INCEST

All that we have said about the trauma of rape and the need to protect its victims from press attention and identification applies as well to the child or teenager. Traumatic events are often harder on children than on adults. Children who are raped should not be interviewed or identified in news stories. News organizations generally respect this rule.

The rule is no different if the rape occurs within a family. Again, certain numbers are hard to come by, but records of hospitals and child protective services support the claim that fathers, stepfathers, or other relatives commit roughly half of the hundreds of thousands of child rapes each year. Most incest victims are quite young—five or six years is a common age for incest—and the abuse may continue over a long period. News stories about incest cases will depend on information from police and prosecutors, and journalists still will have to decide how to identify the accused.

Anyone who doubts the toll that incest takes on the lives of its victims should consider the reporting by Debra McKinney for the *Anchorage Daily News*. She portrayed the struggles of three women to confront the trauma they had suffered several decades earlier because of assaults by their fathers or an uncle. All three had been unable to cope with the pain, shame, anger, and emotional crippling that followed them into adulthood. For two of the women, not even the deaths of the relatives responsible did much to ease their trauma until the trio bonded in their therapy group. All found that their relatives had a hard time believing their accusations of incest.

In recent years a different sort of story about incest has perplexed journalists and has furious debate raging in medical and legal circles as well. The issue can be illustrated with a fictitious example.

Troubled by emotions, dreams, and unwanted thoughts, a man seeks help from a psychiatrist or therapist. In the course of treatment he appears to remember being sexually abused by his father during early childhood. He had evidently blocked out any memory of the rapes. Supported by this "recovered memory," the man tries to confront the attacker, tell others about the assumed assault, or take part in criminal or civil action against the accused. The discovery may pit the man against his parent or parents, who deny being sexual abusers, and may divide families and friends.

The journalist, whether covering accusations or the legal actions that result from the memory recovery, will be in the middle of a fiercely argued issue. On the one hand, some scholars and clinicians of various backgrounds say memories cannot be lost and then recovered. They often argue that the memory is not actually recovered but is suggested by a cue from the therapist or attorney, a story in the news media, or some other source. On the other hand, other convinced and competent experts argue that memory can be lost and regained, that the trauma to a child that results from sexual abuse may have that result, and that incest and child rape are so frequent that recovered memory cases must be taken seriously.

Some reporters, taking the side of the skeptics of recovered memory, have concluded that most such claims are fraudulent. That stance is a disservice to the many victims of child abuse.

In 1998 a panel convened by the International Society for Traumatic Stress Studies published its conclusions about the recovered memory claims. The panelists, representing the psychiatrists, psychologists, and social workers who work with trauma survivors, offered this evenhanded conclusion:

> While there is some evidence that recovered memories of childhood abuse can be as accurate as never-forgotten memories of childhood abuse, there is also evidence that memory is reconstructive and imperfect, that people can make very glaring errors in memory, that people are suggestible under some circumstances to social influence or persuasion when reporting memories for past events and that at least under some circumstances inaccurate memories can be strongly believed and convincingly described. While traumatic memories may be different than ordinary memories, we currently do not have conclusive scientific consensus on this issue. Likewise, it is not currently known how traumatic memories are forgotten or later recovered.
>
> (1998:23)

The report, *Childhood Trauma Remembered*, should convince reporters that they should not judge claims of recovered memory as right or wrong at the outset. Each case requires the considerable effort of all those involved to reach the truth. The journalist can help by studying that process rather than the bombastic arguments of those organized on either side of the issue.

Moreover, scientists are finding evidence that the brain has a mechanism for suppressing traumatic memories. While it isn't yet known if the brain can bring about complete forgetting, or amnesia, the research made possible by the technology of magnetic resonance imaging (MRI) suggests that journalists—and all who respond to adult accounts of childhood abuse—should keep an open mind about such claims (Anderson et al., 2004:232–35).

Rape at any age robs a person of confidence in life. Recovery is the patient's struggle to come to terms with that loss of confidence. If journalists respect that struggle, survivors will know that it is an honorable one. In a memoir, *Where I Stopped: Remembering Rape at Thirteen*, poet Martha Ramsey wrote about shedding the memory of her trauma. "In each year of my life I can look forward to shedding more. Each time I stumble—at the dentist's, at the garage, or with Eric—the memory grows easier, for I find I can also hold the others—all the men, the witnesses, mother and father, everyone who did not know how to help me—in that river of my awakened heart" (1995:325).

In closing, we offer these suggestions for helpful reporting about rape:

- Put the case in the context of patterns of sexual crimes in the community and state. At times, report these patterns as stories in their own right.
- Avoid ways of describing details that reinforce stereotypes.
- Include details that may help others avoid assault.
- Mention details that get across the seriousness and horror of the crime.
- Name local agencies that help survivors and families and explain state laws on sexual offenses.

DEBRA MCKINNEY

Charting the Course of Recovery

Getting on with their lives. Putting the pieces back together again. With "Malignant Memories," *Anchorage Daily News* reporter Debra McKinney transcends these clichés to give readers an honest look at recovery from childhood sexual abuse.

That she took on the story at all is amazing. McKinney had recently completed "A Story of Incest." The perpetrator was a Baptist preacher, the victims his three small daughters. Six years after sentencing, the entire family—including his wife, who had turned him in—seemed to have been sentenced as well. "They would live the rest of their lives without feeling whole," concluded McKinney. "He had raped their souls." With no comforting end in sight, she felt drained herself: "All I wanted to write about for a while was the latest trend in breakfast food."

Debra McKinney.
Photo by Marc Pingry

Then she met Ezraella—Ezzie—a survivor of incest who told McKinney how she and her friends Margie and Vivian met every week for lunch. They called themselves the Marvellas, a combination of their names. For McKinney its upbeat, you-can't-stop-me spirit was irresistible.

The Marvellas showed what healing could look like thirty years after the abuse. "I needed the Marvellas so bad," McKinney says. So, she reasoned, did her readers.

She took no notes during her first meetings with the Marvellas, letting them get to know her. Without their trust she knew she'd have "a story without a pulse." After some misgivings (Margie was the most concerned, mainly for her kids), the Marvellas included McKinney in about half their get-togethers and—remarkably—Vivian's confrontation with her family and Margie's return to the farm where her uncle had sexually assaulted her.

Trust goes both ways. For her part McKinney offered them the chance to see their story before it landed on neighbors' doorsteps. She had used the same ground rules with the preacher's wife: except for errors, the preview was not about changing the story; it was about easing the shock of seeing themselves in print. As for the possibility that they might, at that point, back down—"That was in the rules too. They understood they were committed before they read." McKinney and her editor defend showing the text of the story to the women. "We felt a strong sense of responsibility to them for trusting us with their stories," McKinney explains, "and it didn't end with the last of the interviews."

Early on she knew the story was recovery—not the incest per se—and such recovery occurs in small steps over a lifetime. McKinney, a fourth-generation journalist, had more than an ear for language and an eye for detail; she had the patience to wait and watch as the Marvellas revealed their stories. Working around other assignments, she also had the luxury of time.

For the actual writing she credits instructors at the Poynter Institute and her editor ("flexible and demanding") for keeping her on track—writing for readers, not her sources. McKinney introduces the Marvellas as she met them, adult women with families, jobs, and a capacity for fun. She describes their lunches—the teasing, the terrors they share, the rich desserts they order. McKinney respects both the anguish of remembering torture no child should ever experience and the difficulty readers have in accepting what they do not want to believe. She continually shifts the focus back to Margie, Vivian, and Ezzie as they are now: celebrating Ezzie's conversion to Judaism with a potluck and slumber party; soaking together in a hot tub after Vivian confronts her family; skipping arm-in-arm like schoolgirls as they leave the barn that Margie's uncle had forced her into.

What McKinney struggled with most was the issue of repressed memories. Vivian's father had confessed, but Ezzie's father and Margie's uncle were dead. In the end, McKinney says, it didn't matter whether she could verify the memories. The story wasn't about the perpetrators or the details of abuse; "it was about getting healthy and reclaiming stolen childhoods."

The vital first step to recovery is remembering, and McKinney invites readers into the process. She braids the women's stories together, letting readers discover with her the extent of the violence. With Vivian, McKinney is able to show memory's elusive nature: Vivian didn't remember her father's barging in on her in the bathroom, as he had confessed, only that she was always constipated as a child. With Margie, McKinney describes the process of remembering as similar to seeing in fog—blurred forms, strained senses, sudden clarity. As Ezzie and Vivian attempt to follow Margie's uncertain directions to her uncle's farm, McKinney notes the wrong turns, the dead ends, the guesses, and doubts. Standing with the Marvellas in the farmhouse, Margie speaks in the voice of a little girl, remembers what her uncle did, cries at long last. Readers, standing there as well, understand.

Though McKinney admits, with relief, that she has never experienced such trauma in her life, she brought considerable knowledge of sexual assault to this story. In addition to the story of the preacher's family, she had covered rape support groups and was familiar with a range of resources: therapists, detectives, attorneys, the head of Alaska's sex-offender treatment program. "Malignant Memories" is infused with solid information.

McKinney has continued to work on similar projects. A recent feature article, "Linda's First Dance," describes a nine-year-old Yup'ik girl who had suffered permanent brain damage when her father fractured her skull a month after she was born. Although she was unable to learn the required dance movements, Linda was nevertheless embraced by her Native Alaskan community and included in this important rite of passage.

Not every story of family violence works out. In what McKinney calls "the best story I never wrote," a woman who had killed her husband in self-defense, in front of her children, seemed eager at first to go public. "But the more she talked, the more I sensed she wasn't ready for the impact on herself or her family." McKinney had already decided not to continue when the woman backed down. "It made me feel good that my instincts were right. Still, it was a hell of a story."

McKinney claims that the strength to write about the aftermath of violence comes from her sources. It also comes from her. Like a reporter who follows soldiers in the field, exposed to combat and the trauma that follows, McKinney bravely follows those who have been wounded—some by the very adults who should have protected them. Carefully charting the course of recovery, she discovers the heroes.

Malignant Memories: It's a Long Road Back to Recovery from Incest

DEBRA MCKINNEY

Debra McKinney's account of the mutual support of three women as they faced down memories of the incest they had suffered was framed by her account of the trip to the farm where an uncle had assaulted one of the women. These excerpts focus on that visit. Although the article emphasizes what McKinney and the women call "the Dark Ages"—the ordeal of opening old wounds—its ending affirms the substantial distance they all have traveled and the optimism they gained in the process. The entire story was published in the Anchorage Daily News on June 6, 1993.

SEATTLE—Twenty-five years have come and gone since Margie last visited the old man's farm. She's not sure she can even find the place. She's not sure she wants to.

The 51-year-old Anchorage travel agent has made a lot of progress lately confronting her fears. But she still has trouble talking about what happened in the barn.

So fragmented are the memories. She remembers her Uncle George carrying her piggyback across the horse pasture, her bony legs, black patent-leather shoes and white-lace socks poking out from under his arms. She remembers staring up at the barn's rafters, and how the hay scratched her skin. She remembers her ankles being strapped down, legs apart.

And then there's the time she was tied by her wrists and hoisted.

Did things like this happen a couple of times? Every visit? Why didn't her aunt come looking for them? Did she not want to know?

Margie wants to remember more. No, she wants to forget. But she knows she has to go back there if she ever wants peace. And so she studies a local map.

Although Uncle George has been dead for more than 20 years, the courage to go through with this comes from two friends.

A year ago they were strangers—Vivian Dietz-Clark, 41; Ezraella "Ezzie" Bassera, 44; and Margie (to protect their own privacy, her children asked that the family name not be used). Now they call themselves sisters.

Their demons brought them together. Within the past few years, memories have surfaced, forcing them to deal with what had long been buried—the sexual abuse they're convinced they experienced as children.

A tremendous amount of energy goes into locking things up inside, Ezzie's therapist, Joan Bender, explained. It's like sitting on a huge, bulging chest to keep it from popping open. Any added stress drains energy from that chore. The lid creaks open. Memories escape.

The three Anchorage women met in a support group for adult survivors of childhood sexual abuse offered by STAR (Standing Together Against Rape). And when that group ended, they continued to meet on their own.

The Marvellas, a combination of their first three names, is what they call themselves now that they're a team. The melding of their identities is a metaphor for the journey they've taken together.

Their efforts took them to the Seattle area this spring to confront family and fears, and to be there for each other.

The first attempt at finding Uncle George's place ended in the Big Brothers Bingo parking lot. Could the farm have been paved over? No, this wasn't right. Margie tried hard to remember. The next hill over looked familiar.

Vivian turned the rental car around, crossed over the freeway, took a left at the top of the hill and ended up in the middle of a subdivision.

What now? They drove on.

At the end of the last row of houses was a gravel road. They took it. Halfway down Margie turned white.

"That's it," she said.

Vivian stopped the car at the top of a long driveway. The three of them sat in silence a moment.

"Let's go down there," Vivian said.

Margie groaned.

"We're going," said Ezzie.

Slowly the car headed down the gravel drive. At the bottom, Vivian stopped in front of a little yellow farm house, the kind you'd expect to have an apple pie cooling in the windowsill.

"Amazing," Margie said.

The place was just the way she remembered it. There was the chicken coop. And the old chopping block. And the big pear tree the guinea hens used to roost in. And there, behind the little house, beyond the gate with the "Keep Out" sign, was the barn.

"I don't want to get out," Margie said.

Vivian put an arm around her and hugged her. Ezzie gently rubbed her back. They all got out of the car.

≈≈≈

At Uncle George's farm, Vivian knocks on the door of the little yellow house, and explains to the woman who answers that her friend used to stay there as a girl. Would it be OK to look around?

Margie, who's stayed by the car, needs a cigarette. She lights one, hoping the woman will say no. She doesn't.

Vivian and Ezzie push because they want their friend to remember. If she can remember, if she can confront her fears, she can learn to be strong.

They escort her to the top of the driveway, as if she were a schoolgirl again just getting off the bus to visit her now late aunt and uncle.

"He would walk with me to the back of the barn like this," Margie said, cinching her arm around Ezzie's waist. "He held me very tight and the horse would follow because he had sugar or something. I'd be squirming because I didn't like being held. And he would tell me if I didn't stop squirming the horse would stomp on me.

"And so I was always afraid of horses."

"But you showed me a picture of you sitting on a horse, and he was next to you," Vivian recalled. "You said you could remember your thighs being chafed after being here because you'd ride your horse."

"No," Margie says.

"From him?"

"Wasn't that just the perfect excuse to be sore down there?" Margie said.

Nothing shocks the Marvellas anymore. They agreed. Yup, the perfect excuse. Then they put their arms around each other's shoulders. Next, they were skipping down the driveway, giggling like kids, not caring what anybody might think.

Margie remembers only bits and pieces of being fondled in bed at night. Vivian decided to walk her through it, using those fragments to pry more memories loose.

"You sleep right here in this corner?" Vivian asked, gesturing toward a small window.

"Uh-huh. I remember times when I was sleeping in that little bedroom and he would go in and stoke the fire, and he'd come in my room and she would call out to him, 'George, aren't you coming to bed? What are you doing?' His whiskers were long late at night."

Margie's cheeks began to flush.

"So, you're laying in your little bed and what's he doing? Touching you?" Silence.

"Kissing you?"

Margie stared at the ground. Her cheeks were now bright red.

"I mean, you're getting whisker burns. And you've talked about his breath. Do you feel his breath?"

Margie couldn't answer.

By then, Vivian had her by the shoulders and was staring into her face. The prodding was more than Margie could handle.

"I just want him to go away," she said in a little girl's voice. She burst into tears, put her head on Vivian's shoulder and sobbed, her body shaking.

At last.

Margie had always said she'd crack a bottle of champagne the day she finally cried. But since she no longer drinks, the Marvellas made do later with chocolate.

"Oh my," Margie said, pulling herself together. "That's enough for me right now."

Later, thinking the Marvellas were on a nostalgia tour, the farm's new owner led them through the barn. While he chatted away cheerfully, Margie systematically looked things over. Looking down on the stalls instead of up, she realized how small she was back then. The barn, which seemed cavernous back then, seemed so tiny.

But no new memories came.

An hour and a half after first pulling down that driveway, the Marvellas were back in the car, debriefing.

"It wasn't scary going into the barn because you were with me," Margie told her friends.

And the scene under the bedroom window?

"I just wanted you to stop," she told Vivian. "I just went, 'No, don't. I don't want to remember this.'"

"I feel a little heavy chested. But I do feel like I went and conquered something."

CHAPTER 11

Using the Searchlight with Precision and Sensitivity

The press . . . is like the beam of a searchlight that moves restlessly about, bringing one episode and then another out of darkness into vision.

WALTER LIPPMANN, *Public Opinion*

An uncle of mine was a wonderful friend in my childhood and teen years, easy going, creative, and caring. He was a veteran of World War I, a fact never discussed in family gatherings. After his death relatives constructed the story of a man sent into combat who emerged physically whole but evidently never spoke to anyone about what he had seen and done. He had grown into adulthood at a time when even speaking about combat experience put one at odds with both medical authorities and other citizens who thought any sign of emotion about war identified "a constitutionally inferior human being," in the words of psychiatrist Judith Lewis Herman. Some physicians argued that war trauma could have psychological effects, but the issue and interest faded quickly when the war ended. Although medical understanding of trauma had become much more sophisticated by 1945 and the end of World War II, veterans' silence remained a hallmark of later wars and of the experience of later groups.

The thesis of this chapter is that journalists' communities and news beats are filled with many silent survivors of traumatic experiences. Not all of them insist on silence. In many cases the survivors are not heard because the media overlook them and their stories. They are not part of any breaking news—no fire, landslide, or shooting brings them to public attention. Eric Schlosser wrote in the *Atlantic Monthly* in 1997: "Americans are fascinated by murders and murderers but not by the families of the people who are killed—an amazingly numerous group, whose members can turn only to one another for sympathy and understanding" (37). Schlosser's remarkable twenty-two-thousand–word article provides a rare account of how the silence of being a homicide survivor pervades the lives of those family members. Many of those people that the news media overlook represent the qualities of character that Americans admire—tenacity, courage, self-sacrifice, strength. Their lives speak to sweeping changes across the globe or in U.S. towns and cities. Yet too often the survivors are left in the shadows of public awareness.

When silence is the result of news media avoidance and not a choice by an individual, journalists can challenge that silence. But the reporting must be respectful, sensitive to private matters, and concerned about recovery and survival more than the awful events that created a victim in the first place. Scott North, a newspaper reporter who is profiled following this chapter, excels at bringing the experience of such survivors to his readers.

Poet Peter Balakian explores another kind of silence in his memoir, *Black Dog of Fate* (1997). Some of his relatives had escaped the Turkish government's genocide of hundreds of thousands of Armenian people early in the century. Yet Balakian describes a childhood with grandparents, parents, and aunts who never spoke of the massacres by Turkish authorities between 1910 and 1915. The book was the poet's assault on the silence produced by the trauma of the genocide experience. Survivors of the Holocaust, the Cambodian genocide of the early 1970s, the Balkans wars, and the Rwandan slaughter in the 1990s know about those silences. Balakian wonders how a state action that killed so many and scattered many others to refuges throughout the world could become lost to memory. As the survivors committed their suffering to silence, the genocide of Armenians faded from the world's collective awareness.

Other people have sought to understand silences of different kinds. Judith Lewis Herman writes that social mores silenced the traumatic sources of women's suffering in the nineteenth and early twentieth centuries. "The cherished value of privacy created a powerful barrier to consciousness and rendered women's reality practically invisible. To speak about experiences in sexual or domestic life was to invite public humiliation, ridicule, and disbelief. Women were silenced by fear and shame, and the silence of women gave license to every form of sexual and domestic exploitation," Herman writes in *Trauma and Recovery* (1992:28). Grasping her own critical need to speak about what happened to her, Nancy Venable Raine, a rape survivor, titled her 1998 memoir about recovery *After Silence*.

Today people talk more openly about domestic violence than ever before, yet they often fail to see the oppressive character of many relationships. Herman writes:

A man's home is his castle; rarely is it understood that the same home may be a prison for women and children. In domestic captivity, physical barriers to escape are rare. In most homes, even the most oppressive, there are no bars on the windows, no barbed wire fences. Women and children are not ordinarily chained, though even this occurs more often than one might think. The barriers to escape are generally invisible. They are nonetheless extremely powerful.

(1992:74)

Conflict that appears to be rooted in differences of skin color or ethnic origin is often noisy, confrontational, and violent. Once the conflict subsides, those who fought may choose silence because of weariness or because of symptoms of trauma. The great and effective civil rights actions in American history took place in the 1950s and 1960s. Yet those activists can be found today among the many silent victims of prejudice and social conflict in every community. U.S. Rep. John Lewis of Georgia, in his 1998 memoir, *Walking with the Wind*, describes the summer of 1964 in Mississippi when he and other African Americans and their allies physically challenged the brute force of southern resistance to desegregation. The summer gave civil rights leaders "a purpose, a goal, an object of hope," writes Lewis (1998:274), who was beaten by a mob in Montgomery, Alabama, in 1961 and knocked unconscious by Alabama state troopers in March 1965 in Selma. Of the veterans of the civil rights action, Lewis writes: "Like the soldiers who would begin coming home from Vietnam within a year, the veterans of Mississippi Summer were affected for the rest of their lives by what they went through and what they witnessed. Their spirits, as well as many of their bodies, were broken. Some remained casualties from then on. Many simply dropped out of the system. Others surrendered to overwhelming anger and irrational behavior" (273). Unlike the veterans who might have asked for and found clinical help in the 1960s, civil rights activists found little help and scarcely any understanding that they too had been in combat. "Get over it, their friends and families would tell them," Lewis writes (273).

THE LEGACY OF WAR

Paul Fussell, the war historian, has written that most of us do not want to hear about the horrors of war. Yet in 1998 director Steven Spielberg created a remarkable film about the Allies' 1944 invasion of France that included nearly an hour of simulated but horrifying and realistic images of men in the landing force being killed and maimed. Did people see the film because, as a whole, it was another entertaining story told in cinematic form or because they wanted to know more about the violence of war? Critics praised Spielberg for the gritty honesty of the film, but few, if any, used trauma knowledge in appraising the film. And none that Coté and I found appeared to be aware that some of those who survived the assault would continue to experience its effects long afterward. After the war the traumas of both combatants and civilians were dismissed far too readily. Civilians suffered more than half the casualties in World War II (compared with only 5 percent in World War I), but even those who came through it without physical injury lost homes and possessions as well as friends and relatives.

Peacetime is a good time to report on war, because the searchlight does not stay focused on the day-to-day action of a particular conflict. When the searchlight can sweep around more and seek out those who are often missed, what stories might journalists be able to tell?

The pessimistic accounts are already there in such great numbers that they have become clichés. Some veterans of Vietnam and the Gulf war who were ignored in their communities turned to drugs and crime. The suicide rate among veterans is stunningly high for people in those age groups. Decorated veterans turn up in homeless shelters, sleeping in parks, or dead in city alleys. If the story is about one person, it is likely to describe a slide from success and achievement into weakness and failure, if not death. The stories feed on a stereotype about veterans, the Hollywood notion that war survivors are destined to find success after the war ends. Those who fail to return to conventional lives must somehow be flawed, an echo of the strange thinking in the medical profession at the time of World War I.

Yet the struggle—the real story—for some men who fought in Vietnam was to recover from the traumas of combat and the subsequent emotional assaults of rejection at home and failures in their postwar lives. Although a failure to survive these pressures, represented by a suicide or committing a crime, is a sure-fire story, the recovery story gets little attention. The omission is not due to a lack of information; veterans and therapists will readily tell journalists what it entails. Since the United States invaded Iraq in March 2003, few newspapers or television news programs have provided information about how to recover from a war, the day-by-day effort whose results are scarcely noticeable, the two-steps-forward, one-step-back character of the process. Veterans with PTSD who have taken our classes have been able teachers, reminding us from time to time that a traumatized person may have difficulty dealing with course material that will spark no special emotional reaction in most students.

Jonathan Shay, a psychiatrist for a group of Vietnam War combat veterans in the Boston area, describes the barriers they faced in recovery in his book *Achil-*

les in Vietnam (1994). For years, as he counseled the veterans, he considered the similarities of their combat experience to that described by Homer in the Greek classic *The Iliad*. Interweaving the stories from *The Iliad* with those told by the Vietnam veterans suffering severe post-traumatic stress disorder, Shay tries to find ways to prevent psychological injuries.

What the former combatants faced each day, Shay writes, was a set of symptoms that ruined the character and personality of the victims most affected. The litany of effects includes loss of authority over mental function; persistent mobilization for danger; a persistent focus on survival; persistence of betrayal, isolation, thoughts of suicide, and meaninglessness; and destruction of the capacity for democratic participation (1994:170–81).

Shay does not offer recovery as a guarantee. But, he says, "recovery is possible in many areas of life, perhaps in the most important ones for a fulfilling existence" (186). Yet some of the most active veterans "remain highly symptomatic." The veterans, then, dare to regain their place in their families and communities despite the long-lasting effects of trauma. The journalist who approaches the war survivor must be alert to both the dangers and opportunities in asking for a narrative. Do not assume that asking the veteran about combat experience will be therapeutic. Telling the story under the wrong conditions may be terribly harmful.

Journalists and therapists educe the stories of war trauma for very different reasons, and their ways of eliciting the narratives differ in important ways. Whereas therapists working with veterans often encourage them to tell their stories, the narrative of war experience is a delicate instrument. "Narrative heals personality changes only if the survivor finds or creates a trustworthy community of listeners for it," Shay writes (1994:188). Often, those listeners have endured similar traumas but not always. Indeed, Shay argues for more sharing of veterans' narratives in a wider community. Any audience for the narratives must be able to listen without being injured by the accounts and without blaming the victim or denying the story's reality, according to Shay. A good listener will refrain from judgment, respect the narrator, and be willing to experience some of the terror, grief, and rage.

How do these expectations apply to a journalist whose reporting of the war narrative will be passed on to an audience and who cannot assure that any of these standards will be met? Should the reporter, whose own capacity to listen with respect and without judgment may be limited, even solicit such stories? Because Coté and I believe that news reports can be a bridge for understanding between those who fought in U.S. wars and the public, we encourage reporters to write about combat veterans but in ways that do no further harm.

In casual interviews or those in which the reporter and the subject of the story meet only once, reporters should not ask victims of violence, including combat trauma, to recount what happened to them during the trauma. A Vietnam veteran who spoke at the University of Washington said he would talk freely about the history, policies, and aftermath of the war but would take no questions about what happened to him during the war. He had learned on many occasions how troubling it can be to tell that story to an audience that is not prepared in the way Shay describes. And it can also prompt unwanted memories for the veteran. (When the veteran and the reporter have time to come to trust each other, the veteran may make disclosures about trauma.) But, of course, there are exceptions to this advice. Some veterans can recount their combat history in extensive detail. If you are interested in a compelling example of a combat narrative, read Robert Kotlowitz's *Before Their Time* (1997). Kotlowitz, one of three in his platoon who survived an irrational and failed assault on an entrenched German unit in France during World War II, tells the story of his survival and the aftermath in fascinating detail.

But the news story can tell how a person found his or her way back into civilian life or moved further toward personal goals after the war. And it can explain what recovery involves.

In 1998 a Seattle reporter compiled an extraordinary account of war experience in World War I, based on the recollections and letters of her 105-year-old grandmother. Trust was not an issue when Carol Smith, the *Seattle Post-Intelligencer* reporter, interviewed Laura Frost Smith, who had served as an army nurse on five of the bloodiest fronts of the war. The nurses witnessed the many amputations, brain and head injuries, and deaths even as they, the first women to participate in the U.S. military, fought prejudice and bureaucratic pettiness at the front. Carol Smith writes that her grandmother rarely mentioned the war after she returned to the United States. "Though many of the nurses' experiences were more dramatic than those of their husbands, boyfriends or brothers, they didn't talk for fear of embarrassing the men. Social pressures against women doing 'men's work' also enforced their silence. But the war's imprint remained. It would influence my grandmother's outlooks and actions for the rest of her life" (1998:E5). Smith's story, which her newspaper presented on three full pages, went on to describe the many connections between war experience and later actions, emphasizing not the trauma but its importance in a person's later life.

Communities are rich with the contributions of veterans of Vietnam, the Gulf war, the wars in Afghanistan and Iraq, or older conflicts. One Vietnam veteran who lives in a Seattle suburb spends his time working with scouts and applies the lessons of the war in a remarkable way. Alarmed by the overuse of violent video games by boys, he developed a program of working with parents and boys who are observed using such games compulsively.

SURVIVORS OF GENOCIDE

In 1946 the United Nations General Assembly passed a resolution on genocide: "Genocide is a denial of the right of existence of entire human groups. . . . Many instances of such crimes have occurred, when racial, religious, political and other groups have been destroyed, entirely or in part." Two years later the UN adopted a convention that identified genocide as acts intended to destroy "national, ethnical, racial or religious" groups. A squabble about terms led to the omission of political groups from the definition, although killing for political reasons was a major form of genocide in the twentieth century. Mass killings may have the same causes but differ from genocide in that they are not part of a campaign to destroy an entire group.

The Holocaust, the extermination of six million Jews by the Germans during World War II, is the example of genocide most studied. The Nazi regime in Germany killed several million other people, including political opponents, Catholics, Gypsies, homosexuals, mentally ill people, and citizens of other nations. The genocide was not part of combat; it was carried out as a policy of the regime.

Other genocides mark the history of the twentieth century. In 1915 the Turkish government carried out the killing of more than 800,000 Armenians in Turkey (Staub 1989:10). In 1975 the Khmer Rouge government of Cambodia targeted potential enemies of the state. Millions of people were taken from cities and forced to build new villages in the countryside under harsh conditions. The death toll from executions and starvation before 1979 has been estimated at two million people. In 1976 the military government of Argentina began wholesale murders of political opponents. Estimates of those killed range from nine thousand to thirty thousand. More recent were the genocide against Bosnian Muslims by the Serb government, the 1994 genocide of 800,000 in the Tutsi minority in Rwanda, and the genocide in Sudan's West Darfur region.

Genocides and mass killings have scattered refugee-survivors throughout the world. They join refugees from combat zones in local communities. Their stories are compelling and need to be told so that everyone can understand the consequences of nationalistic and regional violence. Yet interviewing such survivors and telling their stories with understanding is difficult. When the reporter does not speak the survivor's language, a skilled interpreter can help. The interpreter can also assist the reporter by noting the cultural differences that shaped the survivor's response to the trauma of war or mass killing. Reporters will have to seek the right help or do the research required for an effective interview. They will need to listen for signs that a particular object, act, or event is understood differently by the other person and the reporter. And reporters will need to be sensitive to the likelihood that their questions about a traumatic event may do further harm to the other person.

Anne Fadiman's fascinating study of the treatment of a child in a family of Hmong refugees from Laos offers many examples of how failure to bridge cultural differences caused unwarranted fear and harm. In the book *The Spirit Catches You and You Fall Down* (1997), she recounts how medical personnel in a California hospital asked the child's parents to sign a release before taking the child home to die. The family found the prediction of death offensive. "In the Hmong moral code, foretelling a death is strongly taboo," Fadiman writes (177). An interpreter tells Fadiman, "In Laos, that means you're going to kill a person. Maybe poison him. Because how do you know for certain he's going to die unless you're going to kill him?" (178).

Personal stories give the community a chance to ponder the critical roles played by people enveloped in genocide or mass-killing horrors. Each event confronts the audience with the actions of four kinds of participants: perpetrators, victims, survivors, and bystanders. Historians have little trouble constructing the actions of the perpetrators. Many victims will not be able to tell their stories because they are dead or too severely injured, and few will try. The examples of the survivors and the bystanders may help others to learn how to deal with these unimaginable human atrocities.

The narratives of refugees can illuminate how people in fear for their lives find ways to survive. A Holocaust survivor told the students in one of our classes how she escaped prison camp guards several times by relying on the aid of other prisoners and her own craftiness. Agate Nesaule, now a professor at the University of Wisconsin–Whitewater, tells in a memoir how she and her family had fled Latvia during a Russian advance in World War II and were then captured by brutal Russian troops. During an interrogation Nesaule's mother survived by speaking Russian. "My mother began talking. It is one of the things I most admire about her, that at this moment she could talk, and that she knew what to say," Nesaule writes (1995:72).

The survivors and their stories can be both inspirational and instructive. But what about the bystanders, those who witnessed the killings, who may have tried to halt them or may have assisted in them? Students of genocide have placed the bystander role in the searchlight increasingly in recent years. They argue against an assumption that bystanders can and will do little to prevent violence or mass killing; to the contrary, they say, people need to learn about the potential for moral action among bystanders. Two bystanders whose stories have assumed heroic status emerged during World War II. Oscar Schindler's resourceful campaign to rescue Jews from the German genocide on the pretense of employing them in a factory has been told in books and in a popular movie, *Schindler's List.* Raoul Wallenberg, a Swedish businessman, gained a diplomatic appointment to Hungary in 1944. During the next six months he saved tens of thousands of Jews, relying on bribery, threats, and the issuance of "protective passes" that allowed a safe exit from Hungary to Sweden. (Wallenberg evidently was arrested by the Soviets late in the war and was not heard from again.)

Ervin Staub, professor of psychology at the University of Massachusetts–Amherst, has studied bystander options as part of his effort to understand how to prevent genocide and other group violence. He distinguishes "internal bystanders," members of the perpetrator group who are not perpetrators themselves, from "external bystanders," witnesses who are not members of the perpetrator group. Staub writes: "Bystanders can exert powerful influence. They can define the meaning of events and move others toward empathy or indifference.... Why then are bystanders so often passive and silent? ... Lack of divergent views, just world thinking, and their own participation or passivity change bystanders' perception of self and reality so as to allow and justify cruelty" (1989:88).

For the reporter the lesson in Staub's analysis is that any situation that might result in violence has the potential to be short-circuited by a thoughtful bystander, especially early in the cycle of events. At the same time, if the passive bystander is the model for everyone involved, escalation to violence is more likely. News stories can focus on the interventions of active bystanders. Survivors and refugees from violence elsewhere in the world can be witness to the efforts and failures of bystanders, as well as the acts of perpetrators and the plight of victims. By telling stories that reflect action against violence, reporters also move from passivity to moral action.

SURVIVORS OF DOMESTIC VIOLENCE

When relationships turn violent and violence kills and injures, the news media often report what happened in ways that confuse readers and viewers and contribute to harmful stereotypes. Stories about domestic violence seldom reflect any knowledge of this pathology. Consider two recent stories from the Seattle area. A Cambodian man killed his wife. The second-day story noted a pattern of violence and abuse by the man toward his family yet undercut that key idea by implying, through quoted comments from neighbors, that the killing could be understood as a result of "a clash between traditional Khmer culture and a more liberal American society." In another example newspapers reported that an emergency room physician had killed his wife, staged a car accident to try to cover up the killing, then tried to kill himself. Instead of keeping the focus directly on the killer, his victim, and the problem of domestic violence, news stories offered a bizarre interpretation that would lead readers to conclude that an otherwise normal man had gone berserk one day for inexplicable reasons. One headline said, "Residents Wonder If Small-Town Life Has Left Their Town." The lead of another story began, "In a place the neighbors say is so quiet you can hear a pin drop . . ." Another story emphasized a comment from a neighbor: "'This would be normal for California, but not here.'"

Judith Lewis Herman, the psychiatrist, argues that many people are disturbed by the apparent normality of the killer and his family situation. Perhaps for that reason reporters emphasize the ironies as they try to offer quick answers to the why question. The Cambodian killer, one newspaper said, "was an immigrant success story." Another newspaper described the murderous physician and his wife as "'gentle' and 'generous' people who once lent storage space to a neighbor whose home had been destroyed." A neighbor was quoted as saying, "They just seemed like a real nice couple."

According to Herman, the victim of violent abuse suffers captivity in the same way as a person held in a slave-labor camp. Yet to all outward appearances the man, woman, and children are "real nice" and "normal." Herman describes the batterers as "exquisitely sensitive to the realities of power and to social norms." She adds, "His demeanor provides an excellent camouflage, for few people believe that extraordinary crimes can be committed by men of such conventional appearance" (1992:75). The men in these cases coerce their partners and children into being victims; indeed, the perpetrators thrive on their ability to control other people. Such control requires cutting the victimized family member off from contact with anyone else. "The more frightened she is, the more she is tempted to cling to the one relationship that is permitted: the relationship with the perpetrator," Herman adds (81). The experience traumatizes the victims, fosters changes in identity and emotional responses essential to survival, and burdens victims with intense rage long after the relationship ends.

Deaths from domestic violence are not uncommon. According to the FBI's Uniform Crime Reports for 1995, 26 percent of female murder victims were killed by husbands or boyfriends. Studies of particular cities or regions have placed the percentage as high as 50 percent. Wives or girlfriends killed 3 percent of all male murder victims. Children are often killed along with the spouse or partner. Some children who survive are witnesses to the killings of others.

Reporters can find victims of domestic violence who have escaped abusive relationships throughout the community. But before approaching a woman who has suffered at the hands of a husband or boyfriend, take these ideas into account:

- The threat from the perpetrator may not have ended. Speaking out in any way or being identified in a news story may increase the degree of danger she faces.

- Reporters should take their own identity and physical presence into account. Size, demeanor, and verbal behavior may trigger fear in someone for whom such cues have accompanied violence.

- Domestic violence may create traumatic effects that the person will have to address over a long period of time. Be as sensitive to what this recovery entails as you would be for a person who has been raped.

- The criminal justice system may do little for the abused partner or spouse of a violent person.

- Batterers often coerce others in their family; the relationship is a complex one, never explained simply by a single action that might have provoked a violent response. Do not write about the woman's experience in ways that imply she was responsible for her victimization. Another example from a Seattle-area newspaper illustrates this point. A story about the trial of a man charged with killing his former girlfriend and her baby included this paragraph: "Though they had sex just minutes before he killed her, she apparently told him the relationship was finished, prosecutors have said." While readers may take different meanings from the sentence, some are likely to see the woman as duplicitous, willing to have sex before breaking off a relationship. The sentence has little to do with the power represented by the killer and the gun that he held.

- The story should report interviews with experts on domestic violence. One article included this quote: "I don't think we'll ever know what precipitated this situation." Maybe not, but people who work with victims of domestic violence could make a good guess.

- Careful and sensitive interviewing of a survivor of domestic violence could help to destroy the myths that perpetrators of such acts are normal people and that the victims should take the blame for violence. Amazing insights about this experience appear in newspapers for the homeless, in an array of performance pieces about domestic violence, and in the stories of those who have suffered. Respect all people who are willing to tell their stories about domestic violence.

HOW DISCRIMINATION COMPELS SILENCE AND RESISTS NARRATIVES

This chapter has been about people whose stories have been missing from the news, in part because their suffering encourages their silence and in part because everyone else is too unwilling to take the experience of these groups into account. Each group we have discussed—combat veterans, genocide survivors and refugees, victims of domestic violence—has a high ratio of traumatic exposure and a high risk of post-traumatic stress disorder for some period thereafter. With a good deal of preparation a journalist can help release these personal narratives from the cocoon of trauma in which they are often wrapped.

As we drafted this book, a woman student of color challenged us to extend its reach to include people who live with stress that rarely abates—stress engendered by fear, lack of means, coping with prejudice, and health problems that do not receive adequate attention. In some cases traumatic injury results from, or is complicated by, these conditions. In other instances stress simply reduces the quality of life and erodes optimism and energy. The threat of violence can be so great that its victims rarely experience relief from the stress of living. A climate of prejudice takes its toll in fear, alienation, and resignation from an active life. Writer James Baldwin reminds his white readers of the power of racial terror in the lives of African Americans who regularly confront prejudice and violence. In the fall of 1998 Americans were reminded that lesbian, gay, and transsexual people may face violence and prejudice; a gay University of Wyoming student, Matthew Shepard, died after being beaten fiercely, then tied to a fence and left exposed to the cold in a cornfield. His death, in concert with other murders of gays and lesbians in recent years—including some in the military—was a reminder that violence based on sexual orientation is not uncommon in the United States. Even when violence does not occur, the fear of homophobic prejudice drives some men, women, and teenagers to compromise their own identities and aspirations. Yet the news media often ignore both the violence and the manifestations of prejudice.

We believe that journalists can help remove the veil of silence that surrounds the emotional injuries suffered by these groups. As with the victims of the shock waves of the single horrible event, these people have stories to tell that will help them and inform others. However, journalists have to approach them as wisely and respectfully as they would approach a trauma victim.

We offer these suggestions about how to report these stories:

- Recognize the vitality and resiliency in all communities. Honor the diversity of experiences in every group and disdain easy assumptions about whether people are able to cope with their conditions. Do not assume any particular person suffers either stress or trauma.
- Respect the wisdom represented in often-neglected communities and regularly include their members in stories. Their voices add a dimension of experience often missing in news stories.
- Seek ways to enable people to tell of their experiences. We have read compelling accounts by or about people coping with AIDS or cancer, single parents raising children, and families flourishing in dangerous neighborhoods. Yet such stories are rare enough that when they do appear, they receive unusual attention. Such stories are not routinely reported.
- Trust the authentic voice of a person who has experienced difficult conditions. The *Seattle Times* invited a young man with AIDS to write a regular column; the personal perspective was both fresh and startling in its candor. Homeless people write for and sell newspapers. Many articles are compelling stories about the experiences of homelessness.
- Report about subtle as well as obvious forms of prejudice, but learn about both from the perspective of people who see them as threats in their own lives.
- Beware of news conventions that routinely provide a political or religious "balance" to stories but end up serving only to demean what the victim has said. When a lesbian or gay person is featured in a news report, for example, it isn't unusual for a "balancing" source to be quoted as well, often to provide a negative characterization of the person's identity. The practice is reminiscent of a ploy used by some southern television stations during the civil rights ferment of the early 1960s. After a network news program described a march for economic or political justice, for example, the af-

filiate would present a local segregationist who would provide "the truth" about African Americans' demands for civil equality.

- Respect people's desire for silence, but do more to encourage those who want to speak to tell their stories with your help.

A Witness for the Community

"A murder is an important part of a community's history," says Scott North of the *Herald* in Everett, Washington. "Putting it and the life that was taken into context requires time." North and others on the staff of this daily in Snohomish County, north of Seattle, have succeeded in breaking from "get-it-quick, anyway-you-can" journalism. Using a team approach to reporting, they cover crime with depth, breadth, and an eye for future stories. Most innovative of all, they invite the community into the process.

North started at the *Herald* in 1987 and is quick to credit then-editor Joann Byrd for establishing an ethic of sensitivity to victims. Recognizing that crime coverage was more than police, courts, and perpetrators, she encouraged reporters to seek advice from a local organization, Families and Friends of Victims of Violence, and to listen to survivors.

Scott North.
Photo by Andy Rogers

One of North's first stories was about the murder of a dope dealer. "There was absolutely nothing sympathetic about the victim," North explains, "but every life has something of value." In this case the "something of value" was the victim's wife. "She needed someone to talk to," he says, "and I would spend time with her, just listening. I'm not a cop, and I'm not a therapist. I couldn't do anything for her, really. So I listened."

Just listening, North learned, led to one story, then another, and another, like nesting dolls, like the pages of a photo album turned slowly by the hand of a grieving parent.

"When a parent loses a son or daughter to homicide, they're in a fog," North says. "They hurt so much they can hardly feel, for a while. They're not always ready to talk to me." North is mindful that survivors don't heal on newsroom deadlines. "I tell them that people are going to want to know about their child. 'When you're ready,' I say, 'give me a call.'" It may take months. It may take a year. "The fact is," North emphasizes, "a murder case goes on for a long, long time. There's no need to pressure the family."

Even a well-intentioned reporter has to learn the hard way. "You make mistakes," North explains, recalling a man whose seventeen-year-old daughter was murdered by a serial killer. "The interview went well, but the story I wrote portrayed the girl as one of a series of victims, not as a person." North winces as he remembers the letter he received after the story ran, telling him how the father was hurt by what he had written.

Deeply regretful, North called and apologized. He still has the letter. And the "Beacon of Hope" presented to North years later by Families and Friends is the award he is most proud of.

In the early nineties, North got a strong taste of secondary trauma in himself. At that time the *Herald*'s handling of high-profile cases put a single reporter in court all day. "You filed the story that evening and were back in court early the next morning, day after day. By the end of the trial you were a husk," he recalls. A series of such cases included the execution of a rapist and triple murderer after years of appeals. "I thought I had become detached, but witnessing that execution, watching a human die—I kept asking myself why I was there," North says.

The answer that finally made sense led him to realize what was at the core of all his work—he was there as a witness, not for himself or even his newspaper but for the community. And the work had a cost: sleeplessness, flashbacks, numbness. The very detachment he had thought was a sign of strength in a reporter had become corrosive, at home and in the newsroom.

Meanwhile, the *Herald*, under changed editorial leadership, reverted to the "old style." The change backfired when a reporter, responding to directives to be more aggressive, incorporated into the story the name on the mailbox at a crime scene. A practice that is highly questionable when next of kin have not yet been notified was devastating when the father of the young man named learned of his son's murder as he read the newspaper. "It was horrible," North says, "something editors couldn't ignore—a reminder that we shouldn't go back."

The staff was pushing for a reconsideration of newsroom procedures when, in April 1995, seven-year-old Roxanne Doll was abducted, raped, and murdered. The *Herald* was determined to improve crime coverage as this major homicide story was unfolding (pretrial issues alone took a year). Soon after a conference on journalism and trauma at the University of Washington in March 1996, the paper invited representatives of that school's Journalism and Trauma Program to talk with the staff. Faculty affirmed the *Herald's* need to promote coverage that is sensitive to victims and provided basic information about trauma's effects—primarily on victims but also on caregivers, on emergency responders, and—yes—on reporters.

The resulting changes at the *Herald* creatively incorporated this advice. Reporters formed teams of three to five people who alternate or even share coverage. Under this structure a reporter can come up for air now and then to write about something other than crime and disaster.

As the trial of the person accused of killing Roxanne Doll approached, North, teamed with reporters Dale Steinke and Rebecca Hover, made a conscious decision to take the long view. The story—horrific enough on the surface—had additional complications. The accused was a friend of the father's, and, according to testimony, both men were drinking and using drugs together the night of the murder. "We knew we were setting the record now for coverage ten years down the line, when appeals for aggravated murder could still be playing out. We had a huge responsibility to the community to get it right," North says.

To meet this responsibility they made a huge departure from conventional journalism: they requested and formed a panel of community experts and residents for feedback and advice. The panel included a rabbi, a bookseller, an elementary school counselor, child and victim advocates, even a funeral director and a supervisor with the state Department of Corrections.

Every other week reporters and editors sat down with the panel and asked for feedback: How are the stories affecting the community? What effect are they having on Roxanne's schoolmates, friends, and other children her age? The staff sought advice on issues normally raised only in the newsroom, such as how to handle the expected graphic testimony of the medical examiner and how the stories should be played.

"We learned a lot," North says, looking back. "For one thing, the panel didn't have our 'beat' instinct; they respected us when we didn't follow the pack." Nor did panel members want front-page coverage every day of the trial, reminding reporters to keep the Doll case, as tragic as it was, in perspective; other events were important too. They asked for related stories that would help the community grieve, help parents talk to children about sexual abuse, help everyone feel and be safer. These stories turned out to be especially relevant when, during the course of the trial, another seven-year-old girl was killed in a nearby town.

When the panel disbanded after the trial, all agreed that it had been successful. The community members had learned that those who cover the news are grappling with hard decisions and their own emotions, concerned about the effects of their work. The reporters, shedding their usual observer role, gained a sense of partnership and became more firmly grounded in the community itself.

Similar panels have been formed since the Doll case, most recently in May 2003, when editor Stan Strick brought news staff to attend a roundtable on coverage of youths and violence. In addition, senior reporters like Scott North are assigned as mentors for new reporters, to keep up the momentum of improvements in crime coverage.

"I've sunk my roots deep in this place and covered it hard," North says. And though "writing about personal tragedies at a community level usually means writing stories that don't make national headlines," he takes satisfaction in knowing that these are the stories "that become yellowed clippings in scrapbooks."

He cites an example. An Everett couple, Robert and Linda Rule, called to request an interview. They had just learned that their daughter, whose body had been found twenty years earlier, was one of the Green River killer's victims. North began the interview by asking what they were most concerned about. Not surprisingly, it was the way their daughter, Janey, was described when Gary Ridgway pleaded guilty to her murder. It was important to the Rules that the description of her as a prostitute be attributed to the killer, which North sees as fair. "We take the same care when writing about a perpetrator who's been charged with a crime. The killer's perspective isn't necessarily the truth." At the same time the parents agreed that the detail of how the killer had tried to set fire to her hair was necessary to the story—it proved that Ridgway was the killer.

The Rules found the story that North wrote comforting and asked him to write their victim impact statement, which North clearly couldn't do. Robert Rule prepared a statement with the help of Families and Friends and even spoke at the sentencing. "He was the only person who made the serial killer cry," North says.

"One of the great joys of my job is discovering someone like Robert with such a good strong heart," North says. Readers would add that one of the great benefits of someone like Scott North is that, in bearing witness as a reporter, he helps survivors and the community discover their own voice and strength.

Family Supports Decision on Plea Deal; Answers Wait 21 Years

SCOTT NORTH

Scott North saw that his interviews with the parents of Janey Rule, one of at least forty-eight victims of a serial killer, helped them by allowing them to tell their story and that of their daughter. "The story is pretty typical of the work a lot of us do," North says. "I went to their home. I spent time talking with them. We discussed their life history. We went over what the court papers said. We talked about their Janey, and how I could write about her and what happened in a way that would be true and also meet their expectations." The story appeared in the Herald *on November 11, 2003.*

EVERETT—For 21 years the killer had an unholy connection to Robert and Linda Rule of Everett.

The man was never at the front of their minds. But in their quiet moments, he could easily sneak into their thoughts.

Who was he, this stranger, who snatched their 16-year-old daughter from a north Seattle street in September 1982? Why did he discard her body beneath a bush at a hospital construction site?

Above all, why did he pick her?

The Everett couple got answers to some of those questions last week in a King County courtroom as Gary Leon Ridgway, 54, pleaded guilty to killing the Rules' daughter and 47 others.

Linda Jane Rule—Janey to her parents—is now officially a victim of the man who admits he is the Green River killer, a serial murderer now considered the most prolific in United States history.

Ridgway's admissions to slaying Rule and the others came under a deal that spared him the death penalty. In about six months he's expected to be in court again, where he will be sentenced to life in prison without possibility of release.

The girl's parents have no plans to be there.

"I feel we don't have to give him any more time," Robert Rule said.

Until last week, Janey Rule was never officially listed among the Green River killer's victims.

Over the years, her photograph didn't regularly appear among the ghastly lineups of the known dead, images that became all-too-familiar in Washington state as the hunt for the elusive killer, named for the south King County river where he dumped some of his victims in 1982, stretched out across months and years and, eventually, decades.

Robert Rule instead had another image of his daughter. Tucked carefully in his billfold was a yellowing, dog-eared Polaroid, snapped not long after Janey was born in 1966. The camera caught the little girl riding on Linda's hip. Robert Rule had a protective arm wrapped around his young wife's shoulder.

"We were together, and we were walking in downtown Seattle," he recalled. The couple only had enough money to window shop that day, but there was plenty of love to go around.

Within three years, however, the family in that photograph was no more. Linda Rule tossed her wedding ring at Robert in divorce court and they both entered into a series of unsuccessful marriages. Janey shuttled back and forth between her estranged parents, eventually settling into the West Seattle home of one of Robert Rule's brothers.

The Rules said their daughter was one of those young people who seemed intent on putting her life on fast forward. By the time she reached her mid-teens, she'd become a young woman who looked and acted much older than her peers. In time, the street called to her, and despite the love people poured her way, she drifted into what newspapers at the time called a "high-risk lifestyle."

She was last seen alive at 2:30 P.M. on Sept. 26, 1982, on her way to the Kmart on Aurora Avenue in north Seattle. Her body wasn't found until January 1983, in a construction area that is now a parking lot at Seattle's Northwest Hospital.

Although there were suspicions that Janey Rule's death was connected to the Green River murder series, investigators also had their doubts. The killing occurred during the Green River killer's most active period, but it also happened well north of where he was believed to be stalking victims.

Confirmation of how the girl died didn't come until June of this year, after Ridgway had cut his deal.

He agreed to talk with detectives from the Green River Task Force. "During the first day of interviews with the task force detectives in 2003—and prior to any questioning about her case—Ridgway announced that he had killed a woman and dumped her body at Northwest Hospital," King County prosecutors wrote in court papers.

Ridgway claimed he'd picked up the young woman in his pickup truck, paid her to have sex, then strangled her.

Detectives said they knew Ridgway was telling at least most of the truth because he shared a detail likely known only to the killer, Robert Rule said.

Ridgway said he rifled the girl's pockets and found matches. He then lit the back of her hair on fire, twice, eventually extinguishing the flames because he was afraid the smoke would attract attention, court papers show. Ridgway admitted he often molested his victims' remains in worse ways, including necrophilia, according to court records.

Grief over Janey Rule's death was something that her parents shared. So was their love. Both moved to Everett in the early 1980s. They kept in touch. In 1989, they remarried.

The couple now lives in a modest duplex in central Everett. Robert Rule, 63, is a soft-spoken bear of a man who cultivates a long, grizzled beard that comes in handy while working winters as a Santa Claus at the Everett Mall. Linda Rule, 59, barely comes up to her husband's shoulder, but she is feisty, and prods him about with loving verbal barbs.

Their slain daughter's picture hangs on the wall above the television. Linda Rule treasures a coupon booklet the girl fashioned from envelopes in 1980. "This is to the best mom!" it reads on the cover. Inside are carefully penned offers of kindness from a girl who wanted to do good.

"If you don't feel like cooking dinner one night, just give this coupon to any Linda Jane Rule and you won't have to," one reads.

The Rules first learned their daughter's killer had been unmasked on the day before Halloween. A detective with the Green River Task Force called, summoning them to a private meeting in SeaTac. They were surprised because they'd long since thought their daughter's murder had been forgotten.

The meeting occurred the day before Ridgway's guilty pleas. The Rules said they were satisfied with what the detectives told them and the outcome.

A source of pain over the years has been that their daughter's death certificate did not specify how and when she died. Medical examiners simply could not tell. Detectives told the couple that is something they can now set right.

"We are getting a brand-new death certificate," Linda Rule said, dabbing away tears.

The Rules said they support King County Prosecuting Attorney Norm

Maleng's decision to trade away the chance for a death sentence for Ridgway in exchange for the man's dark secrets.

The Green River killer was like a hurricane, Robert Rule said, a storm of evil that ended the lives of at least 48 people and brought injury and misery to hundreds of others who loved them.

Now the storm is passed.

"The justice is he is off the street and can't hurt anyone else, or their families," Robert Rule said.

CHAPTER 12

Oklahoma City: "Terror in the Heartland"

In a single horrific event Oklahoma City illustrates vividly nearly every key point that this book has been making about human cruelty, its ramifications, and the vital role the media play in reporting and interpreting it all. This chapter tells a story that is at once terrible and inspiring. Much of the focus is through the eyes, minds, and hearts of the people at one newspaper and how they affected—and were affected by—a community and nation in shock and recovery.

9:02 A.M.

That morning was sunny. Most newsroom staffers at the *Daily Oklahoman* (today known simply as the *Oklahoman*) were well into their regular routines as they worked on stories for the next morning's edition. At 9:02 A.M. they heard a thunderous noise and the building shook. Joe Hight, the community editor, and reporters Ellie Sutter, Allison Day, Carla Hinton, and Bryan Painter looked out a window to see a fountain of dust bursting into the blue sky from the downtown area a few miles away.

One hundred sixty-eight men, women, and children died on the spot or within hours or days of the blast, which caved in a third of the nine-story federal building. Several structures near the Alfred P. Murrah Federal Building were heavily hit. Other damage was reported as far as fifteen miles from the blast.

The human damage appalled and stunned the city and nation. The final toll included 853 injured. Many victims worked for or were visiting one of the several federal agencies with offices in the building, such as the Social Security Administration, Secret Service, Veterans Administration, and Bureau of Alcohol, Tobacco, and Firearms.

On the second floor, though, most of the occupants in one area were much younger and smaller. They were the preschoolers in the building's day-care center, located just above the spot where the bomb exploded. The center had been built a few years earlier to give government workers a place to keep their children nearby and, they had reason to believe, safe. In addition to the nineteen children killed—fifteen in the day-care center and four elsewhere in the building—police ultimately calculated that thirty were orphaned and more than two hundred lost at least one parent.

INSTANT COVERAGE

The *Daily Oklahoman*'s coverage began literally before the dust had settled. The Murrah building was only about six miles from the newspaper's office, and reporters and photographers rushed to the scene. Staff writer Diana Baldwin went to the site with photographer Jim Argo; in her high heels she circled the smoking and burning building, listening to everything that went on. Reporter Clytie Bunyan already was close to the Murrah building when the bomb went off—too close. She was injured when the blast shook the nearby post office she was visiting. Off-duty reporters and editors automatically went to the office to begin shifts that seemed to never end.

"I have a lasting image of reporters clearing their throats and wiping away tears in order to write, edit, photograph, and create," says Editor Ed Kelley, who was managing editor at the time. "Maybe our readers did get to see that through our stories. They were written not only by talented people but by people who care about their community." Kelley notes that 150 newsroom employees worked overtime—copy messengers and clerks, reporters and editors, the fashion writer and the sports columnist, and management.

Coté and I have emphasized in this book that journalists should respect the privacy of victims and their families in any story. At best, it is a daunting effort to do that when thousands of people are directly or indirectly involved and a whole city and nation want to know what happened. Somehow, the *Daily Oklahoman* did it day after day and week after week, as the horror struck, sank in, and had to be faced in daily struggles for survival and recovery.

Having a formal policy about covering victims is always helpful, but in this case it was not necessary, Kelley says: "There was never any declaration from me or anyone else saying, 'This is how we'll treat these people who have been victimized.' There was a collective sense by our top editors and reporters that these are our people. These are people we send our kids to school with, attend church with."

Still, it was clear that to do their jobs the reporters and photographers had to contact survivors, their families, and friends at precisely the times they were suffering the most and might be most inclined to withdraw. Baldwin says she and her colleagues realized that, took it into account, and still got the necessary stories and pictures. "You have to be patient," she says. "You don't have to beat them over the head to get the story. In fact, you'll probably get the story that others wouldn't if you are patient."

That approach was especially helpful in the sad job of chronicling the deaths. Rather than run standard obituaries, the *Daily Oklahoman* published "profiles of life," one for each of the 168 people who died in the bombing. "We wanted these vignettes to focus more on their lives, not on their deaths," Kelley says.

One of the first profiles, by staff writer Jim Killackey, was of Michael Carillo, a forty-eight-year-old employee of the U.S. Department of Transportation. He was presumed dead, although his body had yet to be recovered from the rubble of the Murrah building. The story focused on his brother's search for dental records to help identify Michael when the time came and on his family and life: "He was a great American . . . who loved his country so very much," the brother told the paper. "Dr. Margaret Louise 'Peggy' Clark loved her horses and loved her kids," read the lead to one of the last profiles several weeks later that noted the life of a Department of Agriculture veterinarian. Between those accounts 166 other tributes told why the man, woman, or child was someone special, someone loved and missed.

The newspaper's staff had been divided into teams, the largest the Victims Team, led by Hight, who is now a managing editor. Reporters from community, sports, business, features, and other beats created the vignettes for each victim, a model followed by the *New York Times* and other newspapers after the September 11, 2001, attacks.

Gathering information for the profiles was part of a style of interviewing that emphasized knowledge of the deceased before contacting the family to ask for the interview and then talking about details of the person's life rather than effects of his or her death, as well as accepting that some people would not want to talk. Some staff members became friends of victims' families, relationships that everyone agreed were appropriate, so long as they were limited by a style of professional responsibility.

One victim who attracted much attention was among the youngest, year-old Baylee Almon. An AP photo that the *Daily Oklahoman* and thousands of other papers around the world printed on Page One showed a firefighter tenderly carrying the limp baby away from the bomb site. Not until the next day did the hospital confirm that little Baylee had died.

Baylee's picture became the most famous Oklahoma City photograph. Many others, though, played important roles in showing not only the massive destruction and grief but also the communal sharing of grief, outpourings of help and compassion, and the informal but heartrending shrines that people erected. Some of the most touching items in the shrines came from children. One photo showed a poster sent by Texas youngsters that read: "We care. For the children who left mommy's, daddy's, family & friends. . . . For the children who were left without mommy's, daddy's, family and friends. Love from children in Texas." It was decorated with pictures of teddy bears and flowers and signed by five children. Another picture showed a drawing by kindergartener Courtney Craig of a sad stick figure that said, "I'm sad because the building blew up."

One photo by staff photographer Steve Sisney even helped solve the mystery of what caused the death of Rebecca Anderson, a nurse. She was not in the explosion but was one of the first medical volunteers to enter the building afterward. She collapsed after leaving the rubble and died four days later in the hospital. The medical examiner finally determined that she had been struck in the head by falling concrete debris. Doctors said the positions of her hands in the photo told them she had suffered a neurological trauma. One more loss, although still painful, was given some closure.

The Daily Oklahoman served as the community's unofficial clearinghouse and coordinator in many ways after the bombing. Most immediately, the paper established a "Searching for Survivors" column in response to pleas from the state health department for help in counting those involved. The more than 225 published responses put the agency in contact with more survivors. Other special columns helped victims' families, survivors, and the public, including "How to Help," "How to Get Help," and "Acts of Kindness." For example, in one of the "Kindness" columns were notes about merchants, organizations, and individuals that provided coffee for rescue workers around the clock for several days and free long-distance phone calls for families directly affected. An internationally known portrait painter offered to paint a free portrait from a photograph of any child killed in the bombing.

Such stories and columns helped ameliorate the immediate immense problems that survivors and local and state officials faced as they tried to cope. The paper also helped survivors, families, and the whole community—however large that became—to understand more about what trauma does to people, especially when it is the result of deliberate human cruelty. Even the *Daily Oklahoman*'s section headings helped convey the information that trauma and recovery are a continuing process.

The first few days after the bombing the heading was "Terror in the Heartland." That was an appropriate label for the initial stages of a severe trauma, especially an intentional criminal act in an environment where people had felt safe from such an attack. For several weeks after that, the heading became "Together in the Heartland," as the paper chronicled how community members and organizations marshaled their resources to help others and themselves. That fits into the longer-term trauma recovery period when survivors of any event search for meaning and help in recovery.

For one of the "Together" pages a story by staff writer Bryan Painter focused on post-traumatic stress disorder (PTSD). Experts told how it can be harder for individuals, or a whole community, to recover from the shock of a violent criminal act than from a natural disaster such as an earthquake or tornado. Bruce Hiley-Young of the National Center for Post-Traumatic Stress Disorder in Palo Alto, California, offered the *Daily Oklahoman* this explanation of the difference: "People were confronted with the tearing away of the illusion of security. We don't generally feel the fear of our mortality. In Oklahoma City, that stopped happening, so people are vulnerable, unlike a natural disaster, because this was an intentional crime. That strikes a chord in people, a deep chord, so I think the recovery process will take longer" (Painter 1995:8).

Hiley-Young notes that dealing with the disillusionment stage varies according to the individuals and how much they are affected: "For the victims, it is not an issue of being mentally ill, rather it's an issue of having a normal response to an abnormal event." Dr. Ken Thompson, a psychiatrist at the University of Pittsburgh quoted in the same story, says: "It's important that the people who need to recover more slowly are not made to feel that there's something wrong with them" (Painter 1995:8).

The story was accompanied by a graphic that showed the four stages in the community's reaction to the disaster—"heroic," "honeymoon," "disillusionment," and "recovery"—and a "coping chart" listed eighteen things people might do to deal with their emotional aftershocks. Some suggestions were highly physical, such as "do strenuous exercise" and "eat well-balanced and regular meals." Others touched on psychological matters, such as alerting survivors that repeated dreams or flashbacks are normal and are likely to become less frequent and painful over time. The paper also told readers about seemingly trivial things that might increase their trauma, providing, for example, warnings about movies that had unusually violent content.

While working to help survivors and the community cope, the *Daily Oklahoman* also heeded the needs of its own people in several big and little ways. The paper made a therapist available to staffers for a year after the bombing, an opportunity that mostly attracted women. The women continued to meet and support each other in the months that followed. Right after the blast the paper relaxed its rules for its state-of-the-art newsroom, allowing pizza and other food to be brought in for those who were working long shifts.

Some staffers talked about their experiences or tried to. Clytie Bunyan, the reporter hurt at the post office who has since become business editor, recalls her anger when she tried to tell a colleague what had happened to her and she realized she "couldn't get through to him." A factual error in the story about her injury troubled her deeply. That happened even though the paper had assigned an editor specifically to avoid and correct errors, saving the *Daily Oklahoman* from publishing mistakes that might have added to distraught readers' trauma.

About two weeks after the bombing, Kelley, the managing editor, issued a staff memo in response to the fear some had that their work was not very important in the great scheme of things and that they were "trafficking in the misery of the victims' families." In the memo he noted that many staff members had had to do things that they were not trained for or prepared for, but he emphasized the kind of volunteer heroism they represented. "But you are among the only 170 or so people in a metropolitan area of 1 million who could, in depth, make sense of what happened, and why, and explain what lies ahead," he told them.

The *Daily Oklahoman* focused heavily and appropriately on the victims and survivors in its coverage, but the paper also demonstrated the need to report on the bombers, especially who they were not. Editors at the *Daily Oklahoman* made it clear that the paper had been determined to own two stories—the victims' story and the crime story. Indeed, the newspaper covered the investigations and trials to the hilt.

The way the paper covered the crime aspect, however, was deliberate. From the start the *Daily Oklahoman* sought not to focus on the culprit at the expense of losing the focus on those dead or suffering. It would have been easy—too easy—to go in the other direction. Much of the coverage elsewhere dwelt on who, or what, might be responsible. The *Daily Oklahoman* and other media in the city might be forgiven for being so angry that they would scream for the arrest and punishment of the bomber or bombers. At times they did and properly so. Whoever killed dozens outright and injured hundreds of others had to be found, both for justice and to ensure they could not strike again.

Early speculation after the bombing centered on a suspicion that Middle East terrorists were probably responsible for the Oklahoma City blast. After all, some Middle Eastern extremist groups had vowed for years to attack Americans. The *Daily Oklahoman* did not jump to that judgment, even when law enforcement personnel detained and questioned some Middle Eastern residents of the area.

Two days after the bombing, police and FBI officials arrested not an international terrorist but Timothy James McVeigh, a twenty-six-year-old former U.S. soldier. The bombing occurred on the second anniversary of the fiery destruction of the Branch Davidian compound near Waco, Texas. Authorities said McVeigh had shown "extreme anger" in regard to the government's handling of that situation, in which about eighty men, women, and children died after a fifty-one-day standoff.

As the story unfolded, the world learned a lot about McVeigh and those who worked with him or knew about his deadly plans. McVeigh's arrest, as well as significant subsequent developments in the investigation, were front-page news for many days. The *Daily Oklahoman* and other local media continued their intensive coverage through McVeigh's trial in Denver, his conviction, and execution. Other stories followed what happened to the two other men convicted in the case: Terry Nichols was sentenced to life without possibility of parole for conspiracy and involuntary manslaughter. Michael Fortier, the government's key witness in the case, drew a twelve-year prison term for not warning anyone about the plot and for lying to the FBI.

OTHER MEDIA

We have focused on the work of the *Daily Oklahoman* because it was the hometown paper and did so many things so well, but other coverage was extensive, of course. The bombing drew throngs of journalists from around Oklahoma, the United States, and the world. Most showed respect for the survivors and their need for privacy. Others did not.

City and state authorities quickly realized, literally before the dust and smoke had settled from the explosion, that media coverage would be intense. Journalists from around the world soon converged on Oklahoma City, seeking news and competitive advantages. The parachutists often push local media out of the way.

Two months later the *Daily Oklahoman* ran a story about a meeting of local officials held to reflect on the media coverage; most concluded it was a positive experience. In Oklahoma City, remarkably, officials said the local media set the stage early for the largely respectful coverage that soon prevailed. Media inquiries from around the nation at first often focused on such questions as how much looting was going on, Red Cross officials said. That tone changed within twenty-four hours, when national correspondents asked more about "the goodness of the community" (Hinton 1995:12).

The officials themselves also were important in encouraging that tone of respect and cooperation. Assistant Fire Chief Jon Hansen said that officials decided soon after the blast that reporters should be closer to the scene, not kept as far away as possible—something that often happens elsewhere. A big reason for the decision was that the public was becoming skeptical that rescue and recovery efforts were proceeding fast enough. "Things were going slow," Hansen said. "We felt it was necessary to get journalists into the building" (Hinton 1995:12). Pool reporters went in and came out to explain the laborious, careful work necessary to clear the debris.

John Cox, deputy press secretary to Frank Keating, then governor of Oklahoma, said that he received two hundred requests for interviews the first day. "This may have been the biggest spot news since the Kennedy assassination," Cox allowed. Police spokesman Bill Citty realized the tremendous media interest when he went to the first briefing and was confronted by seventy-five television cameras. "It scared me," he said. But dealing with the media turned out to be "a wonderful experience" overall. In the midst of the bombing horror "we also saw some of the kindest things" (Hinton 1995:12).

THE FAKE PRIEST AND OTHER FRAUDS

Not all media experiences were so wonderful for survivors and officials. Howard Witt and Hugh Dellios, whose column is syndicated through the *Chicago Tribune*, reported other types in a story that the *Daily Oklahoman* headlined "Local TV Disagrees with Tabloids." As Witt and Dellios put it: "In a city where not a single looter was reported to have ventured inside the five-square-block area of destruction, police were kept busy chasing out visiting tabloid reporters with a lust for exclusive gore" (1995:20). One visiting tabloid reporter donned a priest's vestments to try to sneak into a church where distraught relatives of bombing victims had been brought to await confirmation of the death of their loved ones. The "priest" was caught when someone noticed that he did not have the proper vestment belt in his disguise.

Another tabloid television reporter, Witt and Dellios recounted, posed as a firefighter in an attempt to shoot video inside the bombed-out federal building as workers pulled bodies from the rubble. He was charged with grand larceny, impersonating a firefighter, and obstruction of justice. Another reporter dressed as a firefighter was escorted from the area when someone noticed he was not wearing regular firefighting boots. He even had given interviews to other reporters as part of his ruse. Security guards had to chase out intrusive reporters even at the hospital where most of the critically wounded victims were being treated. As one camera crew from a national tabloid television program was escorted from the hospital, a reporter from a New York City newspaper slipped in behind (Witt and Dellios 1995:20).

By contrast, local and regional journalists had not mimicked the aggressive conduct of many in the national press. Oklahoma City television reporters read homespun poems to calm anxious viewers and skipped reading sports scores because they suddenly seemed frivolous. Jeff Gradney, then a reporter for KJRH–Channel 2 in Tulsa, did a story on his ex-wife's sister that he calls an ode. Her body was one of the first found in the ruins.

"Our philosophy is, we're not going to sensationalize this tragedy that truly happened to our own people," Michelle Fink, spokeswoman for Oklahoma City's NBC affiliate, KFOR-TV, told Witt and Dellios. When its reporters were not invited to funerals for bombing victims, the station stayed away. "We tried to imagine every story in terms of how we would react if we were the family," Fink said.

Even some national media stars came in for some criticism. Connie Chung drew heat from many viewers who thought she sounded condescending in an interview with Assistant Chief Hansen, the fire department's spokesman. The critics complained that Chung, then co-anchor of the *CBS Evening News,* seemed to disparage community leaders' resources and expertise in dealing with the disaster. The fire chief's calm, reasoned reply apparently satisfied many people that officials and the community generally were doing all that could be done.

No staffers at the *Daily Oklahoman* have said they were content with the paper's coverage of the bombing, but their peers have recognized the paper's skilled and compassionate reporting with several journalistic honors for stories, photos, or overall work, including the 1996 Dart Award for Excellence in Reporting on Victims of Violence.

In the weeks after the bombing there were 168 individual funerals, each precious to family and friends. In addition, two other events served in some important ways as funerals for all survivors and the national extended family of Oklahoma City. Both drew heavy, and largely respectful, news coverage.

One news event was the destruction of the remains of the Alfred P. Murrah Federal Building. Indeed, many people who viewed the implosion of the structure on May 24, 1995—about a month after the bombing—said they felt as if they were at a funeral. Some said they realized the demolition marked the end of one stage in the process of grieving and recovery from trauma. That is a milestone familiar to mental health professionals and generally a healthy sign that survivors are coping and functioning better.

Still, other communal "funerals" stirred even more emotions and more symbolism for any people on the long road to recovery from the bombing. In late October 1998 the fence around the building site was removed and ceremonially carried off by hundreds of survivors and family members. The fence had been studded with photographs of victims, flowers, posters, and letters. It was, in a very real sense, a shrine. The removal made way for construction of a permanent memorial, which features 168 empty concrete chairs and an interactive museum exhibit. (The Oklahoma City National Memorial was dedicated by President Bill Clinton on April 19, 2000. Both Coté and I have visited the site and noted the photographs, teddy bears, and other touching items on a remembrance wall.)

Each time, participants and onlookers said it seemed as if they had reached the end of another stage of recovery and the beginning of another. How many stages were still to come, or how long they would take, nobody could be sure.

The day after the fence came down, and about fifteen hundred miles away in New York City, visitors from around the nation were in the crowd outside the studios of a network morning television show. The program daily turns the cameras on the onlookers, most of whom are tourists, who often wave, cheer, or hold up signs addressed to the folks back home. This time the cameras zoomed in on a sign held by one little group. The sign said simply: "Oklahoma City Is OK."

CHAPTER 13

Conclusions

Throughout this book Coté and I have contended that covering violence is a challenging endeavor but one with few journalistic equals in compelling interest and potential benefit to the public and those who suffer physical and emotional trauma. We have provided a framework to help journalists prepare to interview, photograph, and write about people overwhelmed by violence. We have urged attention to those survivors of violence whose stories are often missing from media coverage. And we have emphasized the vulnerability of journalists to the traumatic effects of those they cover in violent events. Indeed, we have endorsed the profession's growing sense that journalists should be recognized as "first responders" in violent situations. Journalists often acknowledge that covering such a story is the toughest and most dangerous assignment they get.

Today's journalists have more potential power than ever. New ways to gather, process, and disseminate news would amaze and make envious journalists from earlier times. The media also now have the benefit of new insights into how people are affected by violence and human cruelty. It would be sad—and, we believe, indefensible—if journalists do not use that knowledge to devise new ways of covering victims and trauma.

We have noted that the public is often angry or bitter about news coverage that tramples and feeds on the raw emotions of people in trouble. Certainly, those critics think it is past time for the media to act differently. Many journalists apparently agree, considering the healthy soul searching and debate within the profession on the ethics and practical effects of such coverage. We have presented troubling examples of what we consider harmful coverage and held up inspiring illustrations of outstanding print and broadcast reporting.

Our aim is not to obstruct or hamper journalists. On the contrary, we want the profession we love to thrive and have the respect, trust, and support of those it serves. Treating with dignity and respect the suffering of people journalists encounter produces some of the most compelling human interest journalism ever crafted and earns the profession respect and trust.

For those already engaged in the "helping profession" of journalism, the knowledge and tools are at hand. For those entering the field, great opportunities lie ahead to influence and shape this important aspect of journalism. In these final paragraphs, we show how the ideas about journalists and trauma are relevant to recent events.

AFTER THE MILLENNIUM AND 9/11

Men and women engaged in journalism since 2001 have shared our sense that the craft faces new demands for excellence. The values of accuracy, thoroughness, and fairness have not lost respect. Twenty-first-century journalists, though, must keep at the forefront of their efforts an awareness that the world they cover, and that they present to readers and viewers, has dangerous new elements. The training and practices of journalists—salaried and freelance—and news organizations now incorporates ideas that likely were given short shrift before 9/11. Let's examine some ideas that will resonate through the work of journalists in the years to come.

DANGEROUS ASSIGNMENTS

Danger has always shadowed the work of journalists. Not until recently, however, has the risk become a topic of national and international news coverage. Daniel Pearl, the South Asia bureau chief for the *Wall Street Journal,* was murdered in 2002 after being kidnapped in Karachi, Pakistan, where he was tracking the terrorism story. For five weeks international media reported on the extensive search for Pearl and his kidnappers and then on the murder, which had been videotaped, shown in part on network television, and moved swiftly to the Internet. Pearl's defiance of his captors provided all journalists with an example of courage. Pearl's widow, Mariane, who traveled into dangerous areas with Daniel in her work as a documentary producer, wrote of his conviction about going into dangerous places:

> War held no appeal for Danny or for me. What interested us was the challenge presented by peace. People often see peace as the simple absence of war, but it

is instead the result of courageous actions taken to initiate a dialogue between civilizations. Both Danny and I saw our profession as a way to contribute to the dialogue, to allow voices on all sides to be heard, and to bear witness.

(Pearl 2003:59)

Journalists learned several lessons from Pearl's death. First, the unfolding drama showed that journalists were risking their lives in pursuit of the many threads of interest connected to terrorist actions around the world. And, in many cases, the reporters and photographers were in dangerous places without direct support from news companies. Freelance journalists lacked even the support that major news organizations were providing to their correspondents in the field. Correspondents going into unsettled regions were taking safety courses, and in a growing number of cases they were learning about the traumatic risks of the work they faced. One of Pearl's most important legacies is a heightened awareness among journalists and the public about the dangers of news work.

Journalists within the United States work in the shadows of both the Oklahoma City bombing and the attacks on September 11, 2001, and with reminders of urban terrorism in recent years in Madrid, London, and Bali, Indonesia. The dangers inherent in working in cities should always have been emphasized in training and staff management; now, they are critical parts of such training—or should be.

Covering War

The U.S. and allied invasions of Afghanistan and Iraq in 2002 and 2003 pressed hometown journalists into war coverage to a degree not experienced in the first Gulf war in 1991. Television stations and midsize newspapers dispatched staff members to the war zone, usually as journalists embedded in military units. Critics contended that journalists attached to military units gained only a limited view of the war experience, while many of those journalists produced or wrote fascinating reports about what soldiers and marines encountered. An author of a collection of oral histories taken from embedded correspondents observed:

Correspondents still found moments of truth and poignancy, even while failing to account for mounting civilian deaths or aggressively challenging the Bush Administration's pretext about taking out those elusive weapons of mass destruction. Some of the best reporting defied whatever spin the

Pentagon tried to achieve when lethal mistakes were made on the battlefield, because an embedded journalist was there taking notes. Nor could the military muzzle its soldiers who spoke openly around embeds.

(Katovsky and Carlson 2003:xix)

The war, expanded by insurgent forces using guerrilla tactics and the potent device of the suicide bomb, drew some correspondents back to Iraq for second, and even third, assignments. In the process some journalists, trained to cover urban beats, not the military at war, found themselves in a new emotional relationship with those serving the United States in the military. Reporters grieved as casualty lists named marines or soldiers they had befriended and respected. Indeed, grief at war deaths and injuries became a theme of news coverage. In city after city journalists reported the life accomplishments of the men and women from their communities who had been killed in military action. Journalists also died covering the war. By January 2006 sixty-one journalists from around the world had died in Iraq, according to the Committee to Protect Journalists.

We suspect that emotional injury among troops got more coverage than in any previous war. Journalists too acknowledged some of the emotional stress of reporting on combat and on the insurgent attacks that often killed and maimed civilians. The war-reporting searchlight fell on torture when floods of still photos showing torture of Iraqi prisoners by U.S. military personnel at the Abu Ghraib prison surfaced. While readers and viewers grappled with the reality that Americans had been torturing prisoners, journalists paid attention to the emotional aftermath of torture for its victims.

More and Better Training

The training of journalists is changing in significant ways in the first decade of the new century. Assignment to Iraq was preceded by hostile-environment training for correspondents and photographers assigned to military units. Information about trauma was generally missing from such sessions or was scarcely mentioned. An important exception was the British Broadcasting Corporation, which provided its international correspondents with detailed information about emotional injury and began a program to expand such training for all personnel. Journalism educators began to teach about trauma, but it appeared that most graduates of journalism schools continued to take their first jobs without special training about emotional risks.

Support for Journalists

The 9/11 attacks in New York and Washington forced news organizations to pay attention to providing support for staff members, especially those closest to the violence, deaths, and destruction. Murders of staff members on international assignment affected domestic colleagues deeply, leading many companies to bring therapists to the newsroom and to address employee needs directly. We have witnessed newsroom gatherings in which staffers talked directly and candidly to editors about the stresses of a recent major event, a healthy response that has been rare in recent years.

A FINAL WORD

The most effective journalist is one who understands the risks of her or his work, has been trained well for that work, and is confident of the support of employers or others during and after coverage of violent events. Those who describe the character of the world for readers and viewers deserve the best training and support possible. The profession has begun to respond to the risks of traumatic injury; there is a long way to go to provide the kind of healthy, resilient news corps that democracy requires.

Hurricanes that thundered across the Gulf of Mexico in the late summer and autumn of 2005 to batter Texas, Louisiana, Mississippi, Florida, Alabama, and Mexico reminded the profession of the dire need for attention to the emotional health of journalists. Hurricanes Katrina, Rita, and Wilma killed hundreds, forced thousands to move elsewhere after their lifelong homes had been destroyed, and left one of the country's most valued cities—New Orleans—under water for weeks.

Journalists rose to the demands of the disaster, some enduring exhausting and dangerous conditions to cover the story. The *New Orleans Times-Picayune*, a newspaper respected for the important role it has long played in the politics and culture of Louisiana, lost its newsroom when the city flooded after Katrina's rampage weakened the levees that guard the low-lying residential areas of the city. Coté and I believe that the storm was one of journalism's finest hours, in large part because photographers and reporters got painfully close to the suffering of people hurt by the storms. Journalism also caught with remarkable clarity the anger of Americans—and not just that of those hit directly by the hurricanes—at the failures of state and federal emergency services. News gatherers linked the failures of leadership and emotional stress in informative ways. Frank Ochberg, the psychiatrist, told us, "Sometimes the story was about those in power and those who were powerless, and sometimes [it was about] the force of nature. I don't think it hurt one bit for news anchors to have tears in their eyes and to be shaken themselves. They were part of the portrait and told the story with humanity and with dignity."

As the last words in this book are written, it is too early to know the impact on the emotions and mental health of people who suffered in the hurricanes, including the journalists who covered the storms even as they lost their homes, possessions, and loved ones and faced the loss of their jobs. The dignity of all who endured those disasters serves the profession as a reminder both the human capacity for recovery and resilience and the moral requirement for journalists to be ready to tell that story.

GUIDELINES FOR JOURNALISTS
WHO COVER VIOLENCE

Understanding Traumatic Injury

- Expect a range of emotional responses from witnesses and survivors.
- Share control with people who have suffered trauma.
- Do not say that a person has post-traumatic stress disorder (PTSD) unless you have a medical confirmation and the person's permission.
- Know the three symptoms of severe emotional injury—intrusive memories, heightened anxiety, and avoidance of reminders.
- Expect that anger and shame may be part of a person's response to a traumatic event.

Coping with Traumatic Events

- Remind yourself that you will see and hear things for which you are not prepared.
- Concentrate on the tasks at hand. Managing details carefully may help alleviate the stress of the event.
- Remember that a calm demeanor will be helpful to people affected by an event; when interviewing or photographing people in this situation, concentrate on their words and maintain eye contact.
- Find a way to talk about what you've seen and heard, and about your emotional responses, after the assignment.
- Consider contacting a therapist if symptoms persist.

Reporting on Terrorism

- Remember that the terrorists want to undermine resolve, create fears, and destabilize life in the civilian population.
- Bear in mind that of all the images that television showed on September 11, 2001, those of people falling or jumping from the towers were most closely associated with self-reported symptoms of PTSD or depression.
- Keep warnings about terrorism in perspective but provide as much information as is available.
- Avoid "scare reporting" of incidents that may reflect terrorist actions when the evidence is not definitive.
- Be respectful when reporting on people who die or are injured in terror attacks; they deserve sensitive accounts of their lives.
- Anticipate the emotional drain of your work if you are assigned to interview survivors and write about the victims. Monitor your reactions.
- Recognize the changes that 9/11 made in Americans' assumptions about life and safety. Be aware of those changes in yourself and the people you report for.

Advance Preparations by Management

- Have a plan for moving a newsroom when it is damaged or threatened; all members of a staff should know alternative contacts in case a newsroom is damaged or unreachable.
- Make advance plans for alternative means of communication. Because cell phones may not work, the staff will need another way to stay in contact with editors and managers. Have a plan—or at least enough fresh batteries on hand to power those walkie-talkies in the closet.
- Identify in advance staffers who would be suited to the task of monitoring their coworkers' emotional state. Prepare for ways to gain relief for overworked reporters (have meals delivered to the newsroom) and to provide activities that can contribute to staff morale (staff gatherings to show how challenges were handled).
- Keep available up-to-date copies of the *Emergency Response Guidebook, 2004: A Guidebook for First Responders During the Initial Phase of a Dangerous Goods/Hazardous Materials Incident*, prepared by the U.S. Department

of Transportation. It lists chemical hazards, recommends distances from the chemical, and provides first aid instructions.

- Arrange for advance safety training and lessons on self-care for reporters who may be sent to assignments in a distant place. These reporters should also be discussing effective ways to cover a changing event with editors and other reporters.

Reporting at the Scene of Violence

- Be aware that local public safety planning for tragic events should consider who will respond, what needs will be urgent, and what long-term help the community will require.
- Discuss with peers and editors how to balance job duties and how to respond to those in need at the scene—whether to help, interview, or leave people alone.
- Recognize the dangers associated with dispersal of chemical or biological agents. Learn about the risks before approaching the scene.
- Be sure that your communication equipment is working and available to reporters and photographers, and the media organization should have a plan for how staffers in the field will communicate with editors and other reporters.
- Take note of your own emotional reactions, appreciate that the intensity of reporting may delay those reactions, and know ways to address emotions when they surface.
- Respect the impact of trauma on people at the scene; they may be disoriented and have difficulty expressing themselves.
- Check with authorities before telling viewers that a devastated area has particular needs; one person's cry for a blanket can lead to mountains of donated but unneeded blankets.

Making the Interview Sensitive and Effective

- Respect the other person's efforts to regain balance after a horrible experience.
- Be careful about conveying secondhand information in the interview—both to the interviewee and to readers and viewers.

- Respect the other person's need to focus on her or his present circumstances.
- Set the stage for the interview by carefully informing the person about your identity, your reasons for doing the interview, and how the interview might be used.
- Explain the ground rules.
- Share as much control with the interviewee as possible.
- Anticipate emotional responses, and allow the subject to make decisions about stopping or temporarily halting the interview.
- Listen carefully.
- Review the salient points of the interview with the subject.
- Take time to assess any personal response to the interview and discuss that response with others.
- Keep these guidelines in mind when doing anniversary interviews.

Writing About Survivors of Trauma

- Bear in mind that accuracy is essential if the reporter on a story about a survivor is to retain his or her trust and that of the survivor's family and friends.
- Avoid repeating the details of an assault or other tragedy weeks or months later unless good reason exists for doing so.
- Avoid the shorthand words—*prostitute, homeless*—that stereotype and detract from the complexity of a person's life.
- Build the story on details carefully chosen to humanize and give dignity to the subject of the profile.
- Consider how graphic details will affect survivors when considering which ones to use. Is the detail essential to telling the story?
- Look for opportunities to tell Act II stories, the accounts of resilient individuals who have found ways to respond to traumatic injury.
- Look for ways to build social context into reporting about individuals.

Pictures and Sounds of Trauma

- Do not knowingly allow a live broadcast of a killing, whether homicide or suicide, especially in close-up and showing wounds and blood.

- Build in a delay of several seconds during live transmissions to allow managers to make a decision about whether to show something.
- Insist that photographers and photo and graphics editors join other editors or news directors in deciding which images to air or publish.
- Be sure relatives have been notified before announcing or showing the identity of a person who has been killed.
- Give viewers of television news reports enough advance warning of what they are about to see so that someone can leave the room, remove children, or change the channel.
- Remember that children may be able to see a photo in a newspaper left lying around or may watch a television report when adults have left the television on.
- Think about the relative effects of photos published on the front page and inside pages of a newspaper, as well as of images in color versus in black-and-white. Something that might be too graphic for someone (especially a child) glancing at a front page could be less troublesome inside.
- Tell the whole story—before, during, and after—of what happened to the human being involved, not just the death, no matter what photos or footage are used.
- Show tape of a death or other traumatic event once if it meets standards, but do not use file tape in subsequent telecasts.
- Discuss the decision, how it affected survivors and the public, and whether the staff should have handled anything differently as soon as deadline pressures ease. The more discussion there is of these experiences, the more likely a news organization is to avoid thoughtless miscues in the future.
- Do not assume that these, or any other guidelines or policies, will save anyone from agonizing about what to show and not show. They will not and perhaps should not.

We also urge news organizations to recognize that their photographers are the most vulnerable of all employees to traumatic injury and that editors endure an emotional wallop when they view a stream of graphic, troubling images, few of which will reach the public. Teams and their managers can agree that it is alright to switch monitors off, or at least to look away, when a particularly graphic feed is coming in. That sensitivity should apply to sound, which can be heard throughout an editing room, as well as images. Finally, those who must view or hear troubling images should be encouraged to take frequent breaks outside the workroom.

Reporting About Children

- Do not assume that children are emotionally well after a traumatic event, even though they may appear to be responding normally.
- Avoid actions at the scene that may frighten children. Cameras and microphones can be intimidating. Even a journalist's scowl may communicate fear to a watching child.
- Avoid making an attractive or available child witness or survivor into a "poster child."
- Involve the child and his or her parents in your discussion about what you are reporting and how you are doing it.

Most victims of abuse find it empowering to tell a reporter about their experience. They may find disclosure uncomfortable in the short term but over time will value being interviewed. Reporters have who covered abuse cases have offered these suggestions for interviewing survivors:

- Decide on a policy about naming victims and apply it fairly. In the priest sexual abuse scandal, the *Boston Globe* promised anonymity to any victim who requested it.
- Find supporting evidence for stories of abuse before publishing the name of an allegedly abusive adult.
- Approach survivors carefully, looking for evidence of ability to cope with the emotional pain of disclosure. Doing interviews will not help some survivors. Indeed, the interview may do more harm than good.
- Begin the interview with a careful explanation of ground rules, including such matters as whether the person will be named and how the interview will be used.
- Allow the survivor to stipulate the rules for his or her participation, including having a therapist or other representative present during the interview.
- Do not revisit courtroom testimony that may cause the survivor more pain.
- Focus the interview on the survivor's efforts to recover from the abuse, rather than on the abuses.
- Provide information about support groups and agencies that assist survivors, because reports of abuse of children move other victims to speak out. Provide lists of books, articles, Web sites, and videos that can help a person find help or decide how and whether to speak about such a personal experience.

Reporting About Rape

- Put the case in the context of patterns of sexual crimes in the community and state. At times, report these patterns as stories in their own right.
- Avoid ways of describing details that reinforce stereotypes.
- Include details that may help others avoid assault.
- Mention details that get across the seriousness and horror of the crime.
- Name local agencies that help survivors and families and explain state laws on sexual offenses.

Using the Searchlight

- Recognize the vitality and resiliency in all communities. Honor the diversity of experiences in every group, and disdain easy assumptions about whether people are able to cope with their conditions.
- Respect the wisdom represented in often-neglected communities and regularly include their members in stories.
- Seek ways to enable people to tell of their experiences.
- Trust the authentic voice of a person who has experienced difficult conditions.
- Report about subtle as well as obvious forms of prejudice, but learn about both from the perspective of people who see them as threats in their own lives.
- Beware of news conventions that routinely provide a political or religious "balance" to stories but end up serving only to demean what the victim has said.
- Respect people's desire for silence, but do more to encourage those who want to speak to tell their stories with your help.

THE DART AWARD FOR EXCELLENCE IN REPORTING ON VICTIMS OF VIOLENCE

Since 1994 the Dart Award has recognized exemplary newspaper reports on violence and its victims. The recipients have included staff efforts—the reporting by the *Daily Oklahoman* of the aftermath of the bombing of the Oklahoma City federal building in 1995—as well as outstanding team and individual efforts. Awards for radio and television reporting about victims were planned as this book went to press.

The $10,000 award is administered by the Dart Center for Journalism and Trauma at the University of Washington in Seattle.

Winners of the Dart Award

2005: "Homicide in Detroit: Echoes of Violence," *Detroit Free Press*. A six-part series that takes a deep look at the impact of homicide on family, police, bystanders, and the city itself. Honorable mentions: *Orange County (Calif.) Register* and *Rocky Mountain News* of Denver.

2004: "Rape in a Small Town," *Providence (R.I.) Journal*. The story of a fifteen-year-old girl raped by a classmate and of the devastating aftermath for her, her family, and her town. Honorable Mention: *Seattle Post-Intelligencer*.

2003: "Legacy of Love & Pain," *Houston Chronicle*. The story of Angela Hudson, who barely survived after her estranged husband set her on fire, and of the effects of the attack on her family. Honorable Mention: *Austin American-Statesman*.

2002: "The Short Life of Viktor Alexander Matthey," *(Newark, N.J.) Star Ledger*. For an article depicting the unhappy life of a Siberian boy whose violent death is told against the larger story of his birth parents, the orphanage in

Russia that briefly shelters him, and his abusive adoptive parents in America. Honorable Mentions: *Detroit Free Press, Orange County (Calif.) Register, St. Paul Pioneer Press.*

2001: "The Joseph Palczynski Story," *Baltimore Sun.* A two-part series on the lives of six women serially victimized by one man's extremes of physical and psychological abuse. A team of writers makes domestic violence—in some ways an invisible trauma—visible to readers. Honorable Mention: *(Newark, N.J.) Star-Ledger.*

2000: "Who Killed John McCloskey?" *Roanoke(Va.) Times.* For its compelling series on the suspicious death of an eighteen-year-old arrested and placed in the care of a mental institution, the cover-up that followed, and the family's grief and confusion. Honorable Mentions: *Denver Post* and *Rocky Mountain News* of Denver.

1999: "A Stolen Soul," *Portland (Maine) Press Herald.* For the sensitive and thorough portrayal of Yong Jones's struggle to bring her son's murderer to justice against the backdrop of her cultural beliefs. Honorable mention: *Palm Beach (Fla.) Post.*

1998: "Children of the Underground," *Pittsburgh Post-Gazette.* For the complex and unsettling account of the hidden network that shelters youngsters escaping from sexual or physical abuse at home—real or alleged—and from a judicial system perceived as unwilling or unable to help them. Honorable mentions: *Westword* of Denver and *Nashville Banner.*

1997: "The Path of a Bullet," *(Long Beach, Calif.) Press-Telegram.* For its chronicle of the toll that a single 22-cent bullet exacted on individual victims and the broader community. Honorable mention: *Sunday (Milwaukee) Journal Sentinel.*

1996: *Daily (Oklahoma City) Oklahoman.* For its extensive coverage of the aftermath of the bombing of the Alfred P. Murrah Federal Building, coverage that helped readers connect to the lives of individual victims, survivors, and families.

1995: "The Test of Fire," *Austin American-Statesman.* For its unsentimental focus on Emmett Jackson's recovery from the arson death of his wife and child and his own extensive injuries. Honorable mention: *(Munster, Ind.) Times.*

1994: "Malignant Memories," *Anchorage Daily News.* For documenting the spirited growth of three women as they transcend the tragedies of incest that have haunted their lives. Honorable mentions: *Orlando Sentinel, Sheboygan (Mich.) Daily Tribune, San Francisco Chronicle,* and *(Long Beach, Calif.) Press-Telegram.*

A NOTE ABOUT TRAUMA TRAINING

Learning about trauma can be stressful, for journalism students as well as working professionals who have experienced violence themselves or seen too much of it as part of their work.

Coté and I want to alert editors and instructors to some problems in training others about trauma and to suggest how to handle stressful reactions.

When we teach about trauma in the university classroom, we tell students that some people may find the subject too intense and may want to leave then or later. We try to take some of the edge off unexpected feelings of anxiety by saying in advance that in any group of fifteen to twenty students, one or more is likely to have suffered some form of trauma. (We also tell the students about the trauma training at least one class session in advance. Those who miss the training often give us some clue to their reasons, and invariably they have gone through a trauma that still troubles them.)

We tell students that if they have unanticipated reactions, we can talk with them informally during or after the session or connect them with someone who can provide formal support. Both of us have experienced a student's suddenly leaving the room in tears or later disclosing a strong, unsettling reaction to the training. It is important to have a training team so that one member can talk to the person who is upset by the training while another instructor continues with the class. A therapist can give that needed support during class sessions or train the instructor to deal effectively with students' emotional reactions.

The Victims and the Media Program at the Michigan State University School of Journalism introduces students in the first-level reporting course to the subject through printed materials, lectures, and videos in which professional actors portray victims. In the advanced news-writing course volunteer survivors appear in person to tell their stories and to be interviewed.

The journalism program in the University of Washington Department of Communication enables all students to do one or more interviews with a professional actor who is playing the part of a person who has experienced trauma. The interviews, carefully monitored by instructors who then offer supportive coaching, follow a session that simply orients journalism students to the nature of trauma and its effects on the people they interview. We know of schools that enlist actors to train drama students to take roles in an unfolding stressful situation.

Both our programs provide time for discussion after each class session. In all these training situations students may suffer unwanted reactions.

Editors who want to conduct in-house trauma workshops for staffers may wish to consider somewhat similar precautions. Even journalists who think they handle stress well sometimes find themselves affected when the topic is discussed openly.

Many newspapers and broadcast stations have a consulting psychologist available who can also be asked to assist in the training. If the company does not have a regular consultant, we recommend one be made available for at least the workshop period.

Introduce the information gradually, allowing ample time for questions and comments. A common reaction when the topic of trauma is raised without adequate preparation is that some listeners simply "close down," overwhelmed by the ideas discussed. Let participants know well in advance what will be discussed and provide breaks in the training for conversation, stretching, or refreshments.

In short, we believe journalists and students need to learn about trauma and violence, but we are equally eager not to harm them in the doing.

RESOURCES FOR JOURNALISTS

Committee to Protect Journalists, www.cpj.org.

Dart Center for Journalism and Trauma. www.dartcenter.org.

———. *Tragedies and Journalists*. www.dartcenter.org/articles/books/tragedies.html (August 10, 2005). Booklet covers risks for first responders, describes traumatic injury, and offers tips for journalists who cover violence.

International News Safety Institute, www.newssafety.com.

International Society for Traumatic Stress Studies, www.istss.org.

Journalism Training, www.journalismtraining.org.

National Center for Post-Traumatic Stress Disorder, www.ncptsd.va.gov.

National Center for Victims of Crime, www.ncvc.org.

National Child Traumatic Stress Network, www.nctsn.org.

Victims and the Media Program, www.victims.jrn.msu.edu.

———. *Reporting on Victims of Violence and Catastrophe*. 1999. Videotape produced by Michigan State University School of Journalism. Available at www.victims.jrn.msu.edu/public/videos.html (October 4, 2005).

BIBLIOGRAPHY

Adams, Eddie. 1998. "Eulogy." *Time,* July 27, p. 19.

Ahem, Jennifer et al. 2002. "Television Images and Psychological Symptoms after the September 11 Terrorist Attacks." *Psychiatry* 65 (4): 289–301.

Aiken, Charlotte. 1996. "Reporters Are Victims, Too." *Nieman Reports* 50 (3): 30–32.

Anderson, Michael C. et al. 2004. "Neural Systems Underlying the Suppression of Unwanted Memories." *Science,* January 9, 2004, pp. 232–35.

Balakian, Peter. 1997. *Black Dog of Fate: A Memoir.* New York: Basic Books.

Benedict, Helen. 1992. *Virgin or Vamp: How the Press Covers Sex Crimes.* New York: Oxford University Press.

———. 1994. *Recovery: How to Survive Sexual Assault for Women, Men, Teenagers, Their Friends, and Families.* New York: Columbia University Press.

Biagi, Shirley. 1992. *Interviews That Work: A Practical Guide for Journalists.* 2d ed. Belmont, Calif.: Wadsworth.

Bloom, S. L. 1997. *Creating Sanctuary: Toward an Evolution of Sane Societies.* New York: Routledge.

Bloom, S. L. and Michael Reichert. 1998. *Bearing Witness: Violence and Collective Responsibility.* New York: Haworth Maltreatment and Trauma Press.

Borden, S. L. 1993. "Empathic Listening: The Interviewer's Betrayal." *Journal of Mass Media Ethics* 8 (4): 219–26.

Brady, John. 1977. *The Craft of Interviewing.* New York: Vintage.

Braestrup, Peter. 1985. *Battle Lines.* New York: Priority Press.

Bragg, Rick. 1997. *All over but the Shoutin'.* New York: Pantheon.

Brownmiller, Susan. 1975. *Against Our Will: Men, Women, and Rape.* New York: Simon and Schuster.

Buchanan, Edna. 1987. *The Corpse Had a Familiar Face.* New York: Charter Books.

Bull, Chris and Sam Erman. 2002. *At Ground Zero: Young Reporters Who Were There Tell Their Stories.* New York: Thunder's Mouth Press.

Bull, Chris and Elana Newman. 2003. "Covering Terrorism." *Dart Center for Journalism and Trauma.* www.dartcenter.org/resources/selfstudy/2_terrorism/index.html (August 10, 2005).

Bureau of Justice Statistics. 1998. *Violence Against Women Survey.* Washington, D.C.: U.S. Department of Justice. Cited in Illinois Coalition Against Sexual Assault, "Adult Victims of Sexual Assault," p. 1n1, available at http://www.icasa.org/uploads/adult_victimss.pdf (October 7, 2005).

Burgess, A. W., ed. 1985. *Rape and Sexual Assault: A Research Handbook.* New York: Garland.

————. 1988. *Rape and Sexual Assault II.* New York: Garland.

————. 1991. *Rape and Sexual Assault III: A Research Handbook.* New York: Garland.

————. 1992. *Child Trauma I: Issues and Research.* New York: Garland.

Burgess, A. W. and L. L. Holmstrom. 1979. *Rape, Crisis, and Recovery.* Bowie, Md.: R. J. Brady.

Butterfield, Fox. 1991. "What the Media All Missed." *FineLine,* July–August, pp. 1, 5.

Butterfield, Fox and Mary B. W. Tabor. 1991. "Woman in Florida Rape Inquiry Fought Adversity and Sought Acceptance." *New York Times,* April 17, p. A17.

Carey, James W. 1987. "Why and How: The Dark Continent of American Journalism." In Robert Manoff and Michael Schudson, eds., *Reading the News.* New York: Pantheon.

Casey, Ginger. 1994. "When a Job Rips Out Your Heart." *Radio-Television News Directors Association Communicator,* September, pp. 37–38.

Casey Journalism Center on Children and Families. 2002. "Coverage in Context: How Thoroughly the News Media Report Five Key Children's Issues." University of Maryland, College Park, February 2002.

CBS. 2002. *9/11.* DVD. Directed by Jules Naudet and Gedeon Naudet. Paramount Home Video. First broadcast March 10.

Collins, P. H. 1991. *Black Feminist Thought: Knowledge, Consciousness, and the Politics of Empowerment.* New York: Routledge.

Coté, William and Bonnie Bucqueroux. 1996. "Tips on Interviewing Victims." *Nieman Reports* 50 (3): 27.

Covering Columbine. 2001. Produced by Marguerite Moritz. Dart Center for Journalism and Trauma and University of Colorado School of Journalism and Mass Communication.

Cox, Christy. 2003. "Abuse in the Catholic Church." *Dart Center for Journalism and Trauma.* www.dartcenter.org/articles/special_features/church_abuse.htm (August 8, 2005).

Crist, Gabrielle 2000. "Eric's Blessing." *Fort Worth Star-Telegram,* October 1–6, 2000.

Crowell, N. A. and A. W. Burgess, eds. 1996. *Understanding Violence Against Women.* Panel on Research on Violence Against Women, Committee on Law and Justice, Commission on Behavioral and Social Sciences and Education, National Research Council. Washington, D.C.: National Academy Press.

Dart Center for Journalism and Trauma. 2005. "Covering the Tsunami: A Frontline Club Discussion." www.dartcenter.org/articles/special_features/frontline_tsunami.html (August 10, 2005).

De La Cruz, Ralph. 1996. "Path of a Bullet." *(Long Beach, Calif.) Press-Telegram,* November 10, pp. K1–12.

Deppa, Joan, Maria Russel, Donna Hayes, and Elizabeth Flocke. 1993. *The Media and Disasters: Pan Am 103.* London: Fulton.

Dezern, Craig. 1993. "The Miracle of Philip Chandler." *Orlando Sentinel,* December 26, *Florida* magazine special edition.

Dorfman, Lori, Katie Woodruff, Vivan Chavez, and Lawrence Wallack. 1997. "Youth and Violence on Local Television News in California." *American Journal of Public Health* 87 (August): 1311–16.

Fadiman, Ann. 1997. *The Spirit Catches You and You Fall Down: A Hmong Child, Her American Doctors, and the Collision of Two Cultures.* New York: Farrar, Straus, and Giroux.

Fancher, Michael. 2004. "Powerful Photograph Offered Chance to Tell an Important Story." *Seattle Times,* April 18, p. 2.

Feinstein, Anthony. 2003. *Dangerous Lives: War and the Men and Women Who Report It.* Toronto: Thomas Allen.

Feinstein, Anthony, John Owen, and Nancy Blair. 2002. "A Hazardous Profession: War, Journalists and Psychopathology." *American Journal of Psychiatry* 159 (September): 1570–75.

Figley, C. R., ed. 1985. *Trauma and Its Wake.* New York: Brunner/Mazel.

———. 1995. *Compassion Fatigue: Coping with Secondary Traumatic Stress Disorder in Those Who Treat the Traumatized.* New York: Brunner/Mazel.

Figley, Charles, Brian Bride, and Nicholas Mazza, eds. 1997. *Death and Trauma: The Traumatology of Grieving.* Washington, D.C.: Taylor and Francis.

Fischer, H. W. III. 1994. *Response to Disaster: Fact versus Fiction and Its Perpetuation: The Sociology of Disaster.* Lanham, Md.: University Press of America.

Forster, Stacy. 2002. "As It Became Ground Zero." In Chris Bull and Sam Erman, eds., *At Ground Zero: 25 Stories from Young Reporters Who Were There.* New York: Thunder's Mouth Press.

Freedom Forum. 1998. *Jonesboro: Were the Media Fair?* booklet, n.p.

Freinkel, Andrew, Cheryl Koopman, and David Spiegel. 1994. "Dissociative Symptoms in Media Eyewitnesses of an Execution." *American Journal of Psychiatry* 151 (September): 1335–39.

Fussell, Paul. 1989. *Wartime: Understanding and Behavior in the Second World War.* New York: Oxford University Press.

Gaffney. Donna. 1999. "Interviewing Children: How to Capture Their Words and Tell Their Stories." *Children's Beat,* Summer, pp. 24–26.

Gannett Foundation Media Center. 1991. *The Media at War.* New York: Gannett Foundation.

Gassaway, Bob. 1989. "Making Sense of War: An Autobiographical Account of a Vietnam War Correspondent." *Journal of Applied Behavior Science* 25 (4): 327–49.

Gavit, John Palmer. 1903. *The Reporter's Manual: A Handbook for Newspapermen.* Albany, N.Y.: Author.

Gilbert, Allison, Phil Hirschkorn, Melinda Murphy, Robyn Walensky, and Mitchell Stephens. 2002. *Covering Catastrophe: Broadcast Journalists Report September 11.* Chicago: Bonus Books.

Gilliland, Mary A. 1998. Letter to the editor. *TV Guide,* Flint-Lansing, Mich., ed., May 23, p. 86.

Glaberson, William. 1991. "Times Article Naming Rape Accuser Ignites Debate on Journalistic Values." *New York Times,* April 26, p. A14.

Goldstein, Arnold P. 1996. *Violence in America.* Palo Alto, Calif.: Davies-Black.

Goldstein, Tom. 1998. "Dramatic Footage, Yes—But Is It News?" *TV Guide,* May 23, 1998, p. 41.

Goleman, Daniel. 1995. *Emotional Intelligence.* New York: Bantam.

Gordon, M. T. and Stephanie Riger. 1989. *The Female Fear.* New York: Free Press.

Greenfeld, Lawrence. 1997. *Sex Offenses and Offenders: An Analysis of Data on Rape and Sexual Assault.* Washington, D.C.: U.S. Department of Justice, Bureau of Justice Statistics. Cited in Illinois Coalition Against Sexualt Assault, "Adult Victims of Sexual Assault," p. 10n75, available at http://www.icasa.org/uploads/adult_victimss.pdf (October 7, 2005).

Guillén, Tomás. 1990. "Privacy and the Media amid the Serial Killer Phenomenon: A Case Study of the Green River Serial Murders." Master's thesis, Communications Department, University of Washington, Seattle.

Halstead, Dirck. 2004. "Bill Biggart's Final Exposures." DigitalJournalist.org. www.digitaljournalist.org/issue0111/biggart_intro.htm (October 5, 2005).

Hansen, Jane. 2001. "From Investigation to Print." *The Final Analysis.* Georgia Bureau of Investigation, Division of Forensic Science Newsletter, April.

Harrigan, Jane. 1997. "On the Other End of the Story." *American Journalism Review,* January–February 1997, p. 46.

Haviv, Ron. 2000. *Blood and Honey: A Balkan War Journal.* New York: TV Books.

Haws, Dick. 1997. "The Elusive Numbers on False Rape." *Columbia Journalism Review,* November–December, pp. 16–17.

Herman, Judith L. 1992. *Trauma and Recovery.* New York: Basic Books.

Higgins, Marguerite. 1955. *News Is a Singular Thing.* New York: Doubleday.

Hight, Joe and Frank Smyth. 2004. *Tragedies and Journalists; A Guide for More Effective Coverage.* Seattle: Dart Center for Journalism and Trauma.

Hinton, Mick. 1995. "Group Reviews Media Coverage after Bombing." *Daily Oklahoman,* June 22, p. 12.

Howe, Peter. 2002. *Shooting under Fire: The World of the War Photographer.* New York: Artisan.

Huston, Aletha et al. 1992. *Big World, Small Screen: The Role of Television in American Society.* Lincoln: University of Nebraska Press.

Ignatieff, Michael. 1985. "Is Nothing Sacred? The Ethics of Television." *Daedalus,* Fall, pp. 57–78.

———. 1998. *The Warrior's Honor: Ethnic War and the Modern Conscience.* New York: Metropolitan.

International Society for Traumatic Stress Studies. 1998. *Childhood Trauma Remembered: A Report on the Current Scientific Knowledge Base and Its Applications.* Northbrook, Ill.: Author.

Katovsky, Bill and Timothy Carlson. 2003. *Embedded: The Media at War in Iraq.* Guilford, Conn.: Lyons Press.

Kauffman, Jeffrey, ed. 2002. *Loss of the Assumptive World.* New York: Brunner-Routledge.

Kelley, Tina. 2003. "Writing Portraits of Grief." *Dart Center for Journalism and Trauma.* www.dartcenter.org/articles/oped/2003_09_05.html (August 10, 2005).

Kessler, R., A Sonnega, E. Bromet, M. Hughes, and C. Nelson. 1995. "Posttraumatic stress Disorder in the National Comorbidity Survey." *Archives of General Psychiatry* 52:1048–60.

Kleber, R. J., C. R. Figley, and B. P. R. Gersons, eds. 1995. *Beyond Trauma: Cultural and Societal Dynamics.* New York: Plenum.

Koehler, Elizabeth. 1995. "Emergence of a Standard: The Rape Victim Identification Debate Prior to 1970." Master's thesis, Communications Department, University of Washington, Seattle.

Kotlowitz, Robert. 1997. *Before Their Time: A Memoir.* New York: Alfred A. Knopf.

Lachowicz, Steve. 1995. "Learning to Cope with Tragedy." *Wenatchee World,* July 16, p. 2.

Ledingham, John A. and Lynne Masel Walters. 1989. "The Sound and the Fury: Mass Media and Hurricanes." In Lynne Masel Walters, Lee Wilkins, and Tim Walters, eds., *Bad Tidings: Communication and Catastrophe.* Hillsdale, N.J.: Erlbaum.

Lewis, John, with Michael D'Orso. 1998. *Walking with the Wind: A Memoir of the Movement.* New York: Simon and Schuster.

Libow, Judith. 1992. "Traumatized Children and the News Media: Clinical Considerations." *American Journal of Orthopsychiatry,* July, pp. 379–86.

Lichty, Lawrence W. 1984. "Comments on the Influence of Television on Public Opinion." In Peter Braestrup, ed., *Vietnam as History.* Washington, D.C.: University Press of America.

Lisberg, Adam. 2003. "9–11 Journalists Share Memories, Support." July 11. *Dart Center for Journalism and Trauma.* www.dartcenter.org/articles/oped/2003_07_11.html (August 10, 2005).

Lombardi, Kristen. 2003. "Clergy Abuse and Public Trauma." Lecture to International Society for Traumatic Stress Studies Conference, Chicago,November.

Maass, Peter. 1996. *Love Thy Neighbor: A Story of War.* New York: Alfred A. Knopf.

McKinney, Debra. 1993. "Malignant Memories." *Anchorage Daily News,* June 6, pp. A1–11.

Meili, Trisha. 2004. *I Am the Central Park Jogger: A Story of Hope and Possibility.* New York: Scribner's.

Mencher, Melvin. 1997. *News Reporting and Writing.* 7th ed. Dubuque, Iowa: Brown and Benchmark.

Metzler, Ken. 1989. *Creative Interviewing: The Writer's Guide to Gathering Information by Asking Questions.* 2d ed. Englewood Cliffs, N.J.: Prentice-Hall.

Nader, Kathleen. 1997. "Treating Traumatic Grief in Systems." In Charles R. Figley, Brian E. Bride, and Nicholas Mazza, eds., *Death and Trauma: The Traumatology of Grieving.* Washington, D.C.: Taylor and Francis.

Nathanson, D. L. 1987. *The Many Faces of Shame.* New York: Guilford.

National Child Traumatic Stress Network. n.d. "Understanding Child Traumatic Stress" in the section entitled, "How Development Influences Posttraumatic Stress Responses" www.nctsnet.org/nccts/nav.do?pid=ctr_gnrl (August 10, 2005).

National Television Violence Study. 1997. Thousand Oaks, Calif.: Sage.

Nesaule, Agate. 1995. *A Woman in Amber: Healing the Trauma of War and Exile.* New York: Soho Press.

Newman, Elana, Roger Simpson, and David Handschuh. 2003. "Trauma Exposure and Post-Traumatic Stress Disorder Among Photojournalists." *Visual Communication Quarterly* 10 (1): 4–13.

New York Times. 2003. *Portraits 9/11/01: The Collected Portraits of Grief from the New York Times.* New York: Times Book/Henry Holt.

Ochberg, Frank. 1987. "The Victim of Violent Crime." *Radio-Television News Directors Association Communicator,* December, pp. 12–13, 41.

———, ed. 1988. *Post-Traumatic Therapy and Victims of Violence.* New York: Brunner/Mazel.

———. 1993. "Post-Traumatic Therapy." In John P. Wilson and Beverley Raphael, eds., *International Handbook of Traumatic Stress Syndromes.* New York: Plenum.

———. 1996. "A Primer on Covering Victims." *Nieman Reports* 50 (3): 21–26.

———. 2000. "Bound by a Trauma Called Columbine." *Washington Post,* November 19, pp. B1, B4.

Overholser, Geneva. 1989. "American Shame: The Stigma of Rape." *Des Moines Register,* July 11, p. 6A.

———. 1990. "A Troubling but Important Set of Stories." *Des Moines Register,* February 25, p. 1C.

———. 2003. "Name the Accuser and the Accused." July 23. *Poynteronline.* http://poynter.org/column.asp?id=54&aid=42260 (August 10, 2005).

Painter, Bryan. 1995. "Emotional Recovery Varies, Expert Says." *Daily Oklahoman,* May 29, p. 8.

Pearl, Mariane. 2003. *A Mighty Heart: The Brave Life and Death of My Husband, Danny Pearl.* New York: Scribner.

Peterson, April and Meg Spratt. 2005. "Choosing Graphic Visuals: How Picture Editors Make Their Choices." *Visual Communication Quarterly* 12 (Winter–Spring): 4–19.

Pinsky, Mark I. 1993. "Covering the Crimes." *Columbia Journalism Review,* January–February 1993, pp. 28–30.

Pliego, Joan. 2004. "The Reality Had to Get Out: Tami Silicio on the Photograph That Cost Her Her Job." *Real Change,* October 28–November 10, p. 1.

Quarantelli, E. L., ed. 1978. *Disasters: Theory and Research.* Beverly Hills, Calif.: Sage.

———. 1989. "The Social Science Study of Disasters and Mass Communication." In

Lynne Masel Walters, Lee Wilkins, and Tim Walters, eds., *Bad Tidings: Communication and Catastrophe*. Hillsdale, N.J.: Erlbaum.

Quindlen, Anna. 1991. "A Mistake." *New York Times*, April 21, p. E17.

Rainey, James. 2005. "Unseen Pictures, Untold Stories." *Los Angeles Times*, May 21, p. 1.

Raftery, Mary, prod. 1999. *States of Fear*. RTE (Irish Television Service) documentary.

Raftery, Mary and Eain O'Sullivan. 2001. *Suffer the Little Children: The Inside Story of Ireland's Industrial Schools*. New York: Continuum International.

Raine, Nancy V. 1998. *After Silence: Rape and My Journey Back*. New York: Crown.

Rainey, James. 2005. "Unseen Pictures, Untold Stories." *Los Angeles Times*, May 21.

Ramsey, Martha. 1995. *Where I Stopped: Remembering Rape at Thirteen*. New York: Putnam.

Ricchiardi, Sherry. 1999. "Confronting the Horror." *American Journalism Review*, January–February 1999, pp. 35–39.

Robertson, Lori. 2003. "High Anxiety." *American Journalism Review*, April 2003, pp. 19–25.

———. 2004. "Images of War." *American Journalism Review*, October–November, pp. 44–51.

Rose, Suzanna, Jonathan Bisson, and Simon Wessely. 2003. "A Systematic Review of Single-Session Psychological Interventions ('Debriefing') following Trauma." *Psychotherapy and Psychosomatics* 72:176–84.

Rosenblatt, Roger. 1983. *Children of War.* New York: Anchor/Doubleday.

———. 1994. "Rwanda Therapy." *New Republic*, June 6, 1994, pp. 14–16.

Rynearson, E. K. n.d. "The Story of a Trauma: Collage or Chronicle?" Unpublished manuscript.

———. 2001. *Retelling Violent Death*. Philadelphia: Brunner-Routledge.

Santana, Arthur. 2001. "Helping and Hoping, a Man Resolves to Rescue His Wife." *Washington Post*, September 13, 2001, p. A01.

Scanlon, Joseph. 1998. "The Search for Nonexistent Facts in the Reporting of Disasters." *Journalism and Mass Communication Educator*, Summer 1998, pp. 45–53.

Scherer, Migael. 1992. *Still Loved by the Sun: A Rape Survivor's Journal*. New York: Simon and Schuster.

———. 2003. *Back under Sail: Recovering the Spirit of Adventure*. Minneapolis: Milkweed Editions.

Schlosser, Eric. 1997. "A Grief Like No Other: Parents of Murdered Children." *Atlantic Monthly*, September, pp. 37–67.

Schorer, Jane. 1990. "It Couldn't Happen to Me: One Woman's Story." *Des Moines Register and Tribune*, February 25–29.

Seidel, Jeff. 2004. "Death on the Doorstep." *Detroit Free Press*, December 5, p. 1G.

Shapiro, Bruce. 1995. "One Violent Crime." *Nation*, April 1995, pp. 445–52.

Shay, Jonathan. 1994. *Achilles in Vietnam: Combat Trauma and the Undoing of Character*. New York: Maxwell Macmillan International.

Shepard, Alicia C. 1999. "Covering the Big One." *American Journalism Review,* July 1999, pp. 22–29.

Siegel, Jessica. 1999. "Hugging the Spotlight." *Brill's Content,* July–August, pp. 80–85.

Simpson, R. A. and J. G. Boggs. 1999. "An Exploratory Study of Traumatic Stress Among Newspaper Journalists." *Journalism and Communication Monographs* 1 (1): 1–26.

Sitarski, Kathy. 1996. "The Wheel of Violence." *Humanist,* May, p. 23.

Sites, Kevin. 2004. "Open Letter to the Devil Dogs of the 3.1." November 21. *Kevin Sites blog.* www.kevinsites.net (August 10, 2005).

Sloan, William David and James D. Startt, eds. 1996. *The Media in America.* 3d ed. Northport, Ala.: Vision Press.

Smith, Carol. 1998. "Witness to War: World War I Left Its Enduring Mark on the Life of Laura Frost Smith and Generations of Women." *Seattle Post-Intelligencer,* September 24, pp. A1, E5.

Smolkin, Rachel. 2003. "Thinking about the (No Longer) Unthinkable." *American Journalism Review,* May 2003, pp. 52–56.

Snyder, Louis L. and Richard B. Morris, eds. *A Treasury of Great Reporting.* New York: Simon and Schuster, 1962.

Snyder, Robert W. 2001. "Solidarity in a War Zone." *Dart Center for Journalism and Trauma.* www.dartcenter.org/articles/headlines/2001/2001_09_19.html (August 10, 2005).

Spratt, Meg, April Peterson and Taso Lagos. 2005. "Of Photographs and Flags: Uses and Perceptions of an Iconic Image before and after September 11, 2001." *Popular Communication* 3 (2): 117–36.

Stanush, Michele. 1994. "The Test of Fire." *Austin American-Statesman,* September 4, sec. G, p. 1.

Staub, Ervin. 1989. *The Roots of Evil: The Origins of Genocide and Other Group Violence.* New York: Cambridge University Press.

Stevens, Jane Ellen. 1994. "Treating Violence as an Epidemic." *Technology Review,* August–September, pp. 23–30.

Sylvester, Judith and Suzanne Huffman 2002. *Women Journalists at Ground Zero.* Lanham, Md.: Rowman and Littlefield.

Temple, John. 2004. "It's Impossible to Ignore Pain of Columbine." *Rocky Mountain News,* February 28, p. 2A.

Terr, Lenore. 1990. *Too Scared to Cry: Psychic Trauma in Childhood.* New York: Harper and Row.

———. 1994. *Unchained Memories: True Stories of Traumatic Memories, Lost and Found.* New York: Basic Books.

Virginia Department of Fire Programs. 2000. "Emergency Response to Terrorism; Job Aid." Edition 1.0.

Walters, L. M., Lee Wilkins, and Tim Walters, eds. 1989. *Bad Tidings: Communication and Catastrophe.* Hillsdale, N.J.: Erlbaum.

Watkins, Audrey Lott. 2000. "How Covering Jonesboro Changed a Reporter." *Dart Center for Journalism and Trauma.* www.dartcenter.org/articles/special_features/jonesboro1.html (August 10, 2005).

Windrem, Robert. 2001. "'They Are Trying to Kill Us': On the Receiving End of an Anthrax Attack." *Columbia Journalism Review,* November–December 2001, pp. 18–19.

Witt, Howard and Hugh Dellios. 1995. "Local TV Disagrees with Tabloids." *Daily Oklahoman,* April 30, p. 20.

Ziegenmeyer, Nancy, with Larkin Warren. 1992. *Taking Back My Life.* New York: Summit.

INDEX